# Mindful Moment

52 weeks of Mindfulness
Exercises and Reflections

# Mindful Moment

52 weeks of Mindfulness
Exercises and Reflections

Bonnie (Sumanā) Ryan-Fisher

*For my parents,*
*who taught me the value of faith, inquiry and determination*

*and*

*For Ajahn Sona,*
*dear teacher and guide on this practice path*

*and*

*For my Dhamma friends,*
*too numerous to list, too precious to neglect*

*and*

*Always, for Jim*

**MINDFUL MOMENT**
**52 Weeks of Mindfulness Exercises and Reflections**
Bonnie (Sumanā) Ryan-Fisher

Text © Bonnie Ryan-Fisher, 2017
All rights reserved

Book design by Karma Yönten Gyatso
Back cover author photo by Des Illes Photography

Published by
**The Sumeru Press Inc.**
301 Bayrose Drive, Suite 402
Nepean, ON
Canada K2J 5W3

**You Can't Roller Skate In A Buffalo Herd**
Words and Music by Roger Miller. Copyright © 1964 Sony/ATV Songs LLC. Copyright renewed. All Rights Administed by Sony/ATV Music Publishing, 424 Church Street, Suite 1200, Nashville, TN 37219.
*Reprinted by Permission of Hal Leonard LLC*

Library and Archives Canada Cataloguing in Publication

Ryan-Fisher, Bonnie (Sumanā), author
    Mindful moment : 52 weeks of mindfulness exercises and reflections / Bonnie (Sumanā) Ryan-Fisher.

ISBN 978-1-896559-36-0 (softcover)

    1. Buddhist meditations.  2. Meditation--Theravāda Buddhism.
I. Title.

BQ7280.R93 2018        294.3'4435        C2017-906990-X

For more information about The Sumeru Press visit us at *sumeru-books.com*

# Contents

How this book came to be  *9*

1  Busy-ness  *11*
2  Brief Meditations  *17*
3  Check ins  *21*
4  Metta  *27*
5  Bored and Restless  *33*
6  Distractions  *39*
7  Body Knowing  *45*
8  Point of View  *49*
9  Anger  *55*
10  Senses  *61*
11  Reminders  *65*
12  Renunciation  *69*
13  Attention  *75*
14  Memorizing  *81*
15  Watching  *87*
16  Making Change  *93*
17  Gratitude  *99*
18  Expectations  *105*
19  Self-talk  *111*
20  Difficult exchanges  *117*
21  Goodwill  *121*
22  Sharing Practice  *127*
23  Complaining  *133*
24  Intentions  *139*
25  Negative Thoughts  *145*
26  Generosity  *151*
27  Forgiveness  *155*
28  Breathe  *161*

29  Silence  *167*
30  Ceremony  *173*
31  Presence  *179*
32  Walking  *185*
33  Autopilot  *191*
34  Immersion  *197*
35  Pause  *203*
36  Listening  *209*
37  Frequent Action  *213*
38  Morning Intention  *219*
39  Naming  *223*
40  Joy  *229*
41  Kindness  *235*
42  Continuity  *239*
43  Blessings  *243*
44  Right Now  *249*
45  Well Wishes  *251*
46  Inner Listening  *257*
47  Peace  *263*
48  Wants  *269*
49  Remembering  *275*
50  Thanks  *281*
51  Moving Meditation  *285*
52  Selfing  *291*

Postscript  *301*
About the author  *303*
Retreat teachers who have influenced my practice  *305*

# How this book came to be

If a writer is someone who writes, that's certainly been a central aspect of my created "self" over most of my life. When not writing with the intention to publish, I am writing letters or in journals of various kinds. So when my exploration of the Buddhist practice path began, I also began journaling/writing about that journey. A few years in, around the time of the new millennium, I had the idea for a book based on these journals. A kind of autobiographical memoir, I suppose, but written with the intention of reaching out to others new to the path who were, like I had been, scrambling for community and feeling isolated in this undertaking. The project barely got started when my mother's passing sent me into enough of a spin that I simply abandoned the formal book idea and went back to my personal journals and the shorter forms of writing usual for me (articles and short stories).

Flash forward: I have been practicing for roughly two decades and I am still journaling. With the encouragement of a dear Dhamma friend, I am also leading a local meditation group. The internet has given me access to many like-minded people and I have found a spiritual home in Sitavana, Birken Forest Monastery, where I retreat regularly. Inspired by conversations with my circle of friends, I decided to launch a blog I call *Mindful Moment*, in 2014, a vehicle for readily sharing my journey as well as more practical matters like meditation schedules, news on retreats, information for a local Dhamma bookclub, or links to relevant teachings.

I have been faithfully posting to the blog at this website on a weekly basis, interrupted by a week or two here and there, most often for retreats. Because of my desire to speak from various places on the journey, I post pieces written not just now, 20 years in as a practitioner, but pieces written along the way. Some reflections here are from the early days when I had young children and a fledgling practice which was relatively solitary except for book teachers and, at one point, the support of an e-mail "tutor" located in Hawaii. I was connected with this tutor through the *Insight Meditation Correspondence Course* developed by Sharon Salzberg and Joseph Goldstein, consisting of cassette tapes of talks and a written guidebook, readily available through *Sounds True*. Later I would travel to take part in various lay retreats, including one in the Tibetan tradition and another in the Zen tradition, but mostly hosted by a group in the Theravada tradition, Light of the Dhamma, in Edmonton, a couple of hours from my home. I was also involved for several years with an on-line women's Zen group, organized by Kuya Minogue, who was at the time in Golden, BC and now is the resident priest at Sakura-ji Zen Centre in Creston, BC. Eventually, I found my way to Birken, my heart home, and my primary teacher, Ajahn Sona, the abbot there.

The daily concerns reflected in the blogs follow the evolution of an ordinary life. Balancing, first marriage and small children, with writing and teaching, and then later, somewhat older kids and our move into a family business as owners and operators of a dog boarding kennel. Eventually, one child and then the other leaving home. Downsizing and moving into retirement. And most recently the discovery of a new career as I took training and began to teach yin yoga at a local studio.

Practice is entwined in daily life and these are the broad strokes that have outlined mine. Through them all, I've been a working writer who found, eventually, that my writing folded into my practice. Mostly publications in the last few years have been Dhamma related. The blog itself is a large element in that.

For a small and simple endeavor, my blog has done well, in that it seems to speak to others on this journey, whether just beginning to develop a more mindful way of living, or seriously committed to the Eightfold path. Bringing it to book form brings me back to that "idea" of nearly twenty years ago. Deep bow of gratitude to John Negru (Karma Yönten Gyatso) at Sumeru Press for his belief in this endeavor and his work in skillfully bringing it to fruition.

### Suggestions for navigating this book

One page on my *Mindful Moment* website is devoted to a listing of mindfulness tips gathered from friends, from readings, from my own experience. This book is set up so that one of these tips or exercises headlines each section. This is then followed by three reflections from the blog. I've tried to choose blogs for each section that mirror in some way the exercise that is the heading for the section.

My suggestion is to work with each exercise for at least a week. Take longer to dwell on one if you like. The reflections that accompany the exercise can be dipped into at any point in that time period. When you're ready, move onto the next. Although numbered 1-52, the order is not really significant and you may want to choose according to what seems relevant to your life situation each week.

It is my sincere wish that each person reading this finds something that is relevant to his or her own journey. May all beings be well, happy and at peace.

*Bonnie Ryan-Fisher (Sumanā)*

# 1  Busy-ness

Our days are full of "tasks" that run into one another in a stream of busy-ness. Place rocks in the stream by pausing for a moment when moving from one task to another, focusing on just one in-breath and one out-breath.

**Daily Practice: Puppies, Pebbles and Weeds**

Doggy Dhamma. Puppy practice. Our little Lenny barks all night and sleeps hard in the daytime except for meals, walks in the yard and play times. He is a delight. Wonderful and exhausting. I'm sleep deprived. Brain given to hiccups in listening and attention. I meditate at 4:00am stroking a sleeping puppy on my knee, sometimes sipping tea. Just here. Just this.

    The test of patience and being with things as they are is certainly evident in parenting a new puppy. There is the pee clean up; the nipping at hands and feet and clothes; water dripping across the floor from a wet terrier beard; and "chase" games around the house when he's bored and won't stay in the kitchen; chewing furniture; barking when he's hungry; and pouncing on the cat. Yet, what I'm finding most challenging is just giving up the "do" mind that keeps wanting to get-things-done, to move on to the study, to do laundry, to bake and clean…always something other than just this, just what the moment holds.

    The human mind is an endless wonder. I look back to a few months ago and remember an extreme sense of fulfillment and ease. And though things are not much different now, there is an underlying sense of something…like a small pebble in my shoe…not enough to stop walking but a bit uncomfortable. Is the pup the pebble? He has changed the day's routines with puppy needs, added a bit of uncertainty and anxiety with our deep wish that he be a good dog, kind with people, gentle and obedient. He is so young (12 weeks tomorrow) and we keep reminding each other of that…the puppy testing of limits and the snappy biting, not just playing too hard but sassing when he doesn't get his way. There's that. So the wishes and desires are layered, rolling into pearls, into pebbles in my shoe, each bringing some element of unease.

And so arise misgivings about the ties I have to the world. In unguarded moments the fantasy stirring of a simpler life of withdrawal. Fewer attachments. Lenny is one of these. A little being taken on willingly. A sense of responsibility there. And this world so vast and problematic. This can bring a sudden bout of world weariness. The news full of problems and unrest. Yet, detaching is not an option. The world is me and I am the world. Whether I'm caught in the haze of sleepiness and small selfish desires or overwhelmed by terrors on a global scale. The answer is not to turn away but to turn inward and toward. To know what I'm feeling. To acknowledge the pebble and look into its make-up. To let the feeling be…while it sweeps through and while it fades. Because it does. All things are impermanent. As evident as this is, it needs to be learned again and again.

Then meditating I find peace clear and deep. I see my own anxiety as if through a shop window. Not mine. I don't have to pick it up. Go in and buy. I can look and walk on. What do I see? The deluded view that the world can be different. That I can be different. It is as it is. Human beings making their own choices, unable to see how their views and desires are the roots of their pain. And in seeing my own part of that, in the shop window, I know my own confusions, feel my heart open and the aching drain away, just tenderness remaining. The day goes on and I am balanced again. So different from letting myself fall weeping into the mud we've churned.

And so I work at moving toward those things that moods sometimes suggest I'd like to jettison from my life. To know the boundaries of the choices I've made. To reconcile those. To keep my practice large enough and stable enough to hold those components that create the doingness of my days, and accept the context of the world I live in, making room for shared elation and the times of grief and terror too. I work to see the yearning for what it is: The root cause of the very suffering it seems to offer escape from. "What if" is a question I'm familiar with as a fiction writer. It is the seed of story making. It's the seed from which fiction flowers, but it can be a weed in living a life.

**Being With Being Sick**

In the *Five Subjects for Frequent Recollection* one of the lines is "I have not gone beyond sickness, I too will sicken." I recite the *Recollections* frequently, as the Buddha advised, but mostly when I say them and I come to this line, I am thinking about life-threatening illnesses. The big ones. It's an abstract idea that relies on either my imagination, or memories of the several times, long ago now, that I've been that ill. But for the last couple of weeks, as a determined but pretty mundane bug took residence in my body, I've been thinking of it all a little differently.

This bug involves aches and pains, clogged sinuses and a persistent cough. And it's been a big reminder that "I have not gone beyond sickness". It has also been an interesting companion during breath meditation. Breathing in, I notice my lungs feel like a cat clawed furnace filter, filaments wagging and waving, bits dislodging and tossing around. There isn't a calming smoothness there. The mind brings in an edge of anxiety waiting for the interruptive cough. The sinuses feel hot and thick. Uncomfortable. Unpleasant. A lot of that. Breathing out, the cough takes its cue, most every time.

Hmmm...time to explore my other meditation options. *Metta* (loving-kindness) seems appropriate, with appropriate care that this beautiful emotion not lapse into self pity, of course. One of my little images of Tara, a Tibetan visualization deity, shows her sitting on the lion of the self. Taking my cue from this image, the self not aggrandized though purring away, I imagine all the small forms of suffering that people are undergoing, just like me. Me, just like them. Suffering is a universal not a personal thing. My heart, tight and small in my congested chest, begins to warm. Not focusing on the breath so much as warmth and light now, I send love to myself in this mundane and ordinary human experience of physical suffering, and then to those others. How ordinary. How fleeting. Yet, how consuming the experience can be. Not allowing the lion of self to strut and roar allows a quiet that lets the truth through. It is not merely this illness that I am suffering from. It's my wish not to be ill, that it not be so, that hurts the most. The doctor can't give me an antibiotic for that. No bottle of syrup on the drugstore shelf will ease it. For this I need the advice of the great physician, the Buddha.

There is suffering. Yet it dissolves as I let go of me in the center. The all-important self that wants to wave its banners and stake its claim. So I make effort in this direction of letting go. Notice worry about what I'm not getting done. Release that worry. Make phone calls, send e-mails, scratch things off the calendar and off the to-do list. Life goes on. Make space for this body to do what it needs to do, taking time to heal. Make space in this mind to just be awhile. In this way, illness might even be a gift.

I've listened to many Dhamma talks over these days. I've lain on the carpet in a sunbeam with my dog. I've read several wonderful novels. I've spent whole nights just feeling my heart beat under my folded hands, breathing with care, coming back to this moment and letting go of the thought "I have to sleep". I've drifted through days with no alarm in the morning and no schedule. Sleep when sleep calls me. Eat when I feel the need. Do a little. Rest a little. Let go of being tied to my usual rhythms of formal practice. Meditate sitting in a kitchen chair, lying on the bed, leaning back on the couch, walking in the yard, head back under the rush of water in the shower. Be embodied and notice how this body feels. Send it love and compassion, but don't get caught, for the discomfort is not all there is.

It's no fun being sick. That is, if I describe it to myself as something that interrupts the way I want things to be. But it has been "fun" in another way. A set of new discoveries, taking paths less traveled by in my usual days. That doesn't mean I'll throw away the calendars and do-lists or stop sitting in the deep dark of the early mornings once I've healed. But I'm grateful for this intense exploration of the changing sensations that breathing with difficulty for awhile has offered. A visceral teaching.

**Stillness**

Before I began meditation practice, I had conversations with people about my intentions. And a common comment was some variation on "I tried that once, but I can't stop thinking." What I had read about meditation suggested to me that stopping thinking was not the point, but I did not know how to express what I thought the process was. I had only read about it. Afraid to venture in, worried about "doing it right".

Eventually, I did begin. And, yes, a restless mind was and is a hindrance I deal with. But beginning again and again, and understanding that this beginning again and again is what the practice of meditation is, I discovered that the first reward of persevering is stillness.

Once, before I began a meditation practice, my sister was visiting. At that time we both had very small children, babies and toddlers. She sat down at the end of the day when they were all finally bedded. And I got out the pail and mop to clean the kitchen floor which had seen its usual number of spills and dribbles that day. Watching me, she laughed with affection and said "You're obsessed." And I smiled, agreed, and mopped the floor. To me this memory moment is symbolic of my behaviors prior to the changes that mindfulness and meditation brought. I did not know how to be still. I even taught "time management" classes from time to time and prided myself on my organizational skills and efficiency in "multi-tasking".

Mindfulness is the practice of being here in each moment. The masters say "When you eat, just eat." "When you do the dishes, just do the dishes." And this seems from outside to be silly and simple, or too profound, a code the ordinary person can't understand. What does it mean? The formal practice of sitting in meditation helped me to experience what this means. To be still. To just breathe. To just listen. To note the restlessness, the itch in my foot, the pressure of my knee on my ankle, the strange strings of thought. And to be still.

This was the first gift of meditation. And the center for me now. A *gatha* (poem) I like very much by Robert Aitken goes like this:

> When I feel I haven't got time
> I vow with all beings
> to light incense, and making my bows,
> touch the place of no time.

When I sit and breathe, I enter that place. And making it familiar, I can call it up again during the day when schedules and chaos, irritations and deadlines intrude. I breathe. And I am connected, still, whole once more.

# 2  Brief Meditations

*Look for spaces for brief meditations in your day as you wait for the coffee machine, sit at a railway crossing, stand in line, sit in a waiting room. Just look inward for a few moments, finding and being with the breath, grounding into the body.*

### Are We There Yet?

On a calendar I had one year, there was a quote attributed to the Buddha: "It is better to travel well than to arrive." Pondering this has been an interesting exercise.

We tend to get caught up in "arrival". "Are we there yet?" isn't just a question kids ask. It's one that we ask ourselves throughout our lives. Is this the place I want to live? Is this the job I want? Is this as well-off as I'll ever be? Have I been everywhere I want to go? Is this person the right partner for me? It shows up in myriad variations. All of them leading to a sense of discontent in the present.

People worry about being contented. They have trouble distinguishing between contentment and ennui or just plain laziness. Isn't it important to keep pushing, to keep stretching, to keep striving and seeking? I think the answer, in harmony with the Buddha's statement on traveling well, is both yes and no.

No, because if we continue to treat life as a means of transportation to somewhere we want to arrive, then we'll miss it. And the one destination we can count on is death. You'll get there, no doubt. It's the when and how that are in question. That's what living a mortal life guarantees. What is born will die. Those other "stops" we think are so vitally important, they aren't "stops" at all really: each becomes its own journey. It may feel like you're stuck when you're going to the same job everyday, don't have enough money to travel, or the kids are always underfoot. But while you think you're sitting still, or spinning your wheels, you are moving forward. You are traveling through the moments of your life to that final, inevitable destination. Do you really want to spend that time watching for the quickest train to the next place?

And the yes part of the answer? To travel well, we need to have harmonious intentions. Does the stretching, pushing, striving and seeking mean you are willing to get what you want in any way you can? Or does it mean you are stretching your idea of self, dissolving the boundaries that define "you"? Are you seeking to understand what motivates you and how your heart and mind work? Pushing your limits in order to stay with what is not necessarily comfortable until you understand where the discomfort comes from? Striving not to be a particular kind of person, but to know and accept all of yourself, even the aspects you would rather not see.

When I think of traveling well, I think of going deeper, not necessarily faster or further or away. Looking into yourself and the moments of your life with the focus of an archeologist. Meticulously brushing away the debris that obscures the treasure, the truth beneath. Staying put in the hot sun and through the long hours of mundane repetition. Looking with deep curiosity and respect.

Every moment traveled this way is traveled well. In this way we see what is in the way and get beneath it, we hold the beauty in our hands and treasure it. Are we there yet? This is a question without relevance in this kind of mindful living. We are here every step of the way.

**Stopping Awhile**

Much of the early reading I did about meditation made it seem complicated and exotic. Mindstates and stages of absorption were often described that seemed beyond comprehension to me, an ordinary person. Yet, a few years into this path, I have discovered a simpler truth. Meditation is not a project, as one of my teachers has reminded me. It is not about achieving something, marking up accomplishments. It need not be fundamentally different from things I did quite naturally before I had any instruction at all. Things so simple I didn't notice them. Meditation is stopping for awhile…and noticing "this".

Meditation is what I do when my young son reaches for me at bedtime for one more hug. I stretch out then beside him and relax and feel his arms about my neck and his breath in my ear. I smell him and soak in his warmth and strength. I let myself be there.

Meditation is what I do when I let my coffee cup grow cool in my hands as I sit at the kitchen table in the morning. I watch the birds rising and falling at the feeders outside the window, the squirrels chattering and warning each other away as they take turns standing guard on the deck rail. I watch the signs of the seasons in the big evergreens that line the back of our yard. Snow gathered in the branches, tops swaying with winds, sun glinting off the deep greens.

Meditation is what I do when I turn a kitchen chair to watch the fish in our aquarium. Listening to the trickle and splash of the waterwheel. Watching the graceful dances and darts of the guppies, the shimmering scales and swift turns of the koi, the fluttering scarf-like fins of the goldfish.

Meditation is what I do when a favorite song comes on the radio and I turn up the volume and stand and sing with this tune and forget the dishrag in my hand.

Meditation is what I do when my husband and I snuggle close or hold hands, breathing together awhile in silence.

Meditation is what I do when I let the water of the shower run over my head and shoulders and stand with my face uplifted and eyes closed relishing the warmth and treasuring the moment.

Meditation is what I do when I close my eyes as I run on the treadmill in the morning and feel the slapping rhythm of my feet, the beating of my heart, the strength and capacity of this body.

These are moments in daily life. Moments when I forget myself and the mental constructs that define who and what I am. Wise teachers remind us such moments are sacred. Our own experience teaches us this.

### Patience

When children are hovering in the kitchen watching the cookies come out of the oven and mom wants to save little fingers and mouths from being burned, she might counsel "Be patient." This kind of patience is a waiting, knowing that desire will be fulfilled. It is full of expectation. It shivers and trembles and leans forward. But eventually it will be rewarded. Eventually, mom will pronounce the cookies cool enough and put one into each outstretched hand.

Unfortunately this is the model of patience that for a long time I took as the standard. I don't think I'm alone. Yearn and wait and bide your time, and there will be a payoff. "Good things come to he who waits." It's polite. It's maybe even saintly. Not pushing and shoving, but waiting. And if the cookies run out, well maybe there'll be a cake in the cupboard.

But this is not the model of patience that fits meditation practice. Here the patience required is still and calm. It's not a waiting but a simple resting in the space of now. No payoff in sight. Not anticipating or expecting, not "just being polite". "Patient endurance" is a common translation of the Pali word *khanti*, yet for me "endurance" implies something grim that is not part of this process. It's a place of serenity, yet a tricky balancing point. It feels to me like a being with things as they are "as if" they will always be this way, and being OK with that, yet knowing, at the same time, there will be inevitable change in some unknown direction and being OK with that too. It isn't an easy thing to cultivate.

I imagine myself as a child standing in front of the oven not knowing whether any of the cookies will be given to me, yet not feeling grumpy or short changed, not a bit like wheedling or manipulating, not falling into planning how to be sure I get one when no one's looking. A tall order for my child-self. Even a tall order for the grown up sometimes. But this is the kind of patience the teachings refer to as a "perfection of the heart."

Patience comes into play in at least two ways in meditation practice. One of these is patience with the practice itself. Sitting with the breath for stretches of time not expecting any bells and whistles. Just this. This breath and then this one. Not being reassured of any kind of progress. Trusting and continuing. Climbing a mountain when we can't see the peak. Entering a tunnel when no light beckons from the other end. And even though this kind of patient persistence does set in place new conditions that ultimately improve life's quality, if we practice with that intention, we may well sabotage the whole endeavor. For me it helps to remember that this is my whole life...this breath and then the next one. The rest is memory/past or imagination/future. Neither exists in the space of this breath. We practice without expectation for the future because this moment is all that we have. We need to begin to feel this deeply. Enter the breath and the body deeply. Dwell here.

The second way patience is related to practice is, paradoxically, in its fruits. Cultivating the skill of being here with the breath allows us to be here when we're on hold on the phone, when someone is late, when we're stuck in traffic or waiting in line, when a flight is delayed, when the cat sleeps on the freshly laundered warm clothes in the basket. The list goes on and on. We lose patience when we live as if some alternate moment were possible. This moment is the result of all that came before it. It is exactly as it has to be. Yet we have a choice in the living of it. Patient acceptance, full attention to what is. Or a yearning that is a kind of self-harm, and often harmful to others as well if we act out unskillfully.

Patience is big-hearted. It includes an acceptance of our own short-fall in this endeavor. We can see our impatience in this moment and accept this, even as we form the intention not to act on it, not to keep the cycle going.

# 3 Check ins

Before rising in the morning, "check in" with body and mind. Asking "how am I today?" will allow you to be aware of when you're feeling weary or ill or sad, and how that might impact what happens in the day. Be kind to yourself when you're vulnerable. Be aware of the need for space to breathe before responding to external triggers.

**Unwelcome Visitor**

Woke up cranky this morning. A couple of late nights…well, later than I'm used to. And the familiar and unpleasant fug of procrastination lingering: there is a neglected manuscript on my desk. Years of work as a freelance writer and editor have made me very familiar with this aroma. There's no wind that will disperse it except the breeze stirred by applied activity…pen or keyboard required. But, whatever the cause of its arrival, crankiness is an unwelcome visitor. I used to just hope it didn't bring a suitcase and plan to stay long. Still, I felt a bit like the innkeeper who is gazing at the vacancy sign over the shoulder of a questionable guest. What are you gonna do? The invitation was extended.

Its presence can color the whole day. The more I push it away, scold myself for getting into this situation, the closer it clings. It leans over my shoulder as I check the outdoor thermometer. Yup…still wintry despite the May blossoms my calendar displays. It growls at my side as I mop up the puppy's throw-up. Too much of a good thing for him before bed last night. Crankiness is stepping on my heels as I hunker against the cold in my pj's waiting for the pup to poop.

And it follows me all the way to my cushion.

I light the incense and the candle, make my bows and scooch over a little way as I settle into sitting, making room. "Invite these unwelcome visitors to tea," wise teachers advise. It's a smart thing to do. When I tell my puppy "no", he gets more persistent. I have to get his cooperation gently. Invite him to show off a trick. Shake a favorite toy in his direction. When I tell myself "no" as I reach for a food I know isn't good for me, I feel my back stiffen and the child inside who won't be denied takes it anyway. But if I breathe and let myself imagine how I'll feel after indulging, well, the errant hand returns of its own accord.

So I bring this wisdom with me as crankiness crowds in. "Here," I say gently, "sit beside me. Make yourself at home. What seems to be the trouble? Too much to do? Tired? Annoyed with yourself for poor planning? That's the way it is, isn't it? Have some tea. Who else is visiting?" And that's when I can see past this unwelcome guest. There's the breath. Reliable. Consistent. There's the sweet drift of smoke from the incense. A sense of release in my shoulders. There's peace. Yes, peace is here too. Less obtrusive than crankiness, but I see it now. And when I do, oh yes, there is gratitude too. And wherever these two are, I can be sure to find joy as well.

Experience is the teacher here. The reflexive reactions to crankiness are twofold: either express it or hold it in, gritting my teeth and wishing it away. Neither of these instinctive responses tend to be very effective. Express it and I'll get the same back. An irritated remark hurts someone's feelings and they snap back. Ouch! Gritting my teeth gives me a headache and I begin to feel like the cork on a champagne bottle ready to blow. Wishing it away makes me feel bad about myself. Not just cranky now, but depressed and guilty too. That's quite a houseful and a bleak gathering.

Practice has taught me a healthier approach. To notice and accept the unwholesome emotions that visit is to open my eyes, my arms and my heart. And that's when I see that there's a lot of room after all. That's when I notice that "I" am this empty space and that the emotions are only visitors. They don't hold me hostage, they don't define me.

By the time I get up from the cushion I can see that crankiness is pretty much ready to move on. I open the door and smile, take the pup and my breath for a walk. And come back to the manuscript. How blessed I am to do work I love. How blessed to be.

**Siamese Twins**

I had a dream one night that I was a Siamese twin. Actually within the dream it was more accurate to say I was both individuals in a set of Siamese twins. The dream was full of a sense of struggle. Of course, being joined at the hip or the side somehow, was awkward. All efforts had to be coordinated and both "selves" had minds of their own and my unfortunate obstinate tendencies. Compromise was necessary. The arguments, well, discussions, were civil. I never have liked raised voices, even in my dreams. But the twins could never agree easily.

I have a blurry recollection of a car that conveniently had two steering wheels, and the chaos that followed from this equal-opportunity arrangement. Most of the dream, however, was lost in the befuddled moment of waking. I was left with an image or two and a sense of frustration and unease.

During the day that followed, I thought about this shadow self, the Siamese twin that would have been beside me were the dream the reality I lived. And in the midst of a moment of indecision over something very simple, I suddenly had to smile. Because, my shadow self, this Siamese twin, really is with me always. I'm seldom of one mind about anything. Options and choices abound.

I'm following a practice path that is built on mindfulness. That is, I strive to be with the moment so that I know what emotional pulls arise and I am able to choose to act in a way that is skillful. One of the twins resists this. She is pulled by emotion, by desire and by aversion, and she'd head for the ditch and ultimate calamity if given the wheel. She isn't going to go away. We're joined at the hip after all. But when I am calm and centered, she'll settle and quit the frantic dance. When I'm calm and centered, she becomes transparent and light and there is no struggle at all.

That calm arises from a strong sense of intention, of knowing how I want to live my life. Of knowing I do not want to carry the burdens of regret or anger and so choosing to act in ways that do not give rise to these. It's not a perfect system. Acting in a way that seems to me to be reasonable, I may find that others react with judgment and anger of their own. But I can let the chain of events stop here by not letting my emotional twin loose to defend our actions and choices. And no matter how "good" we are, there will be times of hurt and loss. That's when she's most prone to think she's all alone and so to get rather self-involved and pouty or sad. Buddhist teachers will often talk of sending metta to ourselves in such times of distress. That's when I need to cradle my emotional twin, opening our shared heart and eyes to the reality that everyone has these experiences. That this is what life brings.

I remember the fuggy and unpleasant feelings I had waking from this dream of struggle: the cloud that was a bit persistent as I started my day. And this was only a dream. When I have gone head to head with my emotional twin in daily life, not relying on the calm of my life's intention, but giving a willing ear to her strident protests and ego-driven worries, unhappiness results. We may in fact get our way, but there is a bitter flavor to such victory and too often disappointment in the outcome.

It was only a dream and I've pushed the metaphor far enough. Yet, to taste its truth is instructive. Mindfulness gives me the ground where it is possible to be of one clear mind, intentionally acting toward the end of suffering for all beings.

### A Certain Kind of Doubt

How do I feel about this enterprise two years into it? I like that the website gives me a place to post notices, keep a schedule for meditation classes, give links to things that might interest people, and then leave it to them to check in or not. Much better than a troublesome e-mail list that might get out of date, that lands messages in people's mailboxes, well-timed or not. A website means readers visit when they choose, read what they choose. Yet, I have mixed feelings about the blog, though that was my prime motivation when I began. That is, I would be writing anyway in my personal journals and it is motivating to share. But I don't know who reads it, if it's read at all, or if it's useful. And it's awfully quiet out there. Despite my "contact me" page on the site, few do, other than those who are already Dhamma friends. Plus, I know the net is a morass of opinions. My purpose is not just to add to that. What I want, what I wanted when I began, was to find a way to share the journey. This is what it was like for me then…a young mother, a beginner to meditation, after a few years, my first retreats, as I was learning and thinking and exploring. This is what it's like for me now. Today. In this moment. Over the last few weeks. As I wrestle with concepts, with mindfulness, with meditation, with keeping on keeping on with this practice that permeates and saves my life. Maybe sometimes it's like this for you too. But is this helpful?

Right speech, the Buddha taught, should be *true, timely, beneficial*. And writing is speech. Honesty and a *true* rendition of how things are for me, through the lens of practice, is always my guideline, whether the content of a blog is "flattering" to me or not, in agreement with prevailing opinions or not.

I trust, I guess, that what is *timely* will hold an individual's attention, will remain in memory, while what is not on target at a certain time for a certain reader will just bounce off or perhaps be stored in memory for when it is appropriate. I know that kind of thing in my own life. Teachings that I read but can't yet relate to so that they glance away and find no landing. A comment from a Dhamma friend that barely registers at the time. But later, something in my experience unearths the thread to what I heard or read and I reel it in and take another look. I'm ready to consider what was said. There is something that suddenly speaks to me.

And what is *beneficial*? Well, that's serendipity too, I suppose, in an enterprise like this. One week speaking to one reader, another week missing the mark altogether for that one, but perhaps speaking to someone else. It's an action based on trust.

Today is a day of a certain kind of doubt. Skeptical doubt, the Buddha taught, is one of the Five Hindrances, obstacles to practice. It's a tricky one. Doubt in the teachings, doubt in ourselves. Doubt in any guise has a heaviness to it. It's like stepping into wet sand. So today a certain kind of doubt is bogging me down. Doubt in the usefulness of what I do each week, sharing my thoughts, sharing my experiences. It's not a plea for everyone to rescue me and go immediately to the e-mail link to send encouragement. It's a place for me to look at, in my own practice. To ask relevant questions: What am I feeling? Why am I suffering? Not distracting myself from what is there. Looking. And in asking, why am I suffering, I get closer to the base. The grasping after results, the need for certainty and the selfing that flows through all human endeavor. "This is mine" includes some measure of pain.

So, it's pretty much exactly two years and I'm prone to assessment. And what assessment means is measuring something, a something, that in this case, is not measureable. Ah...thus the doubt. There's the underpinning of my practice for today. Sitting with uncertainty. The impact and influence of most of our actions and words cannot be measured. Doubt is balanced with trust.

The second factor of the Eightfold Path is Right Intention. I'll come back to that and find a space to breathe and be with uncertainty.

# 4  Metta

Before sending an e-mail or text, take a moment to send metta/loving-kindness to the recipient. Sometimes, if the subject matter is emotionally charged, you may even find this motivates you to edit before pressing send or to save the draft and give emotions time to settle.

**Metta Musings**

As babies we human beings are all feeling and reaction. Cold, we cry. Hungry, we cry. Wet, we cry. Surprised, we startle and cry. But, warm and full, dry and protected, we gurgle, coo and sleep. Gradually we sort out the boundaries, begin to notice a distinction between me and everything else. We discover our own fingers and toes. How things taste. What we like and don't like.

By the time we're toddlers we already have agendas. Locked inside the personal and private nature of experience, we're building an armor called the "self", an idea of who we think we are that we'll use to shoulder through the world. We lay claim and exert control. "Mine" and "no" are early tools in carving out territory and power. Parents and the other adults in our lives have to work at getting across the idea that others have "selves" too. Others have things they consider theirs, and actions they find unacceptable. It's not a concept easy to grasp and those who study developmental phases say it is impossible before a certain stage in mental development. Until then, it just doesn't make sense to us that others have feelings and rights, never mind that they should be considered.

Those early development phases might pass, but we carry mental scars. While we figure out the rules and expectations that allow us to act more appropriately in the world, that is, as if others had selves too, the internal nature of experience always leaves this in question. We can't feel what others feel. We have to take it on faith. And doing this, we begin, gradually, to broaden the sense of what me and mine mean. We let in certain others. Our parents probably. Siblings. Gramma and grampa. The dog. Our best friend. The teacher who treats us kindly.

Later we might include anyone who looks like us, who lives in our town or our province or country. People who hold the same views. Do the same kind of work. Have interests that match ours. It's a gradual thing. The armor expands but it stays in place, probably because we're not even aware that we're wearing it by the time we're all grown up. The armor itself is me and mine. And we believe it keeps "me" safe from everything other. We've created what we accept as a dependable definition of "who I am". This is the mistake. The armor is only an illusion and a trap. Who we are is not something solid and bounded at all. It's the difference between the free-flow of the river and the dam that holds it back.

In English we have a prefix, *meta-*, that added to a base word, has the meaning of going beyond, higher, transcending (according to *Webster*). In the philosophy department of the university I attended, for instance, one could take a course in Meta-ethics, a study of ethics going beyond cultural boundaries and relativity of values. So I'm wondering about how we as human beings develop an understanding of something transcending, more true than, the constructed self. Something meta-. In Pali the word for loving-kindness is *metta*. This quirky coincidence appeals to me. That the development of metta could lead the way to human values that transcend the self.

What if we take it on faith that the armor we see walking around is not who any of us are at all? Given the experiences, the good and the bad we've come up against in the world, the circumstances of our lives, this avatar has a particular shape and demeanor. Inside is the flowing river of experience, just trying to find safety and comfort, maybe joy and peace as we move through. A quirky coincidence, but maybe an insight too: metta is ultimately the door to a meta-view, where we realize the pinch of the armor is the real problem.

## The Precepts

The snow is gone, except for a few unnatural clumps fallen from work vehicles onto the grass and bits of ice caught like crystal ornaments in the the upturned candles of the mugo pines. The rabbits come out at dusk and I invaded their space tonight, hugging the fence as I walked Providence's grounds until I found the secret wooded corner I discovered when I was here last summer. Lost count at six or eight bunnies, though I may have counted some twice after that because they bounce and leap away when I approach, as many as three to a group.

This walking in nature is one of my strategies addressing immediate needs. How to cultivate virtue and lay the hindrances to rest and to be mindful off the cushion. Today I studied the Five Remembrances, recalling them to memory where bits had grown vague or ragged. Another reminder: wake up. Do not waste time. We will age, we will sicken, we will die, and we will be parted from what we hold dear. Facts we mortals strive to ignore. But the fifth is the balance to this. What we do matters. Our decisions, our actions, our speech. We create karma with the choices we make.

Then in tonight's Dhamma talk Bhante gives a list of the Five Spiritual Faculties: Faith, Energy, Mindfulness, Concentration, Wisdom. Mndfulness the pivotal point and the others balancing. Reminding us of the urgency of spiritual practice, balanced by the serene confidence that this path carries us in the right direction.

He tells the story of a learned master who was asked if he has anger anymore. "Yes" the master answered, "but I do not pick it up." Another metaphor: If a pot is heated over a fire and then water droplets are sprinkled on its heated surface, they will dance and disappear. So, too, seeds of anger (or desire or...) will evaporate in the heat of the well-trained mind. OK…I wish it were as easy as lighting a match!

As we leave tomorrow, Bhante will offer the Five Precepts for daily living. And I feel moved, this time, to take them formally. I've seen a variety of wordings, but the ones in the chant book we're using here lists them like this:

> I undertake the precept to refrain from taking the life of any living creature.
> I undertake the precept to refrain from taking that which is not given.
> I undertake the precept to refrain from sexual misconduct.
> I undertake the precept to refrain from false or harmful speech.
> I undertake the precept to refrain from consuming intoxicating drink and drugs that lead to carelessness.

They seem so straightforward and the way I want to live anyway. This commitment will be a support to the mindfulness I am cultivating day by day. I think of the bug in the sink, washed down the drain rather than carried outdoors. I'm inconsistent. The extra box of licorice I gave away without consulting my husband. The wine I like with dinner. The uneasy laughter provoked by a joke or caricature aimed at someone not present. A tendency to sarcasm learned in childhood. What degree of success can I expect? Is intention enough?

When Bhante gives the precepts he reminds us that they are to be taken seriously, but as guidelines, as trainings, not commands. There is value in such a core commitment to the development of virtue. But the commitment is balanced with wisdom and a compassionate heart. As I work to honor my commitment, I have compassion for this less-than-perfect human being intending to live in a way that is harmless, kind and aware.

## Three Mornings

### *The first morning*

This morning I began with reading/chanting the *Loving-kindness Discourse*. Have known this one in English for awhile and trying now to commit it to memory in Pali. This is challenging. May not happen, yet it's beautiful to listen to, beautiful to read and feel the syllables on my tongue.

Afterward, sitting, I watch my mind and body. Noting and letting the selfing dissolve. Asking as I see each thing that grips me and pulls me in, "How can I be with this? How can I make space around it?" Not pushing it away, wishing it away, but opening.

Later still, how much time passes? Twenty minutes, more? Then, perhaps nudged by the loving-kindness earlier, I feel an opening that is sweeping and involuntary. Delicious in the extreme.

One of my teachers has advised me to spend time in reflection after meditation where I let remembering and thinking happen in a limited way. What happened in that time? What was I doing when that happened? What did I learn there? Reviewing the process. This is something new for me in terms of a regular process. It leads to some interesting insights.

Today I think about what people hear when I speak of my practice as "the container" for my life. Does this seem restrictive to them? Yet, each of us lives within a container…that provided by the circumstances, the accident of birth: our parents, this body, this country, these expectations and values and cultural mores. Not seeing the boundaries and just going with this, unaware, is not freedom but the opposite. To see this and choose the container that is meaningful, that is freedom of heart and mind.

This is akin to yin yoga, coaxing the body through gentle moves into postures that are unfamiliar. Opening the body in this way, breaking out of the tightened restrictions of habit and time, allowing new limits and possibilities, greater ease.

Joy from this sitting lingers into an evening of discussion with Dhamma friends and carries into refreshing sleep all the way into the morning and to my cushion again.

### *The second morning*

Then, today, watching body and mind, I feel a shadow flitting through the sunny field of contentment and ease. Is it irritation or impatience? It is a wanting anyway. A wanting to linger in this. Not to have to deal with the world's demands. The mind sways today like long grass in the wind, attention drifting between peace and this pulling desire. "How can I make space around this?" The question is the whole of the sitting, paired with each breath. I continue to feel the tension that is desire's trademark quality. This is what I have to be with today. This is a harder place to be, but no less infused with awareness.

*The third morning*

Now there are tears as I recite the *Loving-kindness Discourse* again and I am surprised by the tears. How the human heart longs for peace. I breathe and soften and open. The pain does not go away but it spreads out, like salt in water. Not just a lump in my heart now but diluted by space, by the ocean of being that I am part of. This is perhaps the real ground of compassion, this vast field of feeling. Swimming through it and not claiming it as only mine. Yesterday's tension dissolves. Yet, the sweet peace of the morning before is tempered, less extravagant and more stable. Here there is an almost dreamlike quality. It seems a trusted voice is whispering, woven into the beating of heart and purling of breath.

# 5  Bored and Restless

When you are feeling bored or restless, close your eyes for a moment and give relaxed attention to what this "feels" like in your body. Let go of the storyline in your mind.

**Staying With Neutral**

In the practice of yoga we are instructed again and again to pay attention to the difference between discomfort and pain. Physical pain in any pose is a warning not to be ignored and so we move out of the pose, recognizing it is not, at least for now, right for us, and for "this body". But discomfort means we have reached an edge, and working that edge, staying with it, can mean growth.

In meditation practice, we learn to recognize the feeling tone of what is passing through the mind, whether that be physical sensation, emotion, or thought. We are taught to note whether the content is pleasant, unpleasant or neutral. One interesting thing about this process is that we begin to see that we pay attention to pleasant or unpleasant, but we don't even notice neutral for the most part. As the Buddha observed, when something is pleasant we try to prolong and hang onto it, when it is unpleasant, we try to escape or end it. Neutral seems like the place in the center of the swing of the pendulum, just that empty space the mind swings through on the way to someplace else. We suffer to the degree that we strain to keep the pendulum up at one end or the other.

Our lives are full of wonderful activities and distractions to assist us in this aim. Few of us ever truly experience quiet. Close your eyes and listen, wherever you are, and there will be sound…traffic, the furnace or air conditioning, voices, music, machinery of many kinds, the whir of the computer and click of the keys on the keyboard, perhaps birdsong or wind in the trees. But sound. And even in sedentary jobs, we are not still. We rotate our chairs, shift our feet, get up to pour a coffee, reach for items, twiddle with things, shuffle things, move things. Our eyes, our hands, our bodies are in constant mini-motion.

Attention deficit is still identified by educators and physicians as a problem that interferes with learning for children. Yet, the context of this culture promotes a constant bouncing of attention. Texting while walking or waiting, talking on the phone while driving, multi-tasking at work and at home. And even the nature of our entertainments caters to this need with loud sound tracks, flashing lights, and fast action cuts in videos. Pages in magazines are cut up with info-bites and colors and pictures. We speak in memos and text-speak.

I don't mean to condemn all this, but it seems to me that we are frantically swinging the pendulum too far in both directions. For most of us, our lives are lacking in balance, in coming back to neutral, in paying attention to one thing, to allowing ourselves to see through into the peace that is possible in that place. If you keep blinking, you miss it. And we're blinking like Christmas lights all the time.

Recently the *Edmonton Journal* carried an article with the title "People uncomfortable alone with thoughts: study". The article states "A new study has shown that being alone with no distractions was so distasteful to two-thirds of men and a quarter of women that they elected to give themselves mild electric shocks rather than sit quietly in a room with nothing but the thoughts in their heads." In other words, we prefer unpleasant over neutral. This doesn't seem healthy to me.

As with all studies, there are things one might question about the conclusions, the methods, etc. but I think it is important here to remember a prime directive in looking for truth. Examine your own experience.

If you've taken part in a yoga class, if you've tried to sit in meditation, if you've sat quietly by a campfire or the ocean, not talking and just breathing and being, what do you notice about your mind? It'll wander. The psychologist quoted in the *Journal* article says "…it's hard for people to direct their thoughts for any length of time." Hard isn't the same as impossible. With patient and persistent practice, we learn to be there with thoughts as they arise and pass away. To watch discomfort as it arises and passes, and pleasure as it arises and passes. If we do not cling and do not push away, the pendulum swings up and then drifts back, and we experience that space in between. We are on the way to finding a peace that we can carry with us. Staying with neutral, like temporarily resting a strained muscle or a broken bone, allows for important recharging, for healing from within.

[Article cited: "People uncomfortable alone with thoughts: study", by Michelle Fay Cortez, *Edmonton Journal*, Saturday, July 5, 2014]

## Going Out of My Mind

What does it mean to be mindful? I'm taking a walk and I am determined to pay attention and to be present. So, this begins with opening the sense doors. Noting the smells in the air. The sparkle of the sunshine or the glitter of the rain. The way drops of rain may pop and splash in puddles, or plop and spread in dust. The sounds that are around me. It means to be where I am, and not in my head working on a problem to be solved, replaying a conversation or daydreaming about the weekend. And this includes awareness of what I might not like so much. The dust and grit thrown up by passing vehicles. The wind blowing rain into my face. The constant hum of traffic. The open-windows of a passing car sharing music.

When I work at this, it isn't so difficult. What is harder is to notice the inner stuff. To be mindful of my reactions and judgments themselves. The voices that move in so quickly with labels and commentary. It's eye-opening to notice these judgments that leap into being about pretty much everything: the weather, the drivers, people passing by, the music overheard, my choices of clothing and footwear, the insects, the mufflers or lack of them, the condition of the road or sidewalk. This mind never experiences the world in a pure form. Each stimulus received is given a label, a category and often an instantaneous story.

> I like this. I don't like that.
> People should....
> People do this because....
> I always....
> I should....
> Why do...?

I'm sure you have no trouble filling in the blanks and adding to the list.

Being mindful, then, means noticing this too. And noticing how this feels in the body and the mind. The wishing, the longing that comes with positive things. The anger and criticism that goes with the negative. The jitters, the tension, the frowns, the clenching, the squinting and hunching. It means asking "how am I with this?" Our attitudes and judgments show themselves in the body.

So being mindful means being willing and able to go out of my mind, moving into my body and seeing what experience is like there. Dropping the stories, dropping the concepts and labels. Stopping with the sense doors as much as I can. Noting and letting go of the jitters, the tension, the frown, the clenching, the squint and the hunch. Relaxing into this moment so far as I can.

Being mindful means paying the same kind of attention to internal triggers. See if this scenario sounds familiar: You're spending some time on your own. You're reading a magazine or watching tv, or opening mail. And suddenly an idea arises – "I need a snack." Most often mind treats this idea the way it treats outside sensory input. It quickly creates an action scenario. So as fast as you'd raise your hand to shield your face from a spray of dust, you find yourself moving toward the cupboard or the refrigerator, looking for something to fill this need. Being mindful means stopping this causal chain at a point where you can assess the reactivity. I need a snack because I'm hungry? Was that really the belly talking? Or I need a snack because I'm bored...the mind's story, looking for pleasant stimulation in the face of too much neutral. These two signals feel different in the body. And when I go out of my mind into my body, I see this. Not a belly rumble then, but that flutter of agitation which is the mind seeking stimulation.

Popular presentation of mindfulness emphasizes that it allows us a fuller life, not missing this moment, or the next. And this is a real and appealing benefit. But its greater value, I think, is in making the space that allows us to choose more skilful actions. Not cursing the driver whose car stirred up the dust. Not eating the chocolate I'll regret later. To the degree that I am present in any given moment I take back freedom: not the simple freedom children crave, to do whatever I want, but freedom from being pulled by blind reactivity into the moment that follows.

## Mind Moments

Reading from *Flower Ornament Sutra*: "In each moment of mind/Are infinite lands produced..."

Mind moments. I've been observing this lately. How a mind moment can produce a whole infinite land. Different lives, different endings. Some spring into the future from this very time and place, and others sweep in like storms from the past, triggered by that futile lightning flash of thought: "if only". In moments of great weariness, the lands I produce in mind moments are beastly. Like some of the verses this sutra goes on to list. Made of dirt, or worse. Pain and suffering. But then a sunbeam or a Lexy-kiss from that darling Newfoundland dog I think of as my own, a devilish grin from my big 12-year-old as he teases me, dimples flashing, or a note from my husband "I love you. Take a nap." Those can lift me into other kinds of lands.

The truth, however, is they're all equally ephemeral. Products of mind. Chemistry and mood. I remember the existentialists that appealed to me in my twenties. The absurdity of all of this. Yes. It is absurd. To recognize the ultimate futility of so much of our effort. But there's something deeper.

A character from Ursula Le Guin's novel *The Dispossessed* says something like: "Suffering is a misunderstanding. The place where the self ceases." But when I look at my own experience I see the contrary here. I see that suffering is a misunderstanding that begins where the self begins. So that when I touch that place where the self ceases, I step out of suffering and perhaps, looking back, catch a glimpse of how it came about. I was disappointed. I was hurt. I hurt another. I yearned. And I could not let this be, let this go. So I cherished it and called it "me".

All of us, we human beings, do this. This is merely our humanity. Soft bodied mortals with feelings more tender still, we live in a world with edges. The physical bumps we may not be able to avoid. But we gradually learn, if we are honest and attentive, that psychological pain, whether deep or trivial, is inflicted by edges we have honed ourselves. Since we crafted them, we know where they are. With awareness, determination, and persistence, we might be able to wend a safe path between.

In reflecting on the mind moments that set me reeling, heedless of what's in my path, I've found my own early storm warning system. When the voice of the inner narrator slips into the "if only's" and the "what if's", I know it's time to turn down the volume and move more carefully, into the infinite land of "what is".

# 6 Distractions

If you work at a computer much of the day, be aware of how it feeds distractability with pop-ups and reminders, always pulling you away. If it is feasible, disable as many of these bells and whistles as possible, allowing more complete focus on one task at a time.

**Observance Days**

Last spring I entered training as an Upasika (lay practitioner), under the guidance of Ajahn Sona at Birken Forest monastery in Kamloops, BC. There are some 30 or more of us, undertaking to deepen our practice in a variety of ways. Having been devoted to ongoing study and a daily sitting practice for years, I was unprepared for the way some simple new commitments have deepened my own practice over these months. One significant discipline has been to designate one day a week as an Observance Day.

The marker of my personal Observance Days is to choose to refrain from entertainments. At first I made this into a mental exercise, worrying about what moments in my day were intended to entertain and distract me...like pausing to rub the dog or pondering what I'd like for lunch. This in itself became a distraction, a useless mental exercise that led into the entertaining world of convoluted internal argument, a mental theme park I'm all too familiar with, having been a graduate student in philosophy. But after a bumpy start, I settled on simple guidelines. In my life, entertainment mostly means books, and though many of these are related to Dhamma, I also have a love of poetry, an interest in sciences, and a passion for novels of many, many kinds. There you go then...no dipping into novels, poetry and scientific ramblings on Observance Days. And no impulsive decision to join my husband watching a movie, which

I generally do once or twice a week. There are obvious addenda: I don't schedule chatty lunches or coffee with friends on those days, or go window shopping. I don't deliberately court "chat" through phone calls or e-mails to friends. And beyond that I don't worry at the details too much. The dog gets his walk and his ear scratches. I don't dash out of the room if music is being played. And I don't force myself to eat something I don't like. This is not about punishment.

The process is about noticing the innate distractability of the mind. The deep grooves of craving and of habit that mark the human mind. Before this I had experienced the boundaries of a retreat for up to several weeks at a time. And I was certainly acquainted with taking windows in each day for meditation, along with building personal "bells" into my days that reminded me to come back to my body. But I still allowed the mind to lead me when it came to downtime, in the evenings in particular. An old habit. I didn't look at the whys or wherefores. Barely considered the impulses. I might mindfully settle with book in hand. Even take moments to reflect on the actions of characters as they related to Dhamma teachings. I generally knew when I was tired and was disciplined enough to choose sleep so as to be able to keep my early morning routine of meditation. But, because I habitually fell into a certain pattern of relaxation in the evenings, I didn't understand how the craving for diversion was working there.

It became very clear early on in the weekly Observance Day ritual. As evening approached, the attention I was able to give to the Dhamma books I was studying or the talks I was listening to, or the degree of stillness I was able to cultivate sitting was undercut by the pull of my whining monkey-mind. "I've only got a chapter left in that great novel." "The new book of poetry looks so delicious." "I'm too tired really. Watching a light movie would be a great way to mellow down before bed."

These, of course, were not new thoughts. The difference was that previously, since they came on cue at a certain time in the day, I didn't hear them at all. Like my dog who goes to sit in his kennel at 5:20 knowing dinner will be served soon, my mind hit pause. No more pondering, no more concentrating, no more "work". It's time for something mind-less.

As a good Dhamma friend says, I've been "teaching the mind who's boss" on Observance Days. I'm noticing what it's up to. Like my dog, it will wait patiently awhile, it might even whimper or bark, but then it goes to lie down with a sigh. Choosing not to do what I want has the indescribable taste of freedom.

### "Not Me" on Retreat

Soon now I leave for retreat. This is, I suppose, a pattern, a habit in my life. To set aside periods of time for this step into an alternate universe. A place where all the things that ordinarily tug at me, brush up against me, tease, taunt or tempt me, are temporarily set aside. Walking through the mirror.

I've always felt this in retreat. Even at the very beginning when I had trepidation and took some of my armor with me. Going off to a retreat at a lay centre, I'd pack good spiritual books, journals, even sketch books and pencils. External aids when the stillness might be too much. And at the beginning, given unstructured time, I'd often turn to these, not yet aware of how I shielded myself from real stillness when I did so. There is an image in the suttas offered by the Buddha of someone trying to start a fire, using a bow arrangement to rub two sticks together. And then periodically becoming weary and taking a break. The tiny bit of heat that had been building, dissipated and so the work had to begin again. Retreats then were like that. Sitting and walking, sitting and walking. Listening to the teacher. Sitting and walking. Then a break from the structure and I'd set down the bow and read or write or draw. Falling back into the familiar. The Buddha instructs us that it is important to keep the effort going.

In ordinary life, this effort is the work involved in not allowing mindfulness to lapse off the cushion. Tough sometimes in the momentum of acting, speaking, doing. And there's a little of that on retreat. But mostly in the silence and dedicated space of retreat, the effort is in keeping the stillness. Noble silence, my teacher says, is not the refraining from speech outside, but the maintaining of silence inside. Refraining from the constant chatter of the mind.

An interesting thing happens when one does this. Not reading. Not writing. Not doing more than the little needed. That is, not seeking distraction and entertainment, the mind continues to quieten even off the cushion. The quiet, associated in daily practice with the formal aspects of sitting or walking meditation, grows. The quieter the mind, the more clear, beautiful and simple the body's needs. On retreat I find myself sitting with hands around a tea mug, not even drinking as minute after minute slides by. A minute, an hour, a day becomes more abstract.

Anticipating retreat these days, I plan my packing differently. Soft, friendly clothes, toothbrush, medications, I tuck into the bag. But I deliberately leave behind books. I allow myself a single journal and one window a day just before sleep each evening to record perhaps those highlights of the day's Dhamma talks or interview with the teacher that I want to re-visit and reflect on later. The rest I will revisit in memory and perhaps record later at home. Here I want to retain the momentum, not set down the bow, allow the heat to grow, perhaps produce smoke or even flame. So along with books, I try to leave behind habits of craving mind, habits of selfing. As much as possible I tuck these into drawers and closets, discouraging them from following me on this journey.

Our practice is a process and it is interesting, arresting to me, to notice how suddenly an image I'd heard so many times becomes relevant. My teacher talks about what can come from being "not you" for a time. I am "not me" when I don't spend hours of every day reading. I am "not me" when I banish anxiety and planning and thinking things over (and over, and over, and over). If retreating several times a year is a habit now, it is one I chose to cultivate. Many of my other habits seemed to choose me, and too often I let them carry me. We are reinforced in this, my teacher says, by others as well as ourselves, for we count on people to be the person we think they are. We expect it. On retreat, we let this go. Each of us is allowed for a time a space where we can be "not me", acting in ways that feel unfamiliar, even artificial.

Noticing how my awareness heightens in these times, I see the relevance of being "not me" for awhile. Walk slowly. Keep silent. Don't make eye contact. Don't seek entertainment. Don't snack. Sit. Walk. Sit. Walk. Do the few chores assigned. Silently. Carefully. No hurry. When the time for chore doing is over, stop. Sit. Walk.

These days, a couple of decades of retreats have created a groove of their own. Is this an alternate "me"? Smiling, "not me" simply sets aside this question that the familiar "me" would never let go. I feel the peeling away from the ordinary begin even as I fold clothes into my bag.

**Choices**

My husband and I tease each other on days when we go from task to task, checking things off the "to do" list, as if when we die our headstones should read "He (or she) got a lot done." We were brought up in households where an underlying assumption was that "busy hands are happy hands". This is not unusual in the upwardly-mobile middle class. It is not unusual for children of the children of the Depression. It is not unusual in a society where success is measured by products and coin.

For much of my life I had disdain for people who were not so busy. People who took time for coffee with friends, for watching soap operas in the afternoon, for naps. But it's not that slowing down and doing less is the problem. Not any more than running on high speed and doing more is the solution. The question is what dimension of life do we allow our time to go to. For mortal life is impermanent and our time in this body and this life is limited.

One year we received a Christmas card from old neighbors who had moved away. The card listed many activities the family was engaged in and then said "but isn't being busy what life is about?" Perhaps it was a plea for affirmation. Or maybe just a rhetorical question, since many will nod in answer. Yet my own unequivocal response was "no".

Whether we spend our time on clubs and committees, meeting work deadlines and redecorating our homes, or whether we instead spend it partying on the weekends, absorbing hours of television in the evenings and exchanging neighborhood gossip with friends in the afternoons, is not the central choice. Both of these choices indicate that we operate within a physical and material view of the world. We are either running to beat the clock…getting more in than time would seem to allow, or we are trying to pretend the clock doesn't exist and simply killing time with trivia. Neither leads to satisfaction. Only desire. For more money, better furniture, more power, the next weekend, another drink, a body like the television star we admire, a car that goes faster.

It is in the recognition of the spiritual facet, the larger context, of our mortal lives that life is given meaning. It is in treasuring and being in each moment, whether busy or still. In recognizing and accepting both the time-bound nature of this body and the place of no-time where all beings are one. The place that allows us to take the perspective of the astronauts, looking down on this little blue jewel in an eternal space. One jewel, unmarked by manmade borders. And knowing each of us is not one alone but a molecule in this greater body.

Having made this larger choice, we can choose to be on a committee if our hearts lead us to that role. We can purchase what we need for our homes and not get caught up in trends and one-upmanship. We can share coffee and talk with our friends without aiming barbs at those not present. We can choose light entertainment and rest without absorbing the dominant messages of our culture. Mindful choice is about opening our eyes to the lines that tug us and not simply allowing the strongest pull to win. We hold our own in the trembling centre so that reflection and wisdom have the opportunity to enter this tugging game.

# 7  Body Knowing

Experiment with a handcraft or physical art that requires you to be with your body, i.e. knitting, painting, carving, pottery.

**Painting Meditation**

If asked how I'd like to spend a summer day, I'd probably describe some comfy spot in the shade, free of mosquitoes, with a jug of lemonade and a book at hand. Yeah…that would come pretty close. And there may be times like that this summer, or a few hours maybe here and there if not a whole day at a stretch: the shade, the book and the lemonade are relatively easy to arrange. However, no matter what my preferences, there will also be days with mosquitoes, days spent on home projects in the hot sun, and rainy days. There will even be days without books, much as this gives me pause.

Recently there have been a few home-project days as we undertake the painting of various sheds scattered around our acreage, as well as freshening up the house deck. I'm not a great painter, but at least outdoors the spills can mostly be cut off the next time we mow the lawn, or buried with a skillful re-arrangement of driveway gravel. And it is an opportunity to engage in painting meditation.

This begins with letting go of preferences. Letting that fantasy of books and lemonade drift away and coming here, to the brush in my vinyl-gloved hand, the liquid strokes on less-than-perfect wood, the drip of sweat running from under the glove as I lift my arm, the flies tasting and tip toe-ing.

I have plenty of time to think about impermanence. We've had to replace some framing pieces on doors and edges and there the wood is smooth and fragrant. In other places, there are deep grooves and crumbling patches where wet and time and insects have eaten into the wood. Spiders scuttle out of corners, their homes disturbed. The skin of my own arm, rising and falling, is a network of fine lines. Age and even the beloved sun at work here. These are not the round, smooth arms of youth.

The hours pass in waves of changing sensation, moving from sun to shade, to sun. The kitten slapping at my ankles for attention, leaving pin-prick holes in heat-swollen feet. Unpleasant. The sharp sweet smell of sun-warmed grass. Pleasant. My hat glued to my head with moisture. Unpleasant. The slow progress of paint strokes. Neutral maybe? Pleasant? Knees creaking and complaining a little, as toes bend and slide uncomfortably in cheap plastic clogs when squatting is required. Gravel digging into flesh, grinding on knee bones when I switch to kneeling. Unpleasant. Then the sweet stretch of a tired back as I stand. Ah! Pleasant. Nerves jangling when I have to climb a ladder unstable on uneven ground, and then reach at odd angles for peaks and corners. But safe on the ground again, admiring my handiwork…yes, pleasant.

Even so pass the moments of every day, but this one measured in the dips and strokes of brush on wood, in the sameness of activity is like placing my mind inside a smaller room for a time. The input is less varied, and so for a bit, like the precious silent days of a retreat, I am held in a space where observation of the moment is simple. The quick arising of aversion and clinging seem to slow down so I catch them easily like lazy flies in the heat. I'm standing in the sands of a just-turned hourglass: the sense of motion a tiny distant vibration rather than the rush of the last grains, which is often the feel of more typical days.

There is satisfaction, yes, pleasant, in the final cleaning-up tasks, in the moments of reflecting on a job completed. And then a moment to notice: the spiders making their wary way back up the walls of the sheds marring the finish or getting mired themselves, the kitten returning to sniff at the paint and leaving tiny blue pawprints on the grey boardwalk as she saunters away. All things are impermanent. This day of painting meditation itself giving way tomorrow perhaps to books, lemonade and shade.

**The Nature of Wind**

In *Golden Wind* by Eido Shimano Roshi, I find this quote: "Whether the wind is a fragrant spring wind or a cold winter wind, or just a gentle wind, after all, the wind is merely a movement of air."

This metaphor explains the mind's true nature beneath the phenomena of thoughts and emotions. New image to me. I suppose it is a different version of ocean depths and waves but it is striking in that it is new. Tonight after supper I was also reading Matthieu Ricard's book *Happiness* and pondering the terse instructions he gives to just look between the thoughts for a moment of clarity and there it is. *Between the thoughts.* This kind of instruction makes we want to laugh or scream. Where is this "between" anyway? Even when I manage to focus on the breath, in, out, it seems to me what I've done is simply slowed down the process. I'm looking at one car closely instead of watching the train whiz by. Am I missing something central here? Where is the teacher when I have a question? Out of a five day retreat just noon today where I could find no clear questions to ask. Now, alone in a hotel, sleeping over before the trip the rest of the way home tomorrow and now I have questions.

No, wait. I've had moments in meditation, perhaps they are more than moments, they're timeless so I'm not sure, when the breath itself fades from view and there is just something. To me it always feels like lifting or pulsing somehow. I've described it as an aura or as if my body is suddenly light as air, as if I'm not anchored. Is that when I'm seeing the air and not the wind, the depths not the waves?

I think what I want is to be able to keep that. And here is where my "clinging" pulls me off track.

Wanting something. That's what may draw us to the Buddhist path in the first place. That is what must be emptied. And in releasing the wanting we find what...peace? Release of self. That wanting was the string that bound us in the first place. For what is the self other than this tight and painful knot of questions and worries and wants?

So this is a way into release. A way of finding, ultimately, nothing. No solid center. The self is only the wanting. And immediately upon writing that I think of a culture built on consumerism. The egos, the selves that result. Teens, in their formative years, so consumed with desire to be "somebody" that their world is defined by it. Children who undertake the task of separating self from the world. "Mine" can be a first word in their vocabulary, in this Western world at least.

Questions and self dissolve together then. Stop asking. Breathe. Release. Make space. Space remains. And settle between. No more restless movement of wind, of the wanting mind.

**Musical Metaphors**

This retreat at Providence is familiar, comfortable. The rabbits are about and I had a lovely gazing session with one tolerant fellow who seemed to sense my admiration. They've barely any white showing yet. Will it be a late arriving winter? Walking the labyrinth and letting the body loosen after a two-hour sit. Feeling amazed and blessed at the inner stillness.

In the private interview we talked a little about the arising of insight from stillness. Trusting my own inner teacher.

Is this an insight? Big smile here. Reconciling "reincarnation" and the idea of no-self has been complicated and problematic for me. Prone to my habit of over-thinking, analysis. I've heard Ajahn Sona's explanation of the falling dice or a candle lit from another candle and I understand the causality link implied life to life as it is moment to moment in this (one) life. But suddenly today, holding the idea of my own insubstantiality, how little I feel connected to previous "me's"( babe, toddler, teen, 20's...beyond) and , at the same time, my deep sense of connection in this life to some few others (like my sister) despite so many changes, I felt, suddenly, the unconscious pulling out what is significant to come to a new understanding. Well, violin tunes have been playing a pretty constant background to any conscious thoughts since a week ago's gig! Another smile. So spontaneously, a metaphor emerges.

It is like a pause, a rest, in music, I'm thinking. Within the same piece of music there may be rests, pauses, changes of tempo and theme. Yet despite these, the whole is identified, externally, as one piece. Conversely, at a concert, an orchestra/artist may play many distinct (separate) pieces and we all agree to their separateness despite how brief the pauses between them may be. In fact, an artist may move directly into one piece from another, using only a transitional chord, yet we claim they are separate. So from this life to the next physical rebirth is a fuller pause/rest, yet the melody, the tune, the theme continues. And within a single lifetime there may be pauses where the theme changes quite dramatically. The metaphor satisfies me intellectually. I'd thought I'd already let go of self as a box and that I also accepted rebirth but some piece fell into place here, completely dissolving doubt today. Of course I've quoted Alan Watts often enough...selves are tunes, not boxes. But I had not expanded it before, considering movement in music, nor the role of rests.

Where'd this come from today and what does it mean, if anything? Just a sense of ease that seems to be the theme of a day that started a bit bumpy. Yet I am very still today. Very settled. The tune that is me running along in a gentle melody. Thank you, universe.

# 8  Point of View

In a conversation where someone is sharing a story or expounding on a point of view, when the speaker pauses, notice how the space feels and resist the impulse to jump in with your own comment or response. Some teachers suggest a 5- or even 10-second rule, waiting that long, giving the speaker space to continue and cultivating your own capacity for deeper listening.

### How We See the World

I'm reading *Zen and the Art of Motorcycle Maintenance*. Liking it. Liking it. Liking the puzzles of new ways of explaining. The author says that such things as gravity, the laws of science, are inventions of the human mind…not things that were "discovered". They represent a way of looking at the world. "All are mental constructions," the *Flower Ornament Sutras* (traditional Zen texts) would say. This rockets me to a different level, a new perspective.

I'm used to thinking this in trying to understand my loved ones, my contemporaries. The way my husband looks at the world, my sons, my sister, a friend. Shaped by their individual experiences, the contexts of their lives. I've even said this sort of thing in trying to explain to my kids things like riots or crime or prejudice. And I've thought it in my passionate study of medieval history, what shapes a period of history. The context of lives.

But something here turned me around to look in the mirror. To consider why I'm both fascinated and made uneasy by talk of ghosts, for instance, or magic, auras and numerology. All that. Why they seem a little silly even as my Celtic heritage draws me to them. This time I live in provides the context of science, which I've often thought of as the religion of our time. Invention. Another way of explaining.

On the level of thought, our minds work within the contexts they have known and accepted. Is there deeper knowing available when we let go of these? This is Zen's territory. The territory of koans, of the sound of one hand clapping. Breaking open the mind. Shaking the ground of reasoning.

I'm running with this now, trying to capture here the thoughts turning. Philosophy, the search for truth. The idea was presented to me in graduate studies that in philosophical inquiry we are trying to move closer to the truth. The idea that truth is somehow somewhere there, then we approach it. Our human hypotheses are tools intended to get us closer. We test different explanations against each other for consistencies. We try to see what explains most effectively. Science uses this method. The triumph of science over what we label as superstition is that it explains more thoroughly. Goes deeper. So the laws of science seem to be truths. Things we discovered.

But now I'm turning this in my hands like a coin discovered in the sand and looking. And I see another side. The laws as our inventions. We make them up to explain what we see. Like the ancient Greeks made up their gods. Like tribes over time have made up myths and stories. And in the context of our lives they explain adequately. Yet, right now, classical physics is undergoing a crisis of faith as the weird world of quantum physics explains things we couldn't see, didn't see or take into consideration before. The ancients couldn't land on the moon or use atom splitters. They had a different point of view to explain from. In another several generations what explanations, what inventions of the human mind, will make most sense?

Inner investigation requires the continuing peeling away of assumptions and contexts. Looking into the things that seem to us to be irrevocably true… the views and opinions we hold dear. Indeed, the views and opinions we come to see as being this self. We polish the mind in meditation and stillness, so that its bright mirror-like surface allows us to look anew and to examine even what we'd rather not see.

I'm trying on a new way of thinking about the closing lines of the *Metta Sutta*: "Without fixed views and opinions, the pure-hearted one, with clarity of vision, free of sensory desire, is not born again into this world." Of course. For this world we are born into moment by moment is formed by our views and opinions, our sensory desires, our less-than-clear vision and less-than-pure hearts. When we're able to shed these, a new world awaits.

## Fun and Games

I was witness to the scene many times as a mother of young children. Small bodies tumbling, running, squealing and laughing. Falling over each other to be first, scrambling for coveted toys, wrestling and rolling in sweet-smelling grass or working industriously together to build some fortress from boxes and blankets and chairs. At first everything is fine. Faces shine with smiles. Brows furrow with concentration. Voices rise in an effort to be heard. Someone pushes too hard, moves a carefully positioned box or toy, ignores someone else's idea. Two reach for something at the same time. A push in a tag game knocks someone to the ground. Whatever it is, the balance tips.

Adolescents carry it further. Dares. Taunts. Teasing and pushing. Roughhousing. Play-fighting. Upping the ante on some risky new game.

Bedtime for little ones can come to the same struggle. Enjoying some game or show or activity and refusing to acknowledge when it has to end. Holding with all their tiny wills and every ounce of being to the enjoyment they're experiencing until it dissolves in tears and tantrums.

"It's all fun and games till someone loses an eye," the old tongue-in-cheek adage goes. Young human beings seem to push the pendulum too far often before letting it swing back. And as we age, though we may refine this tendency a little...leave the party early sometimes because we have to work the next day, bite our tongues when a rough accusation runs through our heads during a friendly debate with a friend, choose not to make another run down the ski hill when we know we're too tired, get a taxi when we've had too much to drink... still, we hold to our pleasures, our sense of being right, our pride in our abilities and our sense of invincibility, often so long that the outcome is painful for ourselves or for others or for all.

Very often, as with children, this tendency to hold on too long and too tightly is made more fierce in an interaction. We're nearly out the door at some party and someone teases that we're getting old. What the heck. One more drink and one more hour. We're keeping our thoughts to ourselves on a controversial subject till someone pushes their opposing opinion and we feel compelled to set them straight. We know it's time to quit, but the playful urging of others leads us to continue.

In solitude, in a quiet rhythm, perhaps of working alone, time slows if we let it. If we do not pump up the pace with a flurry of texts and phone calls, if we really allow the solitude, and turn the attention inward, the mind becomes lucid and clear. We can see the rise and fall of thoughts and sensation. This is possible, of course, and sometimes even easy, in company. In a yoga class, on retreat, spending a day with another with whom one can fall into a space where silence is comfortable, no press for conversation.

But mostly, in interactions things move quickly and we can't always see clearly what our minds are doing, how desire and aversion hook us. We banter, we talk of frivolous things, we play, we race. And we lose our sense of how things are going, of our own motivations, of what right action and right speech might be in the moment.

This is why, I suppose, a good Dhamma friend of mine who spends long stretches in solitary retreat, calls practice in daily life, the "hard work" of this path to peace and freedom. Most of us won't choose to live in solitude, or to enter a monastic community. We'll practice here in the midst of the laughter, the scrambling, the pride and the chaos. As we do, it is good to remember to keep the balance. If no one is going to lose a metaphorical eye, we need to remember the hard work of mindfully monitoring our words and actions. This means committing to a continuity of practice and using our mistakes not to punish ourselves but as reminders that bring us back on track.

**Surrender**

Leading yin classes each week I often remind yogis to allow time and gravity to do the work, to surrender, to give up resistance. It is in this way that the various *asanas* (postures) are effective. We move into a posture that is not typical of our daily living…a twist perhaps, or a backbend or a deep forward fold, and then in the patient waiting, the body is invited to open and release, to test and move toward new edges. In yin, a particular joint and the body wrapping of ligaments are lubricated, activated and opened in this way. We find greater flexibility and strength, protection from injury that comes from stressing tight joints and muscles which are the natural result of immobility and of aging.

Yin meets meditation in a multitude of ways. The most obvious is in the stillness. In yin we are still for several minutes, perhaps only three or five for most asanas in a class, but perhaps as many as ten or twenty or more in personal practice, depending on the posture in question, our intent, our body and our mind. For siddhasana, easy seat, and svasana, corpse pose, are also yin postures and these as well as other gentle postures easily allow the willing body and mind to spend this kind of time.

But stillness is only the most obvious and most externally observable quality that yin and formal meditation share. A necessary condition of stillness is patience. The capacity to surrender our reactivity. To see into the mind and to notice the constant motion there and the way that motion pulls us along with it, compelling us to physically twitch and adjust and express. This may only be in a ripple of small movements perhaps, like a breeze on the surface of a lake, or sometimes in energetic surges of anger or panic or avarice, as when the very rocks divide and the earth and sky open and shift in dramatic and catastrophic ways…earthquakes and hurricanes and tsunamis. The mind is capable of all these things. Training it to stillness is the work of patience.

These similarities between yin practice and formal meditation have been evident to me for a long time. In fact, as a meditator for decades, it was recognizing this overlap that was the seed of my instant affinity with and great love for yin practice.

But over time, another level is revealing itself. When we train in patience and stillness in this way, the impact goes well beyond our formal practice. The capacity for surrender is what takes concentration to a deeper place, and what permits the loosening of ego's hold on all we do, and how we live our lives. I don't think it is stretching things to say that the capacity for surrender is the key to happiness. No longer blockading the door that protects what is mine, I allow it to drift open revealing no threat, but ease of spirit.

It takes a lot of effort, of the unskillful and stressful kind, to maintain a sense of self, the ego that wants everything to be "my way". When we sculpt a self it is a bit like building a sand castle from the yielding, malleable sand near the great ocean. We must protect and refurbish and reclaim in a continual way. This bit of territory is "mine". This solid-seeming wall that contains and guards it. This tower of accomplishment. This bridge of beauty. This is the way we work to protect our body, our feelings, our ideas, our beliefs, views and opinions. Yet, like the wave of the ocean, time itself is inexorable. We age, we change, we lose what we value. Yet gleaming new treasures sweep in, if we have the eyes to see.

When we surrender to the truth of life, without this struggle to maintain an artifice, we find that rather than being only what is within these crumbling walls, we are the entire shoreline and even the ocean itself. Like moving into a yin posture that may at first be uncomfortable, I learn to stretch beyond habit, to be less argumentative and to release my views, to be more generous and less selfish, to be content and less restless. Moving beyond my comfort zone and staying with this, allowing time and inner wisdom to do its work, I create the conditions for surrender and find happiness like a bright seashell surprise.

# 9 Anger

When you feel anger arise, try to touch into the sense of helplessness that lies below it. Send your energies inward, into compassion for yourself experiencing the pain of vulnerability or helplessness, rather than sending the energy outward, contributing to a painful situation.

**Anger**

Anger. It concerns me that anger can show up so quickly, so uncontrollably, from nowhere. It has a physical presence, something I can now identify before the anger itself hits. A prelude. An introduction. A preface. I don't know what, but I feel it. I know it. I'm learning to see it. I used to think that anger came from being weary, from being pressed, from having too much to do. From feeling like a victim, lost in the needs and desires and wants of "others". But I don't think so now. Anger doesn't come from outside. It's just a response. Something I choose to grab onto.

Yesterday was a wonderful day for me. I felt productive. I felt good about me. I felt worthwhile. And so I *was* … all those things. The day began with my run at 6:00AM. And a morning full of things to do. Chores, time for me, obligations. All those things augmented by a call offering a great writing opportunity. So, a day of confirmation.

Then today. I didn't sleep well. Waking. Dreams. Restless. Edgy. Then just before it was time to get up I fell into a coma-like sleep. Too heavy. And so I missed the alarm, the time for my run. My first thoughts were that I would have no exercise this day. I would be still, lethargic and useless and fat before the day was out. And then I just fell back to sleep when I meant to wake and begin then at least. And when I woke, everything was a rush.

Had to dash to get my son to swim class. Leave beds unmade, coffee half drunk and I ate a quick slice of heavy banana loaf instead of something light and healthy. I was impatient on our walk to the pool, and I felt the day dissolving around me, just being eaten up by things I was not choosing and I didn't like me. I confirmed that I was unlikeable by being short-tempered and nasty.

By afternoon when the time came for my son's nap, my head felt full of lead. I was weary and unable to think clearly. I felt lonely and tried to avoid working but somehow I did work a little.

On days like this, anger puts down roots and shoots up when it shouldn't. Unexpected and unpredictable. And the little one who shares my days most often gets the brunt of irritation and impatience that are anger's faces. He is three. All three-year-olds do the things he does yet my actions say he has let me down. I think how this will stay with him in some deep place and then I feel such grief and guilt, I confirm again my worthlessness.

How do I control this cycle? The reading I am doing is showing me a way: By knowing I do not want to be angry and anger is not what I am. I can see what happens in that prelude, that preface I feel; therefore, I can choose not to be angry, to find my patient core, to define myself in a different way. Treat anger like the child it is. Hold it close. Say hush. And then release it. Let it go.

We have so little time. Filling it is not what is important. A schedule with many things to do does not indicate a life well lived. I do not want to live so carelessly. Living carelessly leaves broken dreams and hopes on the floor, it discards old friends, and the feelings of others, and eventually I have to watch my step or I trip on the clutter and mess I've made. Or I'm wounded by some sharp edge of my own making. This isn't healthy. I need to begin to pick up the pieces. Dust the corners and open the windows. Mend what my actions have broken. Create a life with room for breathing. Deeply.

On busy days it's so easy to drop some hasty, thoughtless word and think there'll be time later to make amends. Vigilance is what I'm learning.

**Puddle Monster**

Yesterday, waking at 5:30, I expected that my day would go as planned. A day of space and quiet. The house to myself. A day of writing and study and breaks in the sun with the kitten and the pup.

But as I reached into the refrigerator for my orange juice, my bare toes nudged into a puddle of water. And just like that, the day changed.

So, I'm by myself. Husband, the handy man, gone to work. I read the refrigerator manual and it makes no mention of the current situation. I go to the net, my stand-by source of advice-on-all-things. After reading several chat rooms on similar probems and watching three YouTube videos on solutions, I feel my heart rate accelerating. It could be simple. It could be complicated. And I'm the one who has to deal with it.

Here's where the mind begins its spin: I don't want this. I don't like this. I want it to go away. I want to go back to bed. I want to meditate the way I always do first thing in the morning. I want the day I had planned!

I breathe for a moment and decide to sit and meditate anyway. Clear the mind, settle the voices. So I light incense and candle, I make my bows and I sit. The ritual is comforting. However, the moment I settle on my bench, I hear the voices again. They're gaining volume and speed. There's power in numbers. So the problem seems to be multiplying. It's no longer about a puddle on the floor.

Now they are telling me I am useless and incompetent. That whatever I decide will be wrong. That I'll get into something I can't handle if I start taking things apart. That it is too costly to call a repair man. That my husband may not approve of whatever course of action I take.

I've been a meditator long enough to know all these voices. I've created them all. The whiner, the critic, the procrastinator, the victim. But I also have been a meditator long enough to see when I am buying into the story lines. I may not always see this immediately, but before the story spins too far, I see the power I am giving it by believing it.

So now, I breathe. I come into my body. I consciously relax my shoulders, loosen my hands, smooth my face. I let this experience of ease sink in. And then I touch the problem: There is water on my floor, that's all. Something happened. Things happen.

I let myself sit, enjoying the calm a few more minutes and then I go to the kitchen where I use pencil and paper to make a list, remembering what I've read and watched. The list goes from the easiest "solution" to the most "complex". I start with the easiest one…the one that doesn't require tools I'm unfamiliar with, doesn't cost anything, and may solve the issue.

Here's where I get lucky. Well, the causes and conditions were right, but it feels like luck. The solution works and a few hours later the problem is solved. More importantly, I am not spinning. I do not see the day as if it were in ruins around me. I didn't sit in the sun much. And I didn't have as much time to study or write. But I let myself feel the pleasure of doing what needed to be done.

The liberation meditation can bring may be like this. Just freedom from the demons we create ourselves. The ordinary ones. Adult versions of the monster in the closet.

### Wishing for Harmony

Power. Life's lesson for me lately is strongly centered on this issue. The need for control, the resentment and anger that grow from powerlessness. I think of the resentment that wants so badly to take root in my own heart. Whenever I'm in the presence of anger or tension, it gnaws at me. Only mindfulness keeps it at bay, moves me to see where the tension or anger come from in others and so to begin transforming my own pain into compassion. It is the work of constant vigilance and I succeed only in intermittent bursts. Compassion's flame flickers like a candle, sometimes bright and true, then guttering.

Any communication takes place in the context of relationship and all those involved contribute to the direction it takes. No one is the bad guy. We are all just human. We struggle together in this. The deep sorrow is that we are the cause of our own pain. Anger smothers compassion. I understand so much better, with time, Bhante Pavaro's instruction to direct metta (loving-kindness) to myself first. When I direct it only outward I am misunderstanding metta, I am trying to use it as a kind of power or control of my own. I want my own desires for peace and harmony to be met. I need compassion for myself so that I begin to see where the roots of suffering begin. I need to turn my attention to the anger in my own heart and so protect the tiny flame of compassion. Feed this flame with presence, being here and now, breathing through just this, as it is. My job is only to love and to be present. Wife, mother, sister, friend. Just another flawed and suffering human being.

I have been pondering how when I make space there is more air…more oxygen for this flame. When I hold my own wishes lightly…let them float through, I do not come up against others in conflict. Any wish, held too tightly, hardens and becomes a weapon against those we perceive as hampering its fulfillment. And amorphous worries shimmer like mist in the air. The economy. Wars. Climate. The larger context of these lives we live. I can focus on the mist and feel dizzy and disoriented and lost. Or I can look inward and find stability.

Reading Jack Kornfield's book, *The Wise Heart*, I stop to copy out the bodhisattva vow the Dalai Lama takes. It is based on the words of Shantideva:

> May I be a guard for those who need protection
> A guide for those on the path
> A boat, a raft, a bridge for those who wish to cross the flood
> May I be a lamp in the darkness
> A resting place for the weary
> A healing medicine for all who are sick
> A vase of plenty, a tree of miracles
> And for the boundless multitudes of living beings
> May I bring sustenance and awakening
> Enduring like the earth and sky
> Until all beings are freed from sorrow
> And all are awakened.

I shy away from taking this vow in a ceremonial way, knowing too well how poorly I've kept other vows in my life. But reading this I ponder how intention shapes a life and I place a copy on my altar, adding this to my own haphazard rituals. Then I sit. I begin with metta for myself and visualize the light and strength of the Buddha, in whom I take refuge, flowing into this body, uniting with my own buddhanature within me always...coaxing hidden qualities and capacities, this original self to the surface for this life now.

The bell rings. No me surfaced at all. Just breath moving in this body, through the world of suffering where we all do our best. Breath of all beings. Like wisps of smoke, the anger and blame and the grieving and guilt curl and are absorbed. Inhaled and exhaled. My feet are planted on this path. One step at a time.

A calm carries me back to the kitchen. Tears on my cheeks, bittersweet morning coffee, the turning of the earth and the passing of everything. Now is the only place I live. What intentions will inform that living?

# 10  Senses

*Is there a simple task you can do in the day with eyes closed, going inward? Maybe folding a pile of towels. Doing a few mindful yoga asanas. Washing a bowl of apples. Shelling peas. Taking a shower. Even talking on the telephone. You'll be amazed at how your other senses open.*

**Oracle**

There was no specific question on my mind as I went to my interview with the monk today, so I asked only for further guidance on my practice path. It was like speaking to an oracle, a shadowed figure on his bench with a bank of windows behind him. The bright backlighting I looked into made his face impossible to see and I imagined that same light washing over me, facing him, wrinkled, sagging and age-spotted, rumpled in my sleeping and dish-washing clothes. I laughed and shared this fancy, both of our "roles", both "I's" dissolving as we spoke.

My concern so often is not to be trapped in the discursive, academic and analytic mind that is habitual for me. My teacher's suggestions were clear, precise and practical. His early training was in music and he spoke of the deep pleasure of simple arrangements, of scales. Suggested some composers. And so, gently assisted me in finding space and timelessness in my life, beyond the retreats and monastery visits. Actions and supports in changing directions and my habits of being: Gregorian chants, Japanese haiku, books without words but of black and white photos or eastern block prints and simple line drawings or spare paintings. Coming to appreciate space and emptiness.

He told me of a teacher who advised Western monks to give up reading for five years. I'm sure my jaw dropped. I know my heart hammered. Not this. Not to give up this. And ironically now I record his advice in this self-indulgent and verbose journal. But, baby steps.

He came back to the middle way…just sufficient, just enough. Enough to read, enough to eat…find that and seek no more. OK.

I bow thanks and return to my cushion in the *sala* (meditation hall) for the next hour. I watch words and plans and ideas come and go. I recall "flux" and "emptiness" and I find at last a gentle place where this body breathes and "I" stops its chatter awhile.

Later, on a woods walk, I recall a Dhamma friend's metaphor for the soup of the mind. Experiment with leaving certain ingredients out, he suggested: Like ego? Like expectation? Like planning? So now I think of my interview again, but this time as the companion to this instruction. Experiment with adding certain things: Like space? Like emptiness? Like simplicity? What will these new spices do to an old recipe?

## Suffering

In my daily mindfulness practice I am working to shift inward in intentions. I have let myself weave fantasies and worlds of worry.

Sometimes I feel like I'm turning a corner. The teachings my hands fall upon. The incidents and accidents of people, conversations, and events. But, this is my center right now: Emotions. Relationships. Through the pain and not hoping to dissolve it.

I began on this path through the intensity of grief. The meaninglessness of life…loss, pain, illness. The webs we weave of misunderstanding and confusion. Seeing how I'd wrested control of my life, made deliberate moves and found sorrow or disappointment there. But I see what I wanted was a substitute for the Christian heaven. Yes. A reassurance of something beyond this, something better. And the doctrines of a universal consciousness struck home with me. No man-god on his cloud-throne but a throbbing living universe of which we are just parts. Getting beyond the isolation of "selves" we find this. OK.

But what my heart clung too was the "beyond"…leaving pain behind, feeling the union. A transformation in thinking is slowly happening here with the changes around me, the teachings I'm pondering and practicing with. The meaning of this life is the bearing of suffering as a partner of joy. Not moving beyond it, but into it. Acceptance. Grace. We don't need to seek pain. It is part of living. Of the vulnerability of our bodies, of the changes life brings, of the complexity of building relationships in a world full of others like this very self but in each separate subjective context. There is suffering. We don't escape this. We accept it. And this ennobles us and is the meaning of human existence. Yes.

And over and over again in these past few days the tears sting my eyes and I feel this bittersweet truth as if it were running through my veins. It is. I live. I am human. I suffer. But I also thrill to this world and its gifts. And I can live both deeply and well with the support of this practice path: right view, right intention, right speech, right action, right livelihood, right effort, right mindfulness, right concentration. When I hold to this, attachments fall away and there is an end to subjective suffering which I see now as the suffering of struggle.

I think about the path I've found. This practice path that teaches me to soften. To open my heart and breathe and acknowledge what is. But not to cling to it. Don't hold the pain near and dear. Don't hold the wall between you and the pain near and dear. Breathe it in. Breathe it out. Living. Losing. Dying. It hurts. But joy is possible. Equanimity is possible. Novice that I am, practice has taught me this. The flies struggling in the web. Wishing they had not landed here. Wearing themselves out trying to escape. They suffer more. The fly that stays still. Breathes the air still flowing. Watches the shimmer of light on the web. Accepts even the shadow of the approaching spider. That fly is serene. The metaphor does not imply passivity but active living of what is. Of now. Not wasting time in aversion and desire. But it is a path each of us must come to, to seek. One foot in front of the other. One breath after another. Not something someone can lead me to.

## Opening the Senses

Life can get to be a tangle. In this culture where thinking and planning are encouraged, there is a great danger of becoming caught in a proliferation of thoughts that only make things more tangled. As possibilities arise and alternatives are considered and consequences speculated upon and motives questioned, we can find ourselves feeling boxed in, tied down, tortured by a mind that won't give up this restless pulling in too many directions. The body follows as tension builds in the neck and jaw, the scalp tightens and headaches take root, muscles ache with tension and the healing ease of sleep is elusive. Often the strategies we choose to address these symptoms are wrong-headed.

Beginning by taking a problem or worry to a friend, we may be offered more stories and more alternatives, kicking off greater anxiety. Turning to the internet for advice sources or chat rooms, we may find too many views. Settling in for an evening of television or other entertainment, we may find we are overstimulated by the activity or, if we're able to be temporarily diverted, the issue waits like a ninja to pop out at us as soon as the show or the game ends. Not so short-term in impact is that we may turn to the socially accepted outlets of alcohol or comfort food, adding one more level of complexity to the daily round of coping…clouding our thinking, negatively impacting our health, undermining our self-esteem and perhaps sharpening the inner critic's voice.

The connection between body and mind can be a boon here rather than a snag. It sounds too simple, but coming into the body eases the mind. Runners and swimmers will tell you of this experience, but you don't have to be an athlete. Rather than letting the mind run rampant as the body takes care of automatic routine tasks, we can make a determined effort to be present. This is possible through any of the sense doors, but one that works readily as a type of meditation is sound.

When my mind hurts with the heavy work of thinking and resists settling on the breath, I've often used "listening" meditation. This is not the sort of listening I do when I pull out my favorite CD's by Leonard Cohen or The Indigo Girls, James Keelaghan or KD Lang. Much as I love these gifted artists, they pull me into the lyrics and back into conceptualizing and cycles of thought. What I'm looking for is a doorway out of that crowded performance hall. The best kinds of sounds are random or repetitive and free of language. Sometimes I like ocean waves, or recordings of these. Or just to sit on the deck with closed eyes and allow the sounds of the neighborhood to lift and fall. Or lie on the living room carpet in svasana and let the various sounds of my home fall on my ears. This is an easeful process, my only work is to resist the naming and the questing after particular sounds. To remain a recipient of sound only. The late Michael Stone, a well-known Canadian teacher of meditation and yoga, used a simile of the microphone. It doesn't choose or label or reach for sounds but picks up whatever falls upon it. Letting our ears, then, be microphones only.

Even so, all the senses may open if, for a short stretch of time, we close our eyes and deny the primary sense of sight to take precedence, shift away from words and concepts and let sensation flow. This can be a great part of the magic of a yoga practice or a massage. Surrendering to what the body feels and letting it flow through.

It may be that certain aspects of the problem your life is presenting at any moment do require some planning and thinking. But this is best done when you are clear and focused, not helplessly tumbling in the storm of emotions and speculations. Whether the day just got too busy, or a major event has shaken the habitual patterns of your life, it is wise to rest mind and body awhile, to open the senses and let this body replenish. Things won't fall apart if you stop thinking for awhile. You don't heal a strain by working harder.

# 11 Reminders

Set a random timer on your watch, phone or computer, that rings several times a day. Make these interruptions a reminder to pause and be present. To know where the mind is, what thoughts are pulling. Are you here?

**Stepping Off the Carousel**

It takes effort to make time for a regular meditation practice. But I think it is so worth the work. I remember having the good intentions over and over again to change certain behaviors I was unhappy with. It might be habits, or moods, or actions. But mostly it came down to knowing there was a gap between the life I was living, what I was doing and how I was doing it, and the life I knew I wanted to live. I could not be comfortable where I was. It was a life of "When this..." and "If only this..." not a life of "just this". Not a life of contentment.

What is interesting is that there is still a gap, often, between what I might wish to be the case, the ideal I envision, and what is. But there is contentment now. And mindfulness has made the difference. The more mindful I am in each moment, the more full that moment is. There is no room for "more".

I know what it is like to have a schedule so full that the idea of one more thing to do is just too much. But when I used to think of meditation as one more thing to do, I didn't do it. I thought I could just learn to be mindful and do that. The wanting to be mindful would be enough. I'm not sure why I thought that. Wanting to be strong is not enough. Wanting to be fit is not enough. Wanting to pass an exam is not enough. Wanting to go to the moon won't get me there. There are things to be learned. Skills to acquire and to practice. Things to notice. Things to work on. There is effort involved. The Buddha spoke of "right effort" and it is part of the Eightfold path that he taught.

OK, so why not just learn to be mindful in everyday life? I've tried that too. And I know others who insist they can do it this way. There's certainly enough going on to be mindful of. But that's just the problem. In the normal course of things, thoughts and feelings are whirling by at such a speed that we are like children on a playground carousel. We are holding on to the metal bars and watching the world go by in a blur...either giddy with joy or cowering and crying, depending on whether the sensation is pleasant or unpleasant to each of us. Or maybe we just have our eyes closed and are struggling to endure until the spinning stops. It depends to some degree on the current conditions we're caught in. Is our best friend beside us? Did we just eat too much lunch?

When we do formal meditation, no matter how briefly or for how long, we step off the carousel. We let the momentum drop. We let the world stop spinning. We let the mind return to its natural quiet state. Awareness. Pure and clear.

This is the training ground. Thoughts still arise. Feelings still arise. But instead of spinning by in a blur, they are drifting. We have time to look, to pay attention to each detail as it passes. To notice the insubstantial nature of both thought and feeling. Instead of being a passenger on the carousel, cowering or triumphant, we are the skillful dancer in a spin, gaze fixed on the breath, returning to it in perfect balance after each rotation. We're learning to be still in the midst of movement. This is what it is to be mindful in daily life.

However we meditate, sitting or moving, on a meditation bench or standing in mountain pose, in flowing asanas, or mindful walking, we are training in concentration, wisdom and mindfulness, we are taking control by acknowledging our lack of control. This moment is what it is. Resting in awareness we are here. In daily life then, like the dancer, we can depend on the grace and ease our training has made possible.

**Goodbyes**

There have been a number of goodbyes in my life recently. Loved ones moving away. People who have touched my life passing away. It always has seemed that, like a TV show, periods of my life have themes. Sometimes I'm learning about not having my way. Sometimes I'm learning about joy. Sometimes about patience. Lately, I'm in a season of learning about letting go. A common theme. It has to be, since it's so easily verified by experience that nothing is permanent. No matter what sort of fictions we make up to the contrary. No matter how strong our desire for "forever" and "ever after", the stuff of fairy tales and love songs.

Goodbyes are painful. A short period in an airport illustrates the universality of this. An honest look at our personal experience is like tearing off emotional bandages. Fast or slow? Doesn't much matter. It just hurts. Why it hurts begins to become clear in meditation. The first Noble Truth in the Buddha's teaching is most often translated as "There is suffering". The second that this suffering has a cause. And the cause is clinging or attachment. In the light of this, comparing a goodbye to the ripping away of a bandage is apt. It hurts to be separated from what we've grown attached to, and we attach mightily to the people in our lives. The adhesive there is heavy-duty.

I once glued my hands to a music box I was repairing with *Crazy Glue*. Not only did the removal hurt, but the anticipation, the fear, was pretty painful in itself. I'd gotten myself into a fix (pun intended) and the only way out was going to be unpleasant. My busy mind conjured everything from scalding water to X-acto knives! When we attach to someone in our lives we're inevitably in the same fix. The letting go itself is going to hurt. And knowing this, the anticipation we dwell in hurts just as much. The mind gets busy with scenarios that give rise to fear and sorrow and anxiety, even while the person is still present and suitcases aren't even packed, or no diagnosis has been given.

Meditation is about watching the mind. Watching just these sorts of habitual pain-making patterns. Seems like one wouldn't want to do that. It seems a better "solution" to the pain would be to block it out. And there are certainly a lot of ways to do that. There are TV shows to watch, books to read, parties to go to, friends to call. Sleep is a good escape and drinking might seem like one too. Anything that clouds or closes down the mind, that distracts us from the stories it's telling. The problem with these solutions is that they only work for awhile. And when you wake up, sober up, turn off the TV, close the book, hang up the phone, get back to the empty house, the gremlins are waiting. So the cycle of hurting and numbing gets rolling. This is the way many of us live long stretches of our lives. It's at least as bleak as a bad TV show.

So what if, instead, I choose to watch my mind. I begin to see what happens. Each time I let the mind move into anticipation of parting, lean into the future, suffering arises. Each time I let the mind reach into the past, conjuring up melancholy memories of times I cannot relive, suffering arises. When I succeed in keeping the mind here, in the body, with the breath, in the simple sensations and flickers of passing moments, it is like being in the eye of a storm. Here it is calm and comfortable. Here is ease. Because here the story of "me" and "what I'm losing" doesn't exist. Here I stop the storytelling and creating that makes me a protagonist in my own TV series. Instead there is just experience unfolding.

This is not a grim acceptance of something I don't like but will put up with (like tearing off the bandage). It's clear seeing of this moment as it rises and passes away, impermanent. Rather than writing a script, gathering the material as I reach behind and ahead of this moment, creating a self who suffers, I simply stop and rest. When I do, even these goodbyes don't last. The third Noble Truth tells us that ending suffering is possible. We can taste that in every moment that we're free from the self and its stories.

# Rituals

In the years during which I wandered on my spiritual quest with no path to follow, I often longed for some of the rituals and traditions of my childhood. When we lived in town, on Sunday mornings I used to see from my kitchen window, families preparing to leave for or returning from church, and I would miss that. Just the routine of my childhood. The dressing up, gathering materials, driving together, meeting friends we didn't see during the week, chatter on the church steps, and the Sunday drives and restaurant breakfasts that used to round off the day. There was a comfort in the unspoken coming together of family around something shared, something unifying in a way many other tasks and undertakings were not.

But I had a suspicion of this comfort, as well. The same suspicion that made me unable to hum a remembered hymn without feeling uneasy. That wouldn't allow me to pray no matter what the extremity of pain or need. This all seemed a superficial crutch somehow. Something I shouldn't need.

I did not reserve these reactions for the Christianity of my youth. Statues of the Buddha, the rituals of bowing and lighting incense or candles, bells and robes all seemed to me to fall into this class which caused me a vague unease. The meaning I sought was in none of these things and I was not interested in what I thought of as "mere trappings". But I confess to a different view now.

The change in my perspective, I think, began when I read the suggestion by Rita Gross that religion is more like poetry than science. I hope I have not misrepresented her, but this is how I remember her comparison: it is not so much a matter of proof as of interpretation. No one claims that one poem will be meaningful for everyone, that it will speak to everyone, or even that it will mean the same thing to everyone to whom it does speak.

Beauty, poetry, art, music…they touch something in us that is beyond the limits of words and explanation no matter how we try. And so it is with religion. And, as in the expression of our emotions in poetry we may rely on forms and symbols and in music on tones and rhythms and in art on color and light, so in religion we may choose various expressions. Lighting a candle and stopping to breathe is a ritual which reminds me of that which is greater than those petty concerns I give too much time to. Bowing or inviting the bell to ring slows me down and centers me. Chanting does the same.

And so, I do not gather my family, put on a Sunday hat and sit in a high-ceilinged church once a week to sing and pray. But, I bring a small Sabbath, to use the words of Ram Das, into my day several times a day, through ritual acts that remind me of meaning my heart knows and lips cannot adequately express.

# 12  Renunciation

Experiment with renunciation, setting an intention to take a break from some habitual distraction for a day (or a few hours). This opens an opportunity to get to know how our mind works. What happens when you choose other than the habitual TV program, wine with dinner, phone call when you're lonely?

**Happiness Without Rollerskates**

Perhaps it's just the mood of summer in Alberta, the season of rodeos, but recently I found myself humming an old country song. "Ya can't roller skate in a buffalo herd", composed and sung by Roger Miller, is a classic from my childhood. Many country and cowboy poets, of course, are philosophers. Perhaps that began with the wide open spaces and lots of watching and waiting. Time to ponder the meaning of life. But as I hummed this song and the words came back to me, I got to wondering whether Roger knew he was spouting ideas at least a couple of thousand years old. Long before rollerskates.

The verses of the song outline a number of impossible activities. Besides rollerskating in a buffalo herd, you can't shower in a parakeet cage, swim in a baseball pool, fish in a watermelon patch, and so on. Yet every verse ends with the upbeat assurance that "You can be happy if you've a mind to."

Is it just what the chorus claims then, "All ya gotta do is put your mind to it / Knuckle down, buckle down, do it, do it, do it"? Well, sort of. There's certainly work involved. But much of that work is of the watching and waiting kind that cowboys and poets are adept at and that all of us can master if we're willing to try and see the value in it.

I admit, I'm not all that interested in rollerskating anywhere, let alone in a buffalo herd, but if I look closely at the things I am interested in, that I do want, I see that many of them are even more impossible. I can't protect those I love so that they never experience injury or sorrow. I can't be thirty or even forty again. I can't make everyone like me. I can't eat anything I want and stay healthy. I can't have another conversation with my mom or my dad, both gone for over a decade now. Truth is, many wants have that melancholy flavor of the impossible.

Sometimes, of course, what we want is more mundane…a new car, a holiday, a different job, a different house, new clothes for the season. Or just plain getting my way, winning the argument. And often even these less logically impossible wants are frustrated by obstacles of one kind or another. We think that's what makes us unhappy. "If only I could rollerskate in a buffalo herd, (translation: get that raise) everything would be fine."

But Roger doesn't claim you shouldn't want these things. He says, you can't have 'em, but you can be happy anyway. And this is the simple truth.

The buckling down, though, I would argue, isn't forcing yourself to be happy. It's not gritting your teeth, putting on a smiley face and keeping a stiff upper lip, a little difficult to manage simultaneously. It's buckling down to look long and hard at your own experience. It's not the wanting that is problematic. It's what the Buddha called "clinging". Clinging is when we believe a fiction: I can only be happy when "x" happens.

When we see that happiness is possible, even when we accept that some other things are not possible, it's like a break in the storm clouds. A eureka moment. When we quit longing for something else, what is here is experienced more fully. When we quit longing for something else, we allow gratitude for what is to arise. We see that life is a mixed bag and we choose where to place our attention. But this takes work. It takes mindfulness and presence. So we see the desire for a new car, or to be young again, we sigh and we let it go, and we form the intention to see the happiness that is here right now.

With apologies to both Roger and the Buddha, I'd sing it this way:

> All you gotta do is see,
> Knuckle down, buckle down, and learn to just be.

For those overcome by nostalgia, or those who are asking "Who the heck is Roger Miller?", here's a link to the song:

> http://www.youtube.com/watch?v=skFWsc_-i14

## Retreating From What? To What?

Darkness is falling. The cascades of snow that fell intermittently throughout the day from the roof to the balcony beyond the large window have stopped. Colder then? Wind stirs. It gusts and shushes awhile and then stills. Then all again. A pattern I remember from former visits here to Birken. My stomach rumbles. The first full day is ending. I have found a comfortable way to sit. I am rested, clean and warm. Enough to eat. Retreating from what to what?

When we had the kennel, going on retreat was an odd sort of "vacation". Up early, yes; eating less, yes; no entertainment, absolutely. But a break from the routine of seven days a weeks of dogs, phone and physical labor. Of scheduled days that allowed for no spontaneity. Now at home, no work: Violin. Books. Cooking. Sitting. Turning inward.

So turning more deeply here. Noticing restlessness, noticing boredom, noticing pain and hunger. Walk, sit, read and write a little, sleep. Little else. The breath will do. Even a cluttered mind. Noticing its clutter and mess and wild lack of discipline. Being aware. The gift of retreat right now is that it is cradled in a sense of spaciousness. Not a comma in a run-on sentence, like before. But an empty page in an empty book.

The mind wants entertainment. The Zen teacher in the book I've been reading asks "What is this 'boring'?", and then he laughs. We are all ADD. Stay with this. What's passing now. What is. Don't follow it. Be still. Then carry the stillnes into the day, off the cushion. Let some underling, the secretary part of the mind, take care of planning but let awareness open and rule.

What am I retreating from? From the easy distractions life offers in the form of not just entertainments but duties and obligations, work and even ease. In day to day life the hours rush by in a river of doing, punctuated by the rapids of exhilaration or pools of lethargy. We can become so exhausted from doing that we fall into a kind of numbness when we hit the end of the day. Dragging ourselves through routines with resentment or inattention. Begrudging the moments and wishing for the next.

In retreat there is little to look forward to. The mind does not have the fuel of imagining some "better" time in the next "event" of the day. The food is simple and seldom. The activities pared down. If we are tired or bored, one of my teachers says, it is because we are tired of and bored with our own thoughts. This can be a good thing. We're having to look at them, deal with them, see what's at work. And eventually, noting how unreal they are, these thoughts that rule us, we let them go and come to what is real: this body, this moment, this breath. The heart responds with an opening and ease that is what we'd thought we were trying to create all along. This is the happiness that eluded all our efforts.

But retreat isn't a special place where this kind of happiness is found. This happiness is something we carry. Retreat clears away the clutter that kept it from being found. I always find, following retreat, that for awhile that open space is easier to maintain. There it is, bright and shiny, the peace and happiness I discovered I had all along. But then I get careless. I let a regret drop here, a resentment there, a longing somewhere else, until it's all a mess again. And in the busyness and doingness of the days it gets away on me again, this inner housework. Until I come on retreat.

Teachers advise retreats several times a year. A breathing space for looking deeply and clearing the mind and heart. There is a cumulative effect. Some of the stuff I jettison each time never comes back. And lately I can always see a little, at least, of the gleam of that possibility I uncover on retreat.

## Infatuation

Most often the word "infatuation" is used in the context of romantic love. When we become infatuated with another person, it is as if we put on special lenses. These lenses do not allow us to see qualities we may not find appealing, at the same time as they exaggerate or even invent qualities in the other that we are drawn to. If we think back to romantic involvements that arose in our pre-teens or teens, or even look closely at attractions to singing stars or film idols that we might have as adults, we can see this at work. It's not even necessary for us to know much about the real person. Most of what we think we know is a personal invention, a riff we take off on from the tiniest beginning…a smile, a phrase, a tilted cowboy hat.

Yet, we feel betrayed when something of reality breaks through…a piece of news about the film star, or an action on the part of our "idol" that is drastically out of sync with our expectations and beliefs.

In his book *Living the Compassionate Life*, the Dalai Lama talks about the fragility of marriage in modern times, saying "Marriages that last only a short time do so because they lack compassion; they are produced by emotional attachment based on projection and expectation, and as soon as the projections change, the attachment disappears. Our desire can be so strong that the person to whom we are attached appears to be flawless, when in fact he or she has many faults."

This habit of projection that human beings have, however, is not limited to romantic relationships. In the teachings of the Buddha there are references to the five cords of sensual pleasure. These are simply our five senses: seeing, hearing, smelling, tasting and touching. These are great gifts, of course. We are embodied beings and our senses allow us to fully experience an embodied life. It is not the senses themselves that are a problem, but rather that we can become "infatuated with them and utterly committed to them,...without seeing the danger in them or understanding the escape from them." (MN 26 v32)

When we become infatuated with the senses, we form the idea that satisfying them is the key to happiness. As we did with the TV star, we project the capacity to make us truly happy onto the objects that please us. And over and over again, "our projections change and the attachment disappears" even as the Dalai Lama observes in short marriages. Advertising plays on this by building projections for us. We know this when we pause to evaluate, yet we come to believe that the untainted joy people in the ads seem to experience will be ours as well, if we just own that model of car, smoke that brand of cigarette, drink a particular kind of beer, take our vacation in a certain location.

Our infatuation with the senses leads us to over-indulge, to saturate the senses, and then to become bored and restless because more or different no longer brings the rush it once did. Infatuation leads to the insatiable need for more that is harming us and our world.

This isn't a condemnation. It is the nature of being human. But as human beings we are also blessed with the capacity to see clearly, if we commit to this instead. Careful investigation of our thinking, of how we move from a moment's pleasure to a full-fledged belief in lasting fulfillment, is the beginning. Looking closely, but with compassion for others and ourselves, is vital. Seeing the flaws and accepting them, in ourselves and others.

Ultimately then, we can enjoy the beach while still seeing the abandoned wrappers in the sand, and acknowledging the need for temperance and sunscreen in partaking of its pleasures. We know it is just a beach. It is not the answer to all life's problems. It is just a vacation, not the solution to the difficulties and heartbreak we are working through. It is just a smile from an attractive stranger, not the discovery of the perfect soulmate. When we commit to this investigation, infatuation has no foothold.

# 13  Attention

Next time you are having a conversation with a friend, perhaps over tea or lunch, give the conversation your full attention, turning off your cell phone for the duration of the interaction. Be there fully, body and mind.

**Helpful Acronyms**

Some time ago I read a talk by Ajahn Amaro* that referred to one of those handy memory acronyms I hope I'll recall at important times. The acronym, intended to be of assistance in the pursuit of Right Speech, is simply WAIT. The letters referring to "Why Am I Talking?"

At the time that I read this, I thought how life-changing it could be if I could learn to insert this question into the mental pause that opens in mindfulness before I speak. The pause needs to come first, of course, and anyone training in mindfulness knows that this is an ongoing practice. When we begin, ordinary mind is like an untrained puppy and speech the wagging tail that goes wherever puppy-mind goes. How often do we find ourselves in uncomfortable places because of hasty responses, angry retorts, sarcastic replies, unkeepable promises, exaggerations and humorous anecdotes? As we learn to pay attention to our thoughts and the actions they lead to, speech is just one of the elements of our behavior that becomes a little more disciplined. On a good day, in the right circumstances, we might have reason to be pretty impressed with our well-behaved mind and thoughtful speech. But there are times when the puppy and his tail simply run amuck.

A question like the one this teacher raises though might seem to go a little too far. Do I really need to examine why I am talking every time? Well, if you try this, you'll find it quite revealing. We talk for lots of reasons that have nothing to do with communicating anything at all. We talk because we're nervous or bored, we talk because someone else is not, we talk because someone else is talking too much, we talk to stop thinking. Talking can become as meaningless as the fretful barking of the puppy at the window of a busy street. So, while it is a difficult thing to do, it can be interesting to let this question float through from time to time in the process of practicing mindfulness.

A new aspect of this was opened to me recently on retreat, where speech is not permitted. When talking outloud is so restricted, it's interesting to note how the mind gears up for awhile, and does even more talking to itself. Incredible dialogues may take place within, without any input from anyone else whatsoever. The beauty of this is that, in time, we tire of hearing the barking inside the mind. And somewhere in there the question can be raised again: Why Am I Talking? What purpose does this constant narration of experience, recall of the past, planning for the future, analysis of opinions, listing of accomplishments, whatever we're on about in this internal speech, serve? When the answer arises, a blessed quiet descends. I remember a playschool teacher who would flick off the lights in the room to get the attention of her too excited, babbling young charges. Surprised by the dark, they'd stop their wild chatter. When the chattering mind is surprised by this question (WAIT), it too goes quiet.

In one of his teaching talks on this most recent retreat, my teacher referred to the voices that will arise when conscious mind makes room. When conscious mind, the mind of mundane chatter, makes room, wisdom is permitted to surface. We can be surprised in times of extended silence, outer and inner, by insights and truths that are not heard in words at all, understandings that arise and give clarity where confusion reigned. "Voices" in the stillness. Some mystics have spoken of these voices as being the voices of God or of angels. Rumi would speak of "the beloved". In Buddhist psychology, these voices of wisdom are not "other", but what is known in the luminous mind, the original mind Zen may refer to, before we cloud it over with too much selfing and analytical thinking.

Even if you have never been on a retreat, are not a meditator, you've likely felt such moments. Strolling by the ocean at sunrise, standing in the woods in a gentle spring rain, feeling the tiny fingers of a sleeping infant reflexively wind themselves around your own finger, listening deeply to or making music, reading a poem that moves your heart, lying still under a star filled sky. There are endless moments that arise in life where a natural quiet opens. A quiet of the mind, a peace of the heart. And if we're not in too much hurry, we remember to WAIT, and let this linger and we listen for the wisdom. I've come up with my own acronym for this process. LOL. Oh, I know, it's fitting perhaps that most of us think this means laugh outloud. I suggest it also could mean Listening Opens Learning. It isn't talking, diverting ourselves and others with questions and answers on the level of rational thought, that holds deep answers. It's being quiet. Listening to what the "voices" in the stillness have to say. The joy of that may make us laugh outloud.

\* "Why Am I Talking", in *Beginning Our Day*, Vol. 2, Dhamma Reflections from Abhayagiri Monastery

## Keeping It Simple

Today I had a lovely discussion with Dhamma friends. In the flow of discussion we referred, all of us, not just to various suttas, the Buddha's recorded teachings, but to Dhamma talks we'd heard, books we'd read by Dhamma teachers, and other conversations we'd had with fellow practitioners. Much of this is helpful. Some of it is confusing. And some of it leads to agitation or worry. In the end, the basic guide to practice is to keep it simple.

We set our intention toward the end of suffering and we trust our own experience. If we look carefully at our behaviors and their consequences, we will know what to cultivate and what to abandon. If we look carefully at the methods we employ in meditation, we will know what is carrying us toward peace and understanding, and what is taking us on interesting and problematic detours. The looking carefully is what is incorporated in right mindfulness and right effort.

This does not mean that we should not study or read or discuss. Only that we need to do so with right mindfulness and right effort, as we do everything else. Paying attention to what is going on now for us, and what follows from this. If something is causing struggle and confusion, seek clarification from a teacher if possible or set it aside as unhelpful at least at this time.

The Buddha, roughly paraphrased, said not to merely believe what he taught but to look at our own experience. To see for ourselves. This should likewise apply to whatever we encounter. The greatest effort needs to be in honesty here. What is my experience? Not, what do I think it should be, what do I want it to be, but what is it? How do I feel when I act in anger? What happens to my tranquility in meditation when I wander off into stories or yearn for a "special" experience?

For every factor in the eightfold path, whether it is view, intention, action, speech, livelihood, effort, mindfulness or concentration, we need to be curious and clear about what is happening and what it leads to.

There is a great deal of beauty and value in listening to the experience and wisdom of others. But it is good to listen with the other ear tuned to our own experience. Language is a clumsy tool, and I say this regretfully as one who is a lover of language. It can only approximate experience. And what is spoken or written is sifted further through the filter of my own understanding when I take it in. A word as simple as "dog" conjures different images and emotions for each person hearing it spoken. Embed it in a sentence and the variations escalate. Translate from one language to another and we've added a new dimension of potential miscommunication.

I am a devout follower of the Buddha. And I am grateful for those who have recorded his teachings, translated his words, interpreted and considered every aspect of the path. I am grateful too for my fellow practitioners, at the beginning perhaps of this journey, or further in, struggling to move toward a better way of living, aspiring to an end to suffering. So I will continue to study, to read, to listen and to discuss. And simultaneously to examine my own experience on the journey. Panning for gold is not a high tech process, it doesn't take complicated equipment and years of study, but it does require open eyes, discernment and continuous effort, just keeping it simple.

### What's This?

Both when I lead meditation and when I teach yin yoga, I stress grounding in the body. I think it's kind of interesting that although Western medicine agrees on the location of the brain, there's still a lot of vagueness about the mind. Because the mind, literally, seems to be everywhere. Left to its own devices, it is not contained by time or space, knows no speed limits and isn't troubled by random and odd associations or leaps in logic. How often have you found yourself thinking of something you either haven't thought of in years, or didn't know you even really knew anything about, and wondered "Where did that come from?" Of course, not knowing anything about the subject doesn't stop the mind from embroidering on it. The process is as automatic as water running downhill. The path of least resistance. Drop in a thought or cue and watch it go. The ordinary mind is not grounded. It's freewheeling and often confused.

When we begin to learn to come into the body and to touch a thought not through the words and images generated but through the sensations it gives rise to in the body, we begin to find a place to anchor down. For me, that's often vital to my well-being. Teacher Sylvia Boorstein humorously describes herself as "short, grey-haired and anxious". By that description she and I are almost indistinguishable. The grey is still intermingled with blonde in my case. But I'm thinking a lot of people, no matter their physical stature or hair color, would include "anxious" in the description of traits they feel "belong" to them. Whether there is a person at all to own the traits is another subject. But it seems evident when we look closely that each of us has some kind of theme running through...we tend in certain directions. If I begin from that premise, I have to admit that anxiety is one of my tendencies. Practice has been the antidote to allowing this tendency free rein. Rather than a storm that sweeps through my life and leaves my well-being in shambles after the fact, it is a lurker. Not openly on-line, not out in the open, not so I could point to it, but a subliminal possibility. It is learning to ground into my body that has kept it at this low level of impact on my life. And for that I'm grateful.

Good things happen in every life. Bad things happen in every life. I used to believe that shifting the balance was possible and that in that shift would be the solution to anxiety. Not so. I tried it for a good long stretch and all my moving of mountains amounted to nothing more than lots of grit in my eyes and unstable rubble under my feet. Practice has given me a new approach. Anxiety, like any strong emotion, presents calling cards and I've learned to identify them so that when I open the door, I'm anchored. There are obvious markers like a clenched stomach or a headache. But prior to these, if I'm alert, are less strident symptoms: a sense of unease that trembles through the body and a disjunction between mind and movement so that being with what I am doing is difficult, like a time delay between the command and the action that results. These are the signals to ground. To ask the question: "What's this?"

No naming is required here. Not labels but an examination, rather than ignoring what the body is saying. Noticing how it feels. When I slow down and re-direct in this way, I carry myself away from the mind that has begun to develop stories/excuses/explanations to make sense of the anxiety, handing over the controls. When I come into the body, I nudge narrative aside and return to the physical. I breathe deeply. I soften the tensions that are underneath the symptoms. I place my attention in my feet, in the earth, and know that I am held. Eventually, through these efforts, I make the mental space to notice the mistake that lies lurking: That old belief that being on guard prevents bad things from happening. That being prepared means everything will turn out all right. Instead, grounded in the body and aware of what I feel, I can open the door to what is. I recognize anxiety lurking in the shadows. In the full light of acknowledgment it shrivels a little, less menacing and destructive than I imagined.

# 14  Memorizing

Take the time to memorize an inspiring poem, prose passage, chant or song...choose something a little bit long, a little bit difficult, and work at this with diligence. For several days, repeat it often, outloud or mentally in whatever spaces open in the day. Once it is internalized in this way, you'll find it surfaces and runs through your mind when you need it most. There is a sweetness to this we seldom taste in a society that "records" externally rather than internally.

**Impermanence**

Even if we'd rather not believe the calendar, and if we choose to ignore the school buses back on the roads, it's almost impossible to get through the day right now without at least a sweater, and maybe a pair of socks. Fall has arrived. Green is still the predominant color in the landscape, but its tone is changing. Sliding towards brown and yellow by tiny degrees.

    I haven't had a garden for a number of years now. But I do love to plant big patio pots in celebration when spring arrives and I tend to these lovingly throughout the growing season. Pretty much every morning I water them, turning the pots to keep growth even, clipping dead leaves and flower heads. This year I also apologized to them for the havoc wrecked upon them by my playing puppy and kitten, who themselves are growing rapidly and may be more considerate by next year.

This little ritual is a pleasure. But it is also practice. While I'm working I chant. If I'm alone I do this outloud, if I'm in company I do it in my head. The chant I use is one that is common on retreats, a teaching about impermanence. It has a "tune" to it that I wish I could capture here but the words go like this:

> All things are impermanent.
> They arise and they pass away.
> To be in harmony with this truth,
> Brings peace.

What at first glance may seem like a mournful message, is actually incredibly multi-faceted. I find that repeating this chant often has made it an instinctive default setting for my heart-mind. It is of great assistance in the daily life task of letting go. Letting go of what is delicious, the pleasures and joys of life. And letting go of what is warm, the security and safety we all seek, for ourselves and those we love. It is a truth that our own experience validates over and over. The flower heads that opened from tight buds to surprising points of beauty, one by one droop, wither, and dry. So too each of us. Through the summer I clip the old with a gentle hand and admire the new, lifting petals and paying attention to the butterflies, beetles and bees who appreciate them too.

This time of year, there are only a few new buds to see, and some of these won't ever open and realize their promise. The nights are cold. For awhile, shuffling the pots in and out of the garage at night allows me to prolong their lives, but one night I will forget, be away, or just decide enough is enough. All things are impermanent.

Many years ago I took a particular sorrow to a wise monk during an interview on retreat. This sorrow seemed to fill my life then. I could see no way past it. I was an ant at the foot of a mountain of misery. His advice was not what I expected. He suggested that I add what are called the "Five Subjects for Frequent Recollection" to my daily practice. The part that began to speak to me was this:

> All that is mine
> Beloved and pleasing
> Will become otherwise
> Will become separate from me.

Trusting my teacher's wisdom, and taking on this practice, I found the mountain crumbling. It was not that I got through it but that I saw it for the mirage it was. This was no unique and singular sorrow, visited unfairly on me. It was only the truth. I was not expected not to love, not to be pleased. But rather to know that what I loved and what pleased me could not last. To know this deeply for the universal experience it is. This knowing gives urgency and brightness to this moment. And peace to the heart.

### Housekeeping of the Heart

My first retreat under the guidance of a Theravadin nun. You would think, maybe, that this would not be so unusual when I'm accustomed to the instruction of monastics, but the flavor of this retreat is unique.

When Ayya instructs she has a gentle humor and a soft voice. The microphone provided for her has a dead battery so in this room of some 20 people it takes full attention to hear her. She tells us to be courageous, determined, adamant! She speaks of holding the breath and touching it like a blind person. Getting to know it with that kind of intimacy.

At meal time Ayya sits on the floor with her alms bowl for lunch in a corner of the room. We kneel around her for the blessing in sing-song English and then leave to get our own food in the cafeteria.

The days fill with long hours of sitting practice. With weariness increasing I watch my own doubts in my capacity arise and resolve not to hug them to me, but to watch them and let them dissolve in the passing of this moment and the next. I know how my capacity to come to terms with suffering, how my ability to love well and to move outside of ego have all been strengthened by practice. Serenity and wisdom? These too in time perhaps. I am moved by Ayya's sincerity and humility. Watching her...the fine, long-fingered hands, the quick and fleeting smile, the certainty and kindness in her manner, I am struck by yearning. Not envy. Her teaching and example are gifts and I am grateful to be here. The yearning pulls me like gravity more surely to this path.

Ayya uses a helpful metaphor: Just as a carpenter cannot see how the print of his hand is wearing away the wooden handle of his hammer, day by day, still he will notice when it has worn through. Keep up the practice and do not be despondent at seeing no fruits day by day. The hindrances are worn out through continuous effort, the growth of mindfulness and inward awareness.

Be aware of the workings of the mind. Seeing the wanting. The self-pity. The obstacles that arise. Ayya talks of turning a spotlight inward...watching... "what am I thinking?" And sweeping ego out of the picture. I imagine a poster I could make for the refrigerator door, a visual to keep this front and center, the sweep of a broom in a circle of light.

My share of the world's suffering is little enough. I smile thinking of what's become a joke my husband and I share when we're faced with disappointment. How he told me once decades ago to "Buck up!" Not the words I wanted to hear having confided some complaint about the world. He's a Zen master in the making, I think now, whether or not he knows it. Ayya's way is gentler. Sweeping the self away, the issue itself is gone. We create the problems in claiming them, in taking every disappointment as a personal assault.

I carry these thoughts to the labyrinth, reciting metta verses in this simple walking meditation. Beginning the second stanza of a familiar verse I find a word just gone. "From this protected place I send loving-kindness to all those for whom I feel…" There is a mental blank. The word untraceable. The beginning of the next line waits: "To my family, friends, teachers…" and I know the missing word is one that indicates fondness and bonding but my mind keeps tossing up "aversion" or "animosity". No. I see suddenly how I have been angry. Life's ordinary disappointments, accepted and signed for as mine, have been piling up, a barricade holding closed the door of my heart. I ask simply for an open heart and hold that thought through the walk.

Back sitting I begin the chant again and there it is: "affinity". The word is there as if it were never gone. I feel an involuntary smile. Affinity with all beings. All of us who are imperfect, who suffer. Who try our best, take a step forward, and a step back, and keep on trying. The smile and the thought open a space. This space is the opening of the heart. A little light, a little lightness. This path requires balance after all, balance between the gravity of yearning and the lightness of an open heart.

### Puzzles

When I first felt the falling off of body and mind I thought I had arrived. In some place where peace was complete, where I floated free…no, where I disappeared altogether and achieved some new level of experience. But this seems now to be a place I visit in sitting from time to time, a place that is serene and soothing, but not a place apart from this place at all. And I wonder even if I should be pleased to go there sometimes. Being here…feeling the pen in my hand, the table beneath my forearm, the cold draught at my back, sniffling to avoid reaching for another kleenex, this is where I need to be. Mindfulness, not mindlessness. And so more contradictions and a confusion my discursive thought processes cannot sort out. This is all there is. There are so many of these tangles in the teachings. Tangles in my understanding. This is another place to open, giving up the struggle to understand in the conventional way. It's not about cramming for an exam.

How do we speak of looking within when there is no one looking? It is only a convention of speech then. No referent at all. Though "I" am not, I say "I look", "I sit", "I speak", "I see". When I first began practice with my distance teacher, I recall her suggesting to me to say it differently when I labeled experience: seeing, looking, sitting, speaking, thinking. Drop the "I". Note the "is-ness" of experience alone.

Struggling with this now, my mind settles into a soft state as I lift my head and gaze at the sifting snow on the deck. This morning I had some timeless surreal experience that is like a koan itself. I had set my alarm for 7:00am to allow a rare sleep-in. I was weary when I woke to the bell but I knew that was because of the late working nights I've put in working the kennel alone for awhile with my partner away. The bell tolled again as I tried to talk my body into rising. I turned it off. I showered. With the shower and then sorting a load to wash and making coffee and laying out vitamins and meds for the boys, taking my own, pouring coffee and reading Dogen, I came to 7:47, then nearly 8:00 as I went outside. I fed the cats and gave Jet, our dog, a fresh drink and biscuits. Did the kennel pee breaks and cleaning and breakfasts for the eight dogs here. When I came in, it was still 7:47. I thought my watch had stopped but every clock says the same. And checking the setting of my alarm I found it set for 7:00 as I thought. Where is this hour I'm missing? I feel like Bill Murray in *Groundhog Day*, waking to relive the same day over and over. Is it a mistake or some jump in the snapshots of time? Why does my rational mind not insist on a mistake, an explanation? Instead I feel an odd acceptance of the notion of no time and a clear experience of this.

Dogen again, commenting on our clumsy search for truth. "It is laughable to watch a person tearing apart the boat looking for the sword that fell into the water." To search your pockets for the key you left on the shop counter. To look through the fridge for the apple someone else ate the evening before. How often do we exert our energies in fruitless searches, in the wrong directions, in mistaken assumptions? Yet the person who tears apart the boat in search of the sword must not have known it fell over the side. Didn't hear the splash. What am I missing then? What piece of information did I miss that I look in the wrong way, in the wrong places for the sword of truth. The sword of truth. The image is apt. Swords are beautiful and dangerous. Gleaming and shimmering. Even the plain blade has beauty and the handle, made for grasping, is often intricate and amazing in detail. The way it feels in your hand can be a delight. The weight and molding. Yet a sword's beauty often makes me shiver and shrink away. I cannot deny their beauty. I cannot forget their danger. The pain and injury they can so easily inflict. Like the truth. The truth of impermanence and mortality. Is it this involuntary retreating that makes me close my ears to the splash, turn my back as the metal sinks beneath the water's surface, gazing instead at the solid wooden deck of the boat, straining to find the gleam of metal beneath a coil of rope, jutting out from under a wooden bench.

# 15  Watching

Submerge yourself in a simple "watching" activity. Whether you're watching the fish in an aquarium, the flames of a campfire, the setting of the sun, the leaves moving in the wind, be still for a significant measure of time (15-20 minues at least) and allow yourself to do "just" this.

**Visiting Birken**

Why do I come here? The exquisite silence is a draw. Walking outside on the snowy drives and paths, the placing of each slow step fills all my hearing. No traffic hum. No roaring snow machine engines. When I pause, the tip tapping of dead leaves in the wind, clinging to dark-armed trees is all I hear.

What do I value most here? The silence. Absolutely. But the serenity and harmony too. No sharp words or tones. No tight knot of anxiety in my breast. No being "on". Roles abandoned for a time. Moving task to task in the surreal sense of being no one, going nowhere. When I sit, I'm there. When I watch the birds, I'm there. When I wash dishes, I'm there. Dropping into bed early is fine. Just sleep. No sense of things left undone, of resentment over no time for me. Oddly, "me" retreats when it's given no agenda. No longer protective of the tidbits of private space or time it greedily grasps for in the busy world.

I love the shine and order of this place. The glossy floor of the sala, the tall windows, the gleaming white Buddha, the tiny, organized rooms and the cupboards for shoes at the door, the labels on the coldroom shelves.

All the rooms are simple and pleasant, but I have been assigned a lovely room this stay. First floor in a curving hallway down from a steward's room. The only first floor residents, we will share the large white bathroom between us. I have two long windows on one wall and sliding doors to a balcony, where a note on the glass politely requests the door not be used in the winter.

There is still light filling the room as I write, and all the world of snow and sky and trees beyond. I fit the black jersey sheets I brought over the foam pad on the narrow bed and scrounge two comforters from the hall closet for warmth. The bright red and white one I put on top…its vibrancy pleases me in this room of white pine and white walls. My clothes are unpacked and piled neatly on shelves in the box closet, the white curtain drawn to hide them. The floor is painted wood with a tatami mat under the square desk-table I write at and a pretty white rug with pink and blue borders and flowers. A frame stretched with white canvas separates my half from an unused side where another similar bed and amenities await, but I am told that the rooms are deliberately kept to one occupant for the Great Silence of January through March.

I was picked up at the airport by one steward, then we gathered a second who had been grocery shopping, before driving here. This second steward was a guest here when we met before; he arrived when I was leaving at the end of my last stay. He applied then for an open steward position and was pleased to be accepted. He tells me it took him only three weeks to close shop on his life in Vancouver, get rid of 95% of his possessions and settle in here. He is grateful and pleased with the transition, tentatively refreshing his driving skills to renew the license he let lapse more than five years ago. Driving is a necessary skill for the stewards who must commute to Kamloops for errands and appointments and often taxi guests and monks as well.

I reflect on this capacity and willingness to pare down. The things I love here. The life I have at home and the desire to bring more simplicity to that.

No one appears at teatime. I choose a book from the library shelves and return to my room to read by flashlight. It is not dark enough yet to warrant room lights.

They are conscious here of being off the grid. Producing their own power by solar and supplementing with diesel/propane in the interim. Today, a new experiment means closing down the kitchen fridge and moving food to the cold room and/or the re-freezerator there.

I do not mind this elusiveness of others either. This is a "home", warmer and more inviting than any hotel, and not empty. Yet silent and I have solitude. Quite perfect.

I have been watching my state of mind. I am not lonely or sad at this point. Often I must transition on retreats, feeling guilt over abandoning my family, feeling fear and remorse over the time I am losing with my sons, time that is not available again. Yet, it is simply true that they are growing and leaving me.

At evening meditation, the pull of the room is physical with the soft light, the deep blackness beyond the windows. At the beginning of retreat because of my zeal, I work to remember patience with body and mind. "Come here now, sit and be calm, be quiet awhile." The mind may be unruly for a time, suggesting amusing thought detours, and then suddenly it "agrees" to settle on the breath. This is a pattern I know. I come here for the time retreat allows to make this settling my only task. So that, at home again, in the world, this pathway is so well-worn, the tangle of busy-ness cannot obscure it.

### Being Still

"Be still and know that I am God." This is a biblical quotation I see many places. I'm sorry I have not memorized its verse location. I am reading it now in a non-fiction book by the novelist Sue Monk Kidd. Here she looks at it as an injunction to wait. Move neither forward nor back. Be still. I think of the Quaker way to "pray always" and the Buddhist practice path I am on myself... to be here, now. Present. Mindful. This is like this.

Last night I was weary and exhausted. Dropping one of my medications because of potential longterm side effects and here I am: nauseous, stomach pain, back pain, fatigue. So, as illness does, this slowed me down. I drift. And I began to reflect again, as I need to, on the "doing" that fills so much of my life. I want to learn to be and not to do so much. To be still. In that stillness I find peace. Serenity. Connection. Forgiveness. Tolerance. Compassion. And once more I know why these are so elusive in a world wound up and doing. Going always. Addicted to movement and progress.

Change comes without our pushing. And when we're still we move with it, a petal on the wave, not a motorboat lurching and screaming and beating against the wind and water, smothering sound, polluting water and air. There is a deep yearning in me for stillness. Yet I am afraid of what sometimes seems a tearing away from this life. Looking to force changes. I am beginning to see that being still here, in this life, is what I should allow. Then drift on the wave of change and see what comes. It is not knowing God as I was taught about Him as a child, but touching the mystery inside and outside, encompassing life. Some call this God. Why not? Language and labels are superimposed on what is felt, what is known before it is named. Just be still.

See the fears. In the mirror these days I see the puffy eyelids that always indicate I am tired...often that I'm ill. This is like this. Investigate the body, the feelings. Do not get caught up in concepts and analysis and circles of thinking. For awhile I seem to build a bridge over fear, then I feel the boards shifting and I look down into widening spaces. I have to be careful how I place my feet.

Stillpoint. What does this mean exactly? I find it on the cushion most days. Sometimes at odd moments during the day triggered by a bird song, the light through the trees, the spangle of stars across the clear black sky, even the way a dog snuggles into my neck or the smell of cut grass. A moment that centers and pulls both inward and outward and there it is…the stillpoint.

Exploring not just illness, and always the tangle of family, but the changes of mid-life. Loss of my parents. Both pain and freedom. No need to live to their expectations any longer nor to worry about their being wounded by my choices. Young children grown to the point that they (and I) need the letting go to begin. Stepping off the treadmill/away from the escalator and sitting back to let it be. "Wisdom," Sue Monk Kidd says, " is not a place to arrive at but a way of traveling." OK.

"Do not waste time" is the closing line of the Zen Sandokai. But this does not mean to use every moment in getting things done. Rather, spend the moments, travel, wisely. Find my breath, touch a cold metal gate, see the glint of ice, feel a doggy nose in my bare palm, and know I do not need anything else.

### Particles and Waves

First full day at the monastery. Beginning a couple of retreat days as prelude to Upasika training. I have been thinking I'm more *here* than I've ever been. It's a bit like yin, learning to surrender. In three or five minutes you feel the body release, let go to gravity. In months, then years of practice this is more readily available. So with mindfulness. Years of practice and the surrender deepens.

Birken is like a candle to me. Like an invitation. Yet I absolutely feel something indescribably different this time, with this longed for opportunity opening. From the moment I left home, a spiraling inward, disappearing. For now anyway my stubborn mind gets it, what it is to release.

I went for a walk this morning. The trees here, like those at home, are barely budding, not the full green of Kamloops, of the valley. A chill wind shushing through the trees. Clouds on the move. Such solitude on the walk. My feet crunching sand and gravel. The swing of joints, strength of body, even the discomfort of the cold. Just sensation. Pleasant and unpleasant finding a sweet harmony, only differing voices in the moment's chorus.

Coming back I was pulled down to the marsh. Watching a goose, some ducks. The large goose nearly still, majestic. The ducks noisy and exuberant, dancing and flapping along the surface as if to take flight, though it was all for show. Near the goose, smaller birds. Five of them. I squinted into the light dancing on the water. Are these her goslings? Is this possible? Why don't I know the seasons and times of these things? It seems early to me, but I don't know. Big enough to venture away in circles, though they seemed tethered to her stillness.

The wind pushed the water south in tiny waves or big ripples, depending on your perspective as duck in the water or human on the shore, I suppose. Then no warning and I suddenly felt pinned down while also adrift.

A thought came. In quantum theory the wave and particle conundrum. A wave collapsing into particle when it is observed. That's it exactly, the nature of this "I". A wave of possibility and then pinned down into a particular, a particle, by being observed. Sometimes the observers are external. Our parents, our partners, society. What they see, judge, expect, believe. But sometimes the observer is internal. When we buy into those versions of a particular self, we embroider them…seem to give them dimension. We move in and get furniture and make them "real". So I was thinking of this, and how to step out of it. How to return to the wave of possibility.

All of us, waves of possibility. Consciousness/awareness is just this. Waves. The being aware seeming to collapse this into individuals, into many. One, then many. No. One and many all at the same time, depending on your perspective: This is too difficult to set down in concepts, but on the shores of the marsh Air/wind/breath, water/marsh/blood/tears, earth/grasses/bones, fire/sun/life/heat… it all seemed so completely graspable…even grasped. I am and I am not. The relative and the absolute. Formed and formless. No wonder the writing of Zen poets is so inscrutable.

# 16  Making Change

When you are stuck in a spin cycle of thoughts that wind you further and further into anxiety, grief or anger, try standing on one leg. What you'll notice is that the effort required to do this brings you back into your body and sticks a finger in the spinning wheel of thought. If you're a yogi, you might want to try a balance asana instead. (Tree? Dancer?)

**Joy**

I've been thinking about intentions in my practice. Something that comes to mind is a card I have among the "reminders" near my altar. This card sets out the "seven factors of awakening". It's a sketch of a teeter-totter, with "mindfulness" as the pivotal pyramid on which the horizontal line rests. Each side holds a set of three qualities. On one side are the active ingredients: energy, joy and investigation. On the other the still ingredients of tranquility, concentration and equanimity. This diagram helps me to remember the importance of balance in my practice.

I've been thinking that my current practice leans heavily toward the "still" side. Tranquility, serenity. Both are compelling to me. And equanimity is what I seek when life becomes too much or triggers my innate anxiety response. Concentration, I recognize as having grown over the years of my practice. But on the active side I feel less sense of how to proceed.

I know that making room for retreats, that spending time with others of like-mind are energy making activities for me. And when I am still enough, investigation is more fruitful. Joy, however, can be elusive. Writing this though, I see suddenly that joy is a product of stillness and tranquility for me...just not the "skipping through the meadow singing" joy. Rather a sense of the moment being "right", a sense of calm. Indeed, I suppose that is the very compelling element that draws me to stillness. Why I discovered a surprising affinity with silence and stillness. So perhaps it is a semantic question. How do I define joy?

Years ago I named my violin "Joy" when I bought her. Joy means an untainted happiness to me. By naming her so, I wanted to remind myself not to get too grim and determined and accomplishment centered in taking on this new venture. I wanted to just let joy blossom. But at the same time, joy is not equivalent to pleasure. It is deeper. Steadier. Less fleeting. Joy can accompany sorrow or loss. Watching my children grow I feel this very volatile mix. It is this that can make joy elusive for me, I think. When it is mixed with pain I step back and cannot let it be to its greatest extent. The joy in this world is colored by conflict and threats and fragility. It is joy that is like lovely broken glass glittering in the sun. Dangerous, a little. Deceptive, a little. And I want to learn how to still be openhanded in my holding of it, not passing it by because of fear.

I recognize in my "anxious" nature, my set-point, a kind of fearfulness that undermines joy and perhaps makes the draw to stillness an escape valve...a place not to feel fear and grief and disappointment, rather than a place to feel true contentment. Hmm.

On my shelves is a book by a much loved author, Mary Rose O'Reilly. The book is called *The Love of Impermanent Things*. The title captures thus the painful joy of the sensory world, of loving what cannot last. Coming back again to considering my intention, I see that I am on track afterall. Going deeper with tranquility, with concentration, bounces the end of the teeter totter against the solid ground of experience, gives me stability to investigate and then lifts my heart. When my hands are free, not holding on in fear, not fighting off what I don't want to experience, then my heart lifts in a joy grounded in clarity and truth.

**Life as an Alien**

Into my second decade of practice and I find outside reassurances of spiritual maturing, practice evolving. I have felt these turnings over the years, internally, most often provoked by retreats and more intensive sitting and immersion than daily life seems to permit. And here's the thing: though I value and yearn for these pure practice spaces, I've found that more and more this awareness, this mindfulness is what I do. My thoughts and emotions are accompanied by the observer who looks at them in practice terms.

And so last night, listening to Ajahn Sona's Dhamma talk for my Birken cataloguing work, I find references to the out-of-syncness with the world I am so conscious of now. That watching people in a mall, I could be from some alien planet. That sense of separation, though, is melded to a deep sense of connection, two sides of a coin. Look how we struggle to be happy! Look how we make mistakes again and again!

This lesson repeated in the Zen teachers I've been reading in the last couple of weeks. First Thich Nhat Hanh and now Charlotte Joko Beck. Their practicality and bluntness can be helpful. Joko Beck's reassurance that the seeing of our human-ness, the ego and self-ness that arises over and over is the practice maturing. Living in this awareness constantly. Falling forward into suffering is how I think of it, instead of back...like the progress I made as a teen in water skiing attempts. When I fall so that the pain is clear and in my face, I know the cause, I see the process. She mentions "life as atonement"...not guilt, but refusing to add to the world's suffering.

Knowing the reality of the suffering that is inevitable for human beings, sometimes I feel this little spring of sorrow open. The sorrow is for the realization that things are not, cannot be, as I once thought they were: That romantic love, family love, good intentions would shape a protected universe of unadulterated joy. I think God was in there somewhere too. From this realization at first I fell into a bleak place of no joy. The dark night of the soul so often referred to in literature and in spiritual teachings.

And now, over years of practice, emerging into a realization and acceptance of what is: this world, both paradise and hell. And what it is to be human, the line of good and evil running through each of us. And what it is to be mortal... to know impermanence and its inevitability. And yet to feel the joy in that alongside the suffering. To know that the mistake of imagining separation, obsessing with the pursuit of personal happiness (me against the world), is what causes the pain.

And yet, this body, this human embodiment and these habits of mind, they will "wish". They yearn for a fairy tale world of happily ever after. This is the seed of that sweet sorrow. Now though it is like a pinprick, like a flash of too bright light where tears spring unbidden and my throat clenches.

Yet, recognition of truth brings a smile. This is what I see in the gently upturned lips of the Buddha as he is conventionally shown in pictures and images. Contentment and serenity are possible and only out of reach to the extent that I am unwilling to reach. The central question of the journey: will ego keep hold or awareness allow flight?

## Working With Mantras

I have a habit of keeping index cards near the small altar in my sitting space. I like to write on them short teachings or mantras, or sometimes lists that are helpful in my practice. What I've found is that a particular short teaching will speak to me very strongly for a time, addressing what is going on for me in my life, and being a great aid in working through what life is offering. Then, inevitably, another teaching and/or another phase will take over in the constant change that is life, and I might almost forget the "mantra" that was so fruitful for a time. Paging through these cards periodically I have discovered so often that the path is a loop, or a series of loops, and I will find a time again when what was helpful once before is exactly what I needed reminding of. Lately an interesting coming together has occurred between a previous such "mantra" and a new one.

Some time back I began to work with the phrase "just what the body does". This is a clear and gentle reminder that this body I think of as mine is a biological organism, subject to the laws of living things. That is, despite my efforts to keep it healthy, it will sometimes sicken; despite my efforts to keep youthful vigour and strength, it will inevitably age. And, hardest of all to accept perhaps, despite my inability to imagine my eventual death, the passing away of this body, this will be the case. Human beings have a strong sense of self. And because the body seems to serve and obey in so many ways, we come to think of it as ours and in some way under our control. Me, my, mine…the central error of ego, enters into our lives on many levels, but it is especially strong in the case of our physical bodies. And yet it becomes clear on reflection, that the body is vulnerable in so many ways. And being subject to aging, illness and injury are "just what the body does". This reflection may seem like mere words, but taken as a perspective to work with pain, with grey hair, with wrinkles and scars and limps and unwelcome diagnoses, then carried into meditation as a way of looking at what arises in the body, it can become a lens for truth. We do what we can do, eating in a healthy way, getting exercise that makes sense, not throwing ourselves into danger, but, in the end, the body will do what the body does. It is not a failing or a mistake to grow old nor to sicken. When the mind is still and calm and such a way of observing is used, there is peace with what is.

Yet, for some reason, I never thought to apply this formula to the mind. Recently, reading a wise teacher's account of his own practice experience I came across the corollary that gave me pause: "just what the mind does". The teacher was speaking of the experience we have all had if we have done any amount or kind of meditation. We place our attention on the meditation object and then in a little time or maybe after a good long while, we find that we are "thinking" of other things. We are feeling sleepy perhaps, or we are remembering the lyrics of a song, or we are wishing for the meditation time to go quickly, or we are unable to quit obsessing on an itch in the sole of our left foot. It could be anything. Teachers may give us a variety of instructions but generally it amounts to just noticing what has happened and coming back to the meditation object.

Over time, however, we begin to think we are failing. Once again, caught in the central error of ego, we see the mind as me, my and mine. We fail to acknowledge that thinking is "just what the mind does". When we notice this movement of the mind, it is nothing to be bothered by any more than the aging of the body, which we notice in the mirror, or the illness of the body, which medical tests reveal.

The secret then is no great secret. Everything unfolds according to its nature. Picking up mantras such as these may mean that we are able to observe without clinging to some illusory ideal, and may come back to the meditation object without aversion and judgment. In understanding "what the body does and what the mind does", we relax into an acceptance that contrarily brings peace, and in the case of the mind, may even bring the stillness we were aiming for.

# 17  Gratitude

Remind yourself to be grateful today everytime you turn a tap and water is at hand, every time you flick a switch and light fills a room. These are simple "conveniences" that we forget to notice.

**Storehouse of the Mind**

How many blessings pass us by each day unnoticed? That's a question that mindfulness practice raises. But how many do we note and too soon forget? This second question arises for me today because of my habit of keeping a (nearly) daily gratitude journal. I've been doing this since 2000, marking the new millennium with a new habit, and I've now almost filled my fourth small, thick volume.

I don't often go back to re-read, but it was doing a little of this that got me thinking about memory. Another of those impermanent things all life is made of. My journal entries are simple lists, ranging from three or four to a dozen things, depending on the day. Sometimes each is a few words, sometimes a paragraph. And there are lots of repetitions. For the blessings of a life are often in those things we value and note for periods of time. But these things fold into time and are replaced by others and it takes this physical record to provide the deep probe that unearths those of long ago.

There are the foundational blessings of an affluent and privileged life: A home, reliable water access, electricity, vehicles, plenty of food in vast variety. Those of being a resident of planet earth: blue skies, sunshine, rain, green trees, birdsong, the surprise of a deer on our lawn or a moose in the driveway. Those that come from being encircled by loving family and good friends: phone calls, shared meals, letters and gifts, being cared for when illness visits, help provided when it's needed or asked for, laughter.

But what struck me in looking through these journals were the single, unique moments: A comic strip that touched home and let me laugh at myself and let go a little of something taken too seriously. A movie that brought me to tears or laughter and opened my heart to the wide variety of lives lived. A horse nuzzling my hand or breathing a grassy sigh against my neck. A passage in a novel that had me closing the book to reflect on some new insight. Someone taking time to help with dropped mail. A song on the radio that moved me to tears. My mother's handwriting on a recipe card cracking open my heart with longing shot through with appreciation for her love. One of my small sons bringing me lukewarm instant coffee he'd made and hugging himself with the pleasure of the accomplishment. Earth on my hands, bees buzzing and hot sun on my neck as I gardened. Teaching my sons silly songs as we worked together cleaning ditches in the spring. Missing pets found.

At the time that I wrote these entries and the hundreds more that fill these little journals, these moments were front and center in my mind and heart. The abundance that good days bring or the fleeting moments that softened days of pain or fear, loss or hurt. And now, without these written words, how many of them would come back to mind?

In mindfulness training we learn to be present but to hold the moment lightly, not clinging and wishing for this to last. But most important we are taught to notice the moments as they fly. It is important too, I think, as some teachers acknowledge, to linger deliberately in that noticing, when the flavor is pleasant and sweet. Trauma and pain often lock themselves into our memories. I don't need words on a page to remind me of time spent at the side of each of my parents in their final days and final moments. I don't need to read accountings of the deep hurt of relationships that faltered, of decisions that led to loss or pain. But the moments in each day that are sweet are many and coming day on day they tumble into the storehouse of the mind in the shining disarray of a dragon's treasure trove. How can one little jewel make itself known in the tumble of sparkle and gold?

And so, I like to linger with a sweet moment. Just breathe it in. Know its flavor. And I also value this habit of reflection, setting down the moments that gleam in each day, cataloguing the plenty that is my life.

### Strange Blessing

Over the holidays I was fortunate enough to catch a minor cold bug. Just the niggling sort that makes life a little inconvenient. That reminds you of the great gift of good health, and that slows you down some because it saps your energy. The timing was ideal, really, because there was already some space carved into the usual schedule of the days. Not so many places to be. The temptation in such times, for me, is to fill the time with home-things that I normally haven't time for. Baking, cleaning, sorting, organizing. As well as self-directed writing projects that have been put on hold during busy times.

But a head cold is the perfect antidote to such plans. The mind gets fuzzy. The body gets heavy. It's difficult to stir up the energy to do much that means moving out of a comfortable chair. Especially if that chair is in proximity to a cozy fireplace.

So once the family part of the vacation wrapped up and my darlings went home, I let myself cocoon. Lots of reading, lots of drifting moment to moment, lots of reflection and meditation. And maybe a few yin poses that didn't require bending over and disturbing the sinuses.

Coming out the other side, there is a resurgence of energy that floods into the quiet pool of "just this" that I'd been dwelling in. But perhaps because I'd deepened the pool with meditation and not just vegetation, I find the energy enters like a deep undercurrent of welcome heat, rather than a whirlpool of agitation. I'm thinking it is a shame that life can become so busy in a way that is subtle enough not to be noticed. A commitment here, a meeting there, an appointment, a few errands, a deadline or two. And the day begins to be measured in ticked off boxes in a day-timer rather than the precious breath flow of one's own life, days that won't come again. This even when meditation is part of every day for me, even when mindfulness is an ongoing effort. Still, there can be a false sense of the urgency of "things to do".

Thich Nhat Hanh talks of gratitude for my non-headache, my non-toothache. Today, as the breath I am focused on comes more smoothly, and my closed eyes are without stinging and tearing, I am grateful for my non-cold. Yet, I wonder why it is so difficult to feel this gratitude profoundly when I haven't just been sick. Our memories are both long and short, aren't they? We hold to hurts and losses and preserve them in our mind-cellars, yet we also, simultaneously, seem to forget so quickly some kinds of pain, some kinds of interruptions to the normal. I wonder if by next week my watching of the breath will contain this great pleasure in its ease, or whether by then the ease will be "just what is" until it is interrupted in some way again.

My day-timer pages are busy again. Classes and appointments and errands. When I reflect on this, I think that there are two kinds of clearing I could do. I could clear the pages, an external task, or I could clear my heart and mind, an internal one. I don't have to believe the voices of urgency. I can fall into each moment and be with the driving, the shopping, the waiting, the talking, the listening, the doing. We often hear the injunction to "be" and not "do", but this isn't really the "either/or" it looks like. The days do not have to be lived as a series of busy-tasks, interrupted by mindful breaks, but rather can be lived with full attention, being and doing braided together. I've done a little arm chair retreat over the holiday season. And my wise head cold teacher has been a good guide, bestowing on me this strange blessing to carry forward into the new year.

## What's Cooking?

Where do we live? When we're asked this question, most of us think of the external world, a geographical location perhaps, a place name, a country, or maybe the kind of terrain that characterizes our physical home: mountains, desert, coast, forest, prairie. But even when we are nomadic or rootless in this world, we live, most importantly, in our heart-mind for this is where our personal world is created.

Externally, we may have little control over the weather or conditions. We may not be able to live in the type of dwelling we'd most like, or in a location we prefer. We may not live with or near the people we'd most like to associate with. The Buddha taught about a different kind of dwelling, one we build through skillful effort and attention. This list is most often translated as The Divine Abidings (*Brahma Vihara*). I like this translation because to me the word "abide" means to linger, to stay, and so the list describes places that are lovely to hang out in. So, as a kitchen may be the heart of a home of bricks or wood, Divine Abidings are the product of the heart's kitchen, a place of creativity and nurturing and sharing. A place of warmth and possibility.

*Metta*, or loving-kindness, the first in this short list, is the most familiar. Sometimes translated as loving-friendliness, we know what it implies. The difficulty is nurturing it. How do I create an attitude that is lovingly accepting of myself and others? An inner voice that speaks with patience and in gentle tones. A heart that keeps an open door. This isn't something that happens naturally in a consistent way. Like everyone, I have good-hearted moods and moments, but maintaining this attitude towards myself and others in the midst of mistakes and hurry and disagreement is something quite different. Yet, an abiding is a place to loiter, like the kitchen can be in a physical home. I have to be active and cook up this emotional food served from the heart's kitchen, recognizing the ingredients that will result in success. As moments of loving-kindness arise, I pay attention. What's happening? What is making this possible? What conditions can I put in place to make this last? I am attentive to the process, a metta chef. Tasting the moments and choosing the right ingredients.

*Karuna*, or compassion, is the second in the list. For me, these rooms are adjoining. Like an open-area floor design where kitchen and living room run together. When we cook up enough metta, it overflows into the living space of karuna. There is enough for everyone. I recognize in the difficulties of others, the same difficulties that plague myself. I see in the mistakes of others what I too do or am capable of. I nurture both forgiveness and a wish for well-being.

Compassion is not a gratitude for my own escape from the hardship others experience, a gratitude that might move me to "help" in a way that separates giver and receiver. Instead it is holding to each other in this rocky boat of life. It is seeing the universality of the human struggle, and having a generous and free hand with the fruits of the kitchen's labors.

*Mudita* is translated as sympathetic joy or empathetic joy. It is akin to compassion, the little sunroom annex perhaps off the living room. This is where the more fortunate have found a place in the sun. I can envy them, feel jealousy or craving and be pushed by these dark emotions into a shady corner by myself in my misery. Or I can rejoice in their well being and happiness such that I find the sunshine spreading beyond the alcove to include me wherever I am.

Equanimity or *upeka* is the fourth of the Divine Abidings. This is the place of calm and acceptance. When the metta cake falls, the living room is in shambles and the clouds block the sun, I might be able to abide here. If I'm invited into the best chair in the sunny alcove and served generously from the feast, I might be able to abide here. If I've been mindful and doing the work, both cooking and serving with open heart, this is the place of wisdom that opens for me in good times and in bad. A place where I stay balanced and centered come what may, knowing that I carry my abiding place with me.

To have access to divine abiding is not to stumble on a mystery or to make a lottery win. It is the product of what's cooking in the heart's kitchen.

# 18  Expectations

Is there something in your life that was once a treat but has become something you "expect" or "require"? Ice coffee in the afternoon? A massage every month? A drink before dinner? Try going without this the next time or two the regular time for doing or getting this comes up. Just notice how wanting colors the mind and the moment.

**Big Mind**

Mornings on school days are chaotic from the time I wake the boys until they get on the bus. They are either tired and grumpy with me and each other, or giddy and goofy, unable to focus on any task: eating breakfast, dressing, putting on boots! It is a cycle of prodding and helping and hurrying them along and too often I feel frazzled and angry along the way.

Meditation is teaching me to breathe and look closely during these ordinary times. What do I notice about my feelings when I look closely? Just the volume level and physical play...pushing, hollering, laughing, goofy voices... are abrasive to me in the mornings, my "favorite" time of the day. When left to my own devices, I choose silence, walking, reading, meditation, solitude in the morning. There is pain and loss here beneath the anger as I experience the contrast between what I want and what is. My preferences are not being met. If/When I lose control and am not able to let the intention to chastise them arise without acting on that intention, then I add the emotional tone of blame, feeling immediately guilty for my outbursts.

I am learning, though, about big mind. The "I" who experiences the anger and the guilt is like a closed fist. Big mind is like an open hand.

In opening in this way, and continuing to look closely, I see how much more often (though not always, alas) I am capable of equanimity at these times. Irritation arises, it runs like water over that open hand and it falls away. I let it go, moving on through the steps in getting ready for the day without feeling personally "attacked" by child energy, boistorousness and indifference to schedules. I am often now even able to hear in my head the voices of my own childhood ("be on time", "stay on task") and not act on these directives nor feel less for not having done so.

Anger is an interesting phenomenon. When "buttons" are pushed, I see others as doing this *to me* and my mind narrows around the need to reassert control, to stop the behavior that is triggering my anger. When I can (and it's difficult) pull back and open to big mind, I feel a sense of relief and calm. "I" am no longer under attack and instead of *feeling* anger, I *see* the constant shifting of thoughts and feelings in any interaction.

Strangely, even pleasure can be a button. When my wants are met in a warm memory or happy moment, and I hold tight, I am immediately resentful of interrupting thoughts or needs. Again it is opening to big mind that allows the moment or memory to arise, treasures it, but lets it slip into the next moment as it must. In fact, when I cling to pleasure, narrow in and hold tight, I lose it more quickly to the unpleasant in irritation or anger or regret.

Narrowing in leads to judgement of self and others. I want to "fix" what I am or what someone else is. And suffering then comes as a sense of defeat or pointlessness or sorrow. If I am able to shift to big mind, this does not occur because I allow the feeling or thought to flow through rather than creating a person (me or other) to blame and fix.

Narrowing in is conducive to fear too. I can create whole scenarios when I narrow in, especially regarding my kids: fear for their safety, fear for their futures, their health and their happiness. Big mind prevents this chaining although, I admit, this is the hardest one yet for me, the place where "I" and "mine" take root most readily.

Sometimes people come to meditation as a form of stress relief, rather than thinking about spiritual growth. But practising with opening to big mind makes it clear to me that these are not separate intentions or purposes at all. Learning to notice when I narrow in and learning to move as far as I am able into big mind gives me both a sense of unity with all that is and the immediate experience of a sweet release from negativity, anxiety and pain.

## Sky

There is a half-grown stray cat 60 feet up a pine tree just behind our house. Some possibly food-related scuffle with a jay or squirrel and our own cat popping out of bed for his breakfast frightened him and he climbed the tree without thinking. Straight up. We've named him/her "Sky" though we've only seen him by tipping our heads back and straining our eyes.

We hear him cry. He's been up there three days. He won't respond to our pleas to come down. We can't reach him, not even close, with our tallest ladder. We put tuna on the ground and our cat ate it. We put tuna at the top of the ladder and our cat climbed up, ate it and fell. He landed well, unhurt. He doesn't think before acting. He's never terrified it seems.

Sky didn't think when he was climbing but he's thinking now and he's frozen into place up there. And our fire department says they don't have the equipment to rescue him. And last night it snowed.

When I think of how cold and hungry and miserable he must be, I'm a little overwhelmed with my helplessness. Something happens. That's all. A stray cat went up one of our pines and we don't know how to help him down. That's all.

It's a day later and the Sky has fallen…or climbed down or something and disappeared. And it turns out we now can see how much we'd all invested emotionally in his rescue and hoping he'd become part of our family. More than hoping, I guess. Expecting that would be the case. But things happen. And when he/she finally came down, we weren't around and he must have hit the ground running. Far from here now. And there's something I want to say about this. Something about naming.

How we try to pin things down. Make them understandable, keep them in our control. How laying claim allows us to imagine that we will have something to say about the destiny of that which we name. Whether it's a cat in a tree, our own children, the job we want, the place we live. But in fact it's all in motion, isn't it, and we're in there too. So it's more like billiard balls passing on a table. Odd for one billiard ball to think it has any control over another. They influence each other. Ricocheting. Meeting for split seconds and moving apart. That's all.

I don't know where I'm going with this. It just seemed I was so vastly disappointed when Sky was suddenly not there. Relieved but disappointed. And I saw I'd already imagined a future with him/her in it, already imagined stroking the tigery head and calming him after his descent. Winning his affection. But he's gone. And, as my son said, "that sucks!"

## Something to Look Forward To

It's a habit in our home for my husband and I to compare our agendas for the day as we finish breakfast. This is helpful in case we've forgotten each other's plans (a dentist appointment made months ago or lunch with a friend), if we need to team up for some items on the list (bathing the dog) or we're going in different directions but both counting on using the same vehicle (the truck for hauling, or the jeep for more economical gas use). But I've also noticed there's a tendency in this planning for me to build expectations of the day around some "event". Instead of a flow of moments, in this critical window of time, I am in danger of seeing the day as a page in my daybook, with tidy boxes for various activities. My mind immediately responds to the boxes with emotional labels. I like this, I don't like that. In this mental image, the enjoyable bits appear in highlighted marker and the boxes in between are shadowed grey.

I've been a practitioner for many years and it is my ongoing intention to develop continuity of mindfulness. So in cases like this, I follow the instruction to investigate. It seems a human tendency to think of our lives in segments of some kind: two weeks till a child's birthday, then a week until an uncle's visit, then just three weeks until vacation. We lean forward and rush through the time that is mere filler on the way to the next highlighted event.

Waking, we might be looking forward to that first coffee. We coax ourselves through mundane tasks by anticipating the ones we'll enjoy in the day. During a meal, we anticipate dessert. At concerts we wait to hear our favorite song. On days when we're tired we yearn the whole day for our bed. On nights we can't sleep we yearn for the alarm, and the night to be over. Experts who advise procrastinators and teach time management skills make use of this human tendency by telling us to break large tasks into smaller ones, and to build in rewards when we reach certain points in the process.

My ongoing investigation was nudged recently in reading a novel where a lovable and self-indulgent character justifies her various addictions, from food to cigarettes, by saying "you need something to look forward to". Do we need something to look forward to?

Where does this perceived "need" come from? There is some fallacy at work here about the nature of happiness. When pleasure and happiness are seen as the same thing we form confused priorities and make mistaken choices. It isn't only that we have been conditioned to expect instant gratification, it is also that we have internalized the belief that everything should entertain us. From the food we eat, to the news we watch, to the work we do, we seem too often to be guided by two standards: It should be "fun", and if it can't be fun, it should be over with quickly. Where does this idea come from?

The nature of the mind itself, I think, is at the core of this. It's easy to get a baby to eat candy, much harder to convince him/her to eat oatmeal. Our mind is a baby. What stimulates and entertains, what draws our attention is like candy. TV or study for an exam? Do your taxes or read a good book? Hmmm. We've all been there. It looks like it's a matter of self-discipline, of will power, to learn to do the harder, less appealing thing. But practicing mindfulness reveals that this is not the case. Will power is not at the center, it's seeing how the mind works, so that we break through the confusion that makes us think we're making choices by always doing what we want.

We can be a puppet on the string of impulse for our entire lives. Or we can begin to pay attention. We can see the window of choice. And gradually, seeing this, we are given the opportunity to act in ways that are not instantly gratifying or instantly pleasurable. And here's the thing: When we do this, we discover a deeper happiness. I don't mean passing the exam or avoiding interest on our taxes. I mean discovering the joy inherent in each and every thing we do. The "something" to look forward to is passing by while our head is turned. It's here, in this moment, whatever it holds.

# 19 Self-talk

Sometimes our self-talk, self-judgments can be harsh and debilitating. If you notice this, try keeping a "kindnesses journal"...just a list of the little things you do each day that are kind or helpful to others. Read it over frequently. Realize your goodness.

**Passing Moments**

Watching how experience flows and shifts. These are moments passing: Equanimity. Companion to contentment. So interwoven are these two that the distinction is artificial almost, like sifting blue and yellow out of green: you know both are there when you gaze on the fresh green of the woods on a sunfilled morning, but it's all just brilliant and green to the eye. So, despite life's ups and downs, green is stable for me right now.

\*\*\*

I've been ill. Emptiness this morning following an odd sit. Peaceful. And then plunging into sad regretful memory of bad parenting moments when the boys were young. Loss of patience. Reactivity. Wishing I'd had this calm, this equanimity then. Ah, yearning. The root cause of suffering. So that now, nearly 20 years later, a memory causes pain, pricks tears in my eyes and a turning in my heart. The self. This is the subject of Dhamma study I do the last while. The no-position-taken view of the Buddha. No doctrines of existence or non-existence. Only this. Just this. So the self I create as a solid thing from this memory, in this moment, is a phantom only. An idea. A fleeting thought. How I have to work not to board the train that carries it into a long winding story. To stay here at this juncture, this breath and only note the face in the window, a blur as it whistles by. No nightmare ride then. I have enough presence not to go there. But a dark moment. A shadow. Grief in the window as it passes.

*\*\**

A mood like shifting sands this morning, lingering from the weekend. Not a roller coaster of ups and downs but a sense of unease, not quite sure of my footing. I want to delve and dig and try to figure it out but resist more than a surface dusting. No good reasons. A terrific storm Friday night with torrential rains beating up my coddled flower pots and washing areas of gravel into runnels in the driveway and piles in our "creek bed" laid beside the drive. The constant cloud movement is like a movie scene in fast forward time lapse and it gives rise to a sense of vertigo, human insignificance on this ball floating in space.

*\*\**

On the weekend a bout of world weariness and blues haunted me. The news full of all the problems of the world. The blundering of humans still pursuing ideas and territory as keys to happiness. But Monday morning a peaceful, clear and deep sit. Looking at my own anxiety. How I still hold to some deluded view that the world can be different. It is as it is. Through time human beings make these choices unable to see how their own views and desires are the roots of their pain. And in seeing my own confusion I feel my heart open and the aching drain and just a tenderness remain. The day goes on and I am balanced again. Seeing, but from a place of loving mindfulness. So different from letting myself fall weeping into the mud we've churned.

*\*\**

I lose it with our pup this morning when he scampers across the rug with muddy feet. Shouting at him and sending him to his kennel. Then I am quiet and stunned. There is such a fine line between repressing "bad" emotions and the more skillful holding and non-reacting to emotions that arise. So through the day I see disappointment in my "self" arise and try to hold this. Letting it be and letting it go. Not pushing it away. Seeing my labeling as "bad" but knowing this is labeling, part of the self-making I do that leads to reactivity, the human problem at the core of suffering. I talk to a good Dhamma friend who reminds me this is the work. So much more significant than the verbal tirade I slid into. I did not get lost in it. I saw it. I examine it. This is the path. He offers a lovely metaphor of an old road marked by "danger" signs. We went down there and got in trouble before. And for a long time we note the sign and drive by but one day we are distracted for just a moment and we make the turn again.

*\*\**

Yesterday a Dhamma talk and a poem. The poet said: "If I had my life to live over again I wouldn't change a thing, except to have my eyes more widely open."

### Mirror, Mirror

I can't say I'm familiar with, never mind well versed in, all spiritual traditions, but it seems to me from those I know a little about, that the importance of forgiveness is central to happiness and peace. I don't mean just external peace, as in a treaty or agreement or even a stand-off or cease fire, but internal peace, the state of mind that is perhaps arguably equivalent to happiness of any lasting kind.

Forgiveness is necessary in every relationship, not least of all the one we have with ourselves. When we act in a way that we are ashamed of or feel guilt or remorse around, we tend to add to the burden of the action by being unable to forgive ourselves. We carry a basket of "should haves and could haves" that only serves to weigh us down further in the muck of suffering. How do we move forward to higher and drier ground again if we don't release this weight?

No ordinary human is perfect. And even those of us who are striving to live our lives in a way that runs against the grain of what is ordinary, are ordinary ourselves. We might wish to have the patience of a saint, the courage of a martyr, the strength of a Greek hero and the determination of an Olympic athlete. Perhaps all these traits would be helpful in making the right choices all the time and following through on skillful intentions. Perhaps even one or two would help a lot. But we have what we have. Perhaps intermittent patience and little courage, a modicum of strength and fluctuating determination. Whatever package we have, it is what it is, and here is where we begin. So we train in ways to improve from there without always stopping to assess and scold ourselves. We need to learn forgiveness.

For me this begins with being able to face who I really am and not who I want to be and to love myself anyway. This isn't the natural way the mind works so I have to be willing to keep at it. Not to look away. Recently I've been dipping into watching some of the episodes in a Netflix series titled *Merlin*. Without going into a lot of detail about this fantasy series that takes great liberties with the Camelot legend, it's important to know that they use a film trick regarding "evil" sorcerers in the story. These sorcerers project an image of themselves that is convincing to those who deal with them. However, when sorcerers are glimpsed in a mirror, they appear as they really are. Obviously it's important to the success of the deception to keep mirrors covered.

This is something like what happens for most of us. Mindfulness is the mirror that reveals our true selves to ourselves. Unless we are mindful and deliberate in our investigations of our thoughts, intentions and desires, we are like those that meet the sorcerer, we are under a kind of enchantment. This enchantment is comforting and has its place in terms of self-esteem. It brings a superficial comfort to think of ourselves as the "good guy". The problem is that, just like in TV shows and stories, this simplistic vision of ourselves leads to simplistic visions of others. We are good, they are bad. We are right, they are wrong. When we begin to look into the mirror of mindfulness, we see our scars and wrinkles. That's when we need to be unflinching and love ourselves anyway. A large measure of this is to know that this is so for every one of us. When I see my own flaws and recognize that this is universally true of human beings…each of us is flawed and struggling to pretend it isn't so, then forgiveness begins. For me, and for others. It grows from the compassion of clear insight.

No bad guys here. Flawed humans. And the way out doesn't require the lies of cosmetic surgery and better lighting. The way out comes from looking clear eyed into the mirror. We are not striving to be other than what we are, but to see that beneath mistakes, judgments and actions that are not pretty to look at, there is a pure heart. Loving-kindness and unstinting effort will allow it to shine through.

### Lessons in Metta

A fall retreat. The days passing on winged feet. Meditation, walks, the labyrinth. Settling, not stirring up.

I request an interview and take a couple of practice "bumps" to the monk leading. There I stumble along trying to describe my quandary over metta meditation and those I love most dearly. In traditional metta, there is a progression that begins with sending loving-kindness to one's self, then to those whom one feels affinity with. Thirdly to neutral persons and finally to difficult people. Why, I ask, do I so often find dear ones reappearing in the category of "difficult" people? And why is it here that I find the arising of resentment and blame that block my heart? Not an easy confession.

Bhante touches the right thread immediately and the problem falls away. I need to back up in this progression I follow too hastily. Back up and send loving-kindness to me. Working, thus, on myself, to soften my heart and heal emotional wounds, loosen clinging that is the source of the pain that comes when one feels resentment or blame. Notice the attachment in the guise of love. Build my capacity for loving-kindness where ego-clinging is not a part.

Even before the interview I had given the day over to metta/loving-kindness meditation, but as I return to my seat with a new resolve, settling to the breath and this aching heart, I am surprised to find the fear stories that arise. This is the source, I see, of those blocks. Fear of pain, of conflict, of turmoil of any kind. I move from my head and the thought of fear down into my body. Finding the tension and tight breathing. Stay. Stay. Not creating pretty distractions and not pushing this unpleasant stuff away in the quest for momentary peace. Stay. Observe. Feel. Periodically, I am off on the thought train once again. Old lessons learned over and over. Notice this too, then return. Breath and body.

Thich Nhat Hanh speaks of cradling the wounded self, the imperfect self, as one would a child. "It's alright, dear one. You are loved. You are safe. You are accepted." Allowing these soothing inner voices to contain the pain, I see the struggles of an ordinary person here. No one wants to be miserable. I remember a teacher who said, no one sets that as an intention, yet we find our way there anyway. An inner smile. Back to feeling what I feel. Sending love. Opening the heart. It is a process.

The evening talk is on compassion. Bhante reminds us that when metta is cultivated in regular practice, compassion will naturally arise. Seeing one's own suffering clearly, compassion for the suffering of others finds its beginning. Compassion, he emphasizes, is not grief. Grief debilitates and does not allow us to be helpful so it is not a skillful response. Remembering when grief has overwhelmed me, in the case of my own losses or the losses of others, I know this to be true. Grief is a form of anger and confusion. A struggle against what is. Only seeing, accepting, surrendering, will allow movement toward one's own healing, or an effort to assist another.

And in a flash I see why this loving of myself is so vital in terms of the practice problem I took to Bhante earlier today. How is it possible to classify as "difficult" any being for whom one feels compassion? As ego subsides, there can only be loving-kindness for all of us in this struggle, for every wounded child.

# 20  Difficult exchanges

Expecting a "difficult" conversation with someone? Spend time before sending goodwill to yourself and the other, thus preparing the heart rather than the words. It can also be helpful to carry a pen or a paperclip or such, when you go into the conversation. Before you speak each time, take a moment to "fiddle" with this object, giving yourself time to renew this intention of goodwill.

**Kindly Caring**

A peaceful place to stop reading in the *Flower Ornament Sutra*:

> Arouse your minds to seek enlightenment,
> Kindly care for all living beings,
> Abide by the great vows of universal goodness…

This has the feeling of a prayer and I love the second line, to "kindly care". This is what I strive to carry into my work and in my family. It is easiest with the dogs in the kennel. Mostly it is not difficult to see their needs. The frightened ones that need a kind voice and space to find their own way to me. This works in 99.9% of fearful cases, whether they're tremblers or growlers. I stay around them but not pushing them. And I talk to them. Sometimes my family laughs at the way I talk to the dogs. But for those "guests" who stay often and have become my friends, this has been the foundation for building real inter-species relationships.

There is a big newf who, I swear, understands my needs as I understand hers. It looks like she responds to my words but I know we reach each other through kindess and tone. When she's stubborn I take her face in my hands and rest my forehead on hers and talk to her. I tell her why I'm asking her to come in or out or whatever. And she responds. Kindness.

It's much harder with people, of course. People each have such personal-ego-agendas and such a sense of apartness. Me and the other. It's complicated. I'd like to approach the people in my life in the same way: Forehead to forehead whispering our needs, our reasons. But some would push away, some would be embarrassed and some would be confused. Strangers might think I was dangerous! Some people might hug me, humor me or soften their tone, but we'd go back to a position of space between us. You. Me.

Still, this kindness is a good image. I'd like to keep this in my head. Foreheads touching, whispering. Caring for each other.

It's easiest to keep this as a priority when I am present, tuned into right now. What I need. What you need. Mindful awareness of the moment allows me to open not just to what I want, but to the entire context. What's going on in my mind that gives it urgency? Why I might be encountering resistance from others. What might be going on with them. So compassion, mindfulness, and caring form a tripod of stability from which to act. When I'm here, and you're here with me, we can move forward together, from a place of understanding and not confrontation.

Being present and working to "kindly care for all beings", I do my part to make it possible for such understanding to unfold.

## Opening the Heart

I remember a picture that one of my grandmothers had. It was large and in exaggerated colors. The picture was of Jesus, one hand cupped toward his chest where in a blaze of light the artist had depicted his large and glowing heart. Like the drawings in the cutaway anatomy books my sons are fond of, this exposure of what is normally hidden both intrigued and disturbed me then. Yet, it stayed in memory only subliminally.

The practice of metta or loving-kindness meditation has often provoked this image for me, drawing it out from among so many lost childhood impressions. In loving-kindness meditation there is much talk about opening the heart. So the association, I guess, seems natural. Part of what is disturbing about exposing the heart in pictures like the one I recall is a feeling of vulnerability. This will hurt, won't it? When books on metta meditation describe the pain of compassion, I at first thought I already knew what that was. Feeling sorry for someone hurt. Wishing things were different. Feeling angry about injustice.

But I'm finding that the opening of the heart is one of those subtle changes only apparent at first by the pain it brings. This pain is something I'm struggling to describe. It is not angry. It is a long way from angry. It is not feeling sorry, for it doesn't have that distance, that separation between myself and other. It is not wishing things were different because it is a being in the hurt now, with no room for imaginings.

These are the things I've become aware of as I mindfully watch my own thoughts and feelings moment to moment. A prayer for the pain of animals brings tears to my eyes and an ache to my heart that this is so. Seeing a piece of paper thrown into the garbage rather than into the recycle bin causes a twinge of pain and a welling of sorrow. Piles of magazines whose sole purpose is to sell products and images and desires cause a closing in my throat. And a politician's casual remark revealing deep-seated notions of separation, keeping "our water" or "our resources", triggers those same physical sensations of pain. State of the economy reports which assume the possibility and desirability of unlimited growth. These hurt.

I have felt anger and indignation before in response to some of these things. I have felt hopeless longing for things to be different. I have felt superiority to those who could not see the larger picture. But I am only beginning to understand what it means to not separate myself from this. To know my part in it. To open my heart to the pain of all beings, to the pain of this earth, to the karma we have created and continue to create. I didn't know that the pain spoken of by the wise was real and not metaphorical. I didn't know because I hadn't opened to it.

Not pushing away this pain is part of what I'm learning. To let it be. But also to let it pass as all things do. And to realize that as my heart opens a little more all the time with these experiences, so my actions may begin to reflect that opening.

## Hyphenating Traditions

We are accustomed in North America to hyphenated identities. Women, myself included, not desiring to give up the names of their family of origin, hyphenate their last names, keeping their own surname and adding the surname of their partner. This acknowledges both person and couple and feels right to many people. As well, immigrant Canadians may speak of themselves as British-Canadian or Australian-Canadian or Dutch-Canadian. And those of ethnic origins other than Caucasian may be referred to as Indo-Canadians or Chinese-Canadians or Afro-Canadians.

But I was taken aback the first time I ran across terms likes Jewish-Buddhist, Christian or even Catholic-Buddhist, agnostic-Buddhist. What could this mean, I wondered? Wasn't this some kind of contradiction? My only understanding was by analogy to households with two religions…one partner Jewish and the other Buddhist, but this did not seem right given the context in which these terms were used. And so I took this to mean that somehow a person, once Christian, for example, now considered herself to be Buddhist, but honored that from which she'd come by forming such a dual category for herself.

It has taken awhile to come to a clearer understanding of this. And this understanding illustrates for me what first drew me to Buddhism itself. It is said in traditional teachings that on the subject of "God", the Buddha was silent. Traditional Buddhism is therefore agnostic in nature. While recognizing the sacred unity of all life, and the meaninglessness of "I" apart from all, this tradition does not contain the notion of a supreme being apart from all. My personal understanding has been to take the word "God" to be a synonym for this sacred unity. God is in us all. So, though at first I wanted to change a word I felt was too loaded with images of an old-man-with-a-beard, I am now comfortable with this term. Speaking of the spiritual we must always be satisfied with approximations. This one will do.

But now I see in the hyphenated identities which many other Buddhists claim, that in the Buddha's silence on the subject of God, there is infinite space. Buddhism is, instead of a system of belief, a form of mind training. So, one who is comfortable with Jewish beliefs, or Christian beliefs in any of their myriad manifestations, may also discover truths through this system of internal investigation. The truth of the interdependence of all beings, for instance, is revealed in the stillness and insight of meditation. And meditation supports the practice of mindful living, and the growth of compassion. So that forms of worship, reverence and direct knowing melt one into the other. Hyphenation is an attempt to make this semantically understandable. It is an approximation of this melding of world views.

This is much of what it is to awaken. To know that even in our terms and labels and systems of belief we are all one, all on a shared path. Thus, the discomfort I felt in earlier years with organized religion, perceiving it to cause divisions, is simply released with the breath as we begin again together.

# 21 Goodwill

Stuck at a red-light or waiting in line? Practice sending thoughts of goodwill to those around you and notice how it settles your own restlessness.

**Let It Be**

I heard a speaker once talking about one of the central practices of mindfulness. As we learn to live in the present moment, whether it is watching our breath as we sit, or counting cars at a railway crossing when we're stuck in traffic, or controlling acting out when someone has pushed in front of us in a line-up, we are taught to note what catches the mind (the boredom, the impatience, the anger) and to "let it go". This teacher, Peter Russell. suggested instead that we watch and "let it be". I like this rendering, and not just because I can hear the Beatles' gentle crooning when I think these words.

Letting it go works too, so long as we remember this is not a pushing away. Not a launching ourselves out of there and closing the door. Not giving the feeling a push and turning away. Letting it be is less a matter of me doing anything and that's what mindfulness is about.

In my daily sitting practice I often find serenity. And if I were wishing I'd say that's probably what I'd wish for every day. Finding the mind complacent and obedient. Settling readily on the breath and going with this flow of life, moment to moment. Just as it is. This sort of strong concentration gives rise to a deep feeling of ease that is soothing and healing. When it happens, and the bell rings to end the hour, I carry with me a calm that enhances the day. It gives me access to greater receptivity, allows me to see through to what is important in each moment and not to be side-lined or blind-sided. For awhile anyway.

But on days when the mind is restless or sleepy or full of wanting it is anything but obedient. It moves again and again to being annoyed by itches, drifting into dreams, yearning for the bell to ring. And my task is to be with this. To see what things are like right now and let it be. Not to jump from the cushion, not abandon the effort, not pretend this isn't happening. Watching and being curious about the mind, I see that when I stay with this, let the grumbling continue in the background as I carry the attention gently, like a child having a tantrum, back to the breath, eventually, like the child, it gives up. The tantrum ends. The sleepiness recedes. The restlessness dissolves. The wanting evaporates. And there is just the breath again.

At the railway crossing, I can look at my watch and snort and grumble. I can distract myself by sending a text message or fiddling with the radio. I can annoy other drivers, and cause confusion and possibly danger by trying to maneuver to the shoulder, turn around and find another way. Or I can let it be. Rolling down the window if the day is warm. Loosening a coat and finding my breath in my belly. Letting this moment be a gift. Because it is. Like a shiney coin found in the sand, each moment is available to be discovered as treasure only once. When I can do this, my shoulders loosen and my frown dissolves. My breath comes smoothly and my mind and body are at ease. When the train has passed, I move with clarity, not carrying a burden of pain and resentment with me into the next part of my day.

In the line-up, I can push back and give the other person a piece of my mind. I can get into an argument or even an altercation if the other is also reactive. We can both cause hurt, emotional and physical, that can spin out into the room, the group that is present, and the lives of those we encounter for the rest of the day or beyond. I can step back in silence and let the raving take place in my mind or send messages to the newspaper where cartoon bleeps express my anger and disdain. And in doing this the moment spins out to color my day with tension and anger. I may develop a headache. I may lose sleep composing a rant. I may carry my story to others and bring them on side so that we both carry the burden of anger, and deal with its pain. Or I can let it be. I can breathe and assess whether waiting behind one more person really makes a big difference to my day. I can imagine what things must be like for someone who is willing and able to behave in this way. Was it accidental? A lack of mindfulness we can all be prone to. If intentional, what anger are they already carrying, what are they already suffering? What if I reframe the incident with allowing. What if I invite them, whispering gently in my mind: "Please, go ahead." If I can manage this, I might ease my own sense of injustice. I might find that the smile I bring to my lips also brings happiness and forgiveness to my own heart. Maybe.

Letting it be isn't like lying back in the grass on a sunny day. It's a conscious choice to see what is arising in the moment as well as what I'm bringing to meet the moment. And it requires vigilance and effort. And a lot patience with a human mind prone to tantrums and inattention.

## A Better Self

After so many monastery retreats it is interesting to be at Providence again. A lay teacher here I've not connected with before. A few familiar faces in the crowd. The simple and familiar room and the rituals of making it home for awhile.

The first evening a brief whiff of loneliness when my eyes opened to the dusky day beyond the window, a time for supper and gathering at home. This was palpable for a breath, then I was back, savoring the silence, the freedom from the need to interact for awhile, to turn inward and thus more fully outward to all I am part of.

No Dhamma talk and no chants. Alas. I find myself missing the structure, the rituals, though the group sitting is welcome. Tonight we focus on bare awareness of sound and then move into a compassion meditation. It is soothing, centering, heart opening.

The format for the compassion meditation is taken from teachings by Jack Kornfield in his book *The Wise Heart*. Beginning by thinking of loved ones, allowing thoughts of their unique situations and suffering to arise and following these with heartfelt assurances. "You are held in compassion. You are loved. May your sorrow and pain be eased."

I have used this form before when someone dear is on my mind. But also when some event in the world has sidelined my heart in grieving or sorrow. A headline on the news. A natural disaster. A loss. It is a deep reminder to me of the universality of suffering. Of Bhante Pavaro's wise mantra "Nothing unusual here." And it allows me to open to the suffering that comes home to me in recognizing and fearing pain in the world, in wishing it were otherwise, while merging this pain response with something that is good for the heart. Not just a fear and turning away then, but a recognition and a feeling with and for others. This is so. It hurts. May you know you are not alone. May you know that this too will pass.

I had not planned to seek an interview this time. Thought I would take the solitude deeper, but at breakfast on the second morning, the retreat leader stops me. "You and I should chat today." And so I go. We talk a long time. About lay practice, about marriage and children and aging parents and loss and relationships through the changes life brings, all in the context of Dhamma. When at day's end, I come to write in this pretty journal, a gift from my sister, I find this quote gracing the page in pastels: "I want first of all to be at peace with myself. I want a singleness of eye, a purity of intention, a central core to my life…" The words, as all the quotes in the journal are, are from *A Gift From the Sea* by Anne Morrow Lindbergh, and reflecting on my interview conversation today, I find them apt. The work begins here. At peace with myself.

This does not involve "fixing" myself. But rather developing a kindness, a being and not a doing, observing with care, remaining mindful, exerting right effort. See the unwholesome states and stop them. See the wholesome states and nurture them. And the kindness I show myself does its work without my needing to take control. Thus, through right intention, right effort, and compassion, this better self is something positive I offer my family, my friends and the world.

### Mindful Community

One of the great gifts of retreat for me, and there are many, is the slow withdrawal of anxiety from my consciousness. For me, anxiety is the tag-along partner of care and control, both being features of the climate of my mind. In the ordinary world, awareness of this is primary for me. Noting it. Letting it go. But when I am on retreat, it is as if my mind shifts. It's like a vacation where you leave in a snow storm and step off the plane to beaches and salt air. Over the course of my settling into retreat, the climate of my mind undergoes a transformation, and anxiety melts away.

In these communities, wherever they may be, harmony reigns and there is no harsh speech or sense of prickly irritation surrounding me, as there is in the "world". I am not on hyper alert regarding the judgement and requirements of others. The social "forms" are lifted away. The rules change. There is always an adjustment period when it seems odd not to make polite eye contact, not to say "thank you" or such. But as the flow of kindness and consideration, of harmony and patience and ease begins to become familiar again, I am reminded there is little need for conventions of courtesy where kindness and harmony rule. I have received many glittering false smiles and meaningless directives to "have a nice day" in the world from people in a rush or a self-absorbed fog. Here we are aware of each other more fully, differently, not as other but together. Making way in activity, doing what needs to be done, radiating patience and care. Yes, we are all human, and this picture is not perfect but what I'm trying to describe is that the care is not empty form. It is not just polite action by busy people. I include myself in this. When we are separate and self-absorbed in the world, we require rules to keep our interactions civil. Stop signs. Courtesies. I am grateful for these opportunities to withdraw from the preoccupations and the forms, and hone mindfulness skills without the distraction of anxiety.

Walking meditation is a delight this time. It isn't always so. Walking the smooth grey floor in my heavy socks, I touch the earth gently, enjoying the motion and rhythm. I'm usually alone on the paths. Sometimes I see Ajahn's feet beneath the screen where he walks his own private path. Sometimes one of the young monks or another guest may be there or join in later in the easy silence and movement.

One morning I go out into falling snow and find a royal blue plastic shovel and join Linda in clearing the exit paths and those to the outbuildings. Smiles and bows from a steward and one of the young monks when they pass. When I warm up with the work, I throw back my hood and the thick falling snow fills it. When I raise it again later, I'm showered. Gasping, I turn at a laugh behind me and find Kati, who has joined in with a brilliant canary yellow shovel. It is a lovely time. When the paths are clear, I put away my shovel and head off for a walk. The snow is heavy on my boots now and there's a good climb to the logging road. I stop once and breathe and watch, and life is a great gift that lifts my heart.

Back at the monastery, I shake out wet coat and socks over a bathtub and lay them out to dry in my room. When I go to the sala, some guests are already seated and I slide into my place. Not a cog in a wheel, but a cell in a body. The body breathes each of us in the hour that follows.

Day's end I am grateful for the comfort of my thin foamy on the tatami mat. I reflect on the Buddha's instructions to be mindful in all postures, "sitting, standing and lying down". Breath focus merges into sleep.

First thoughts at the waking bell are of the time to come…my favorite sitting is this earliest one. The bows and soft light, the whisper of movement as everyone settles in the near dark. The day in mindful community begins with ease and joy.

# 22 Sharing Practice

Make an agreement with a friend to text each other at a certain time each day (or even once a week) as a signal that you both will "sit" quietly for 10 minutes watching the breath. During your sitting imagine your friend there beside you, and draw support and joy from your shared intention to be present in the moment as it passes.

**Daily Practice**

It's early and still dark outside. A soft snow is falling. My children are yet asleep. This time of day it can seem, no matter how tired I am or what concerns I took with me to my bed, that all things are possible, and that all is right with the world. It is a time outside of time in that schedules and deadlines have not yet begun to pull, the sun has not begun its journey across the sky reminding us of the passing hours, the phone doesn't ring.

Sometimes I sleep well and other times it may have been a restless and interrupted night, but this factor seems insignificant in the stillness of the early morning before dawn. And this, to me, is an apt metaphor for the peace and gift of no-time that meditation brings.

Sometimes when I sit, I am almost pulled to my cushion with longing. I will take even five or ten minutes if that is all I have, feeling a need draw me. Other times, it is only discipline and memory that cause me to interrupt my day and take time for formal practice. But when I have settled and begin to breathe, it becomes my own dark and silent early morning, my place out of time. And this is so, no matter the quality of that particular day's practice.

There are times when I am so tired that sleepiness overcomes me, perhaps once, perhaps more often as I sit. And the counting of breaths is like the childhood counting of sleep and my head droops. Yet I practice. Coming to awareness a moment later, perhaps even minutes later, I sit tall and begin again.

Sometimes my mind is so restless, I fairly twitch with the effort of remaining still, letting my mind follow for awhile each bodily sensation that distracts me…an itchy foot, a twinge in my thigh, pressure on my ankles, tickling of my nose, tightness in my shoulders, an ache in my knees. Ah! It seems impossible that I can stay with the breath. But I remember a reminder from my many teachers (in the books I read) that anything can be the object of awareness, and so I let each sensation in turn stand in for the breath and little by little I find myself centering.

When the cycles of the furnace, the barking of the dog, the bubble and drip of the aquarium dominate my attention, I use these as well for awhile and then return to the breath. And I have found that the suggestion to count my thoughts on days when these seem too persistent to resist, works to distract me from the content and soon I am able to shift back to my breath.

And so, finally rising from my cushion, whether it be 10, 30 or 60 minutes later, it is like rising before the dawn of a new day, the windows still dark, the world not yet impinging. Time has stopped and all things are possible. It is not that weariness and worry, appointments and deadlines are erased, but that I find in sitting a view that gives all this its proper perspective and importance, for all things pass quickly away.

**Circling Through the Seasons**

Winter's coming again. The long dark nights that mark the season at this latitude. In the summer my early rising is a way of catching more hours of sunlight…beams across the kitchen table, sparkles in the window of my little room as I kneel for my morning bows and chants. At the monastery, the big wooden panels that cover the wall of windows behind the majestic white Buddha in the sala are rolled aside and light patterns the gleaming black floor. It is easy to see the gift of rising early. Easy to roll a still-tired body out of bed with such a world to welcome opened eyes.

But lately I rise in the dark again. The soft sounds of my husband's breathing behind me, the tiny chime of the bell coaxing me across the room. These days, I find my thick socks and sweater in the dark again and soon may add a touque and vest to this morning fashion ensemble as well. At the monastery, others also shuffle sleepily out of their rooms and we sit in a silent circle, the dark floor a deeper black than the shadows, wooden panels closed over the windows to keep warmth in. In awhile, the woodburning stove at the far end of the sala will crackle and snap in the silence of the dark mornings. But not yet, not quite yet.

At the monastery in the dark days on retreat it is cold. But the muffled sounds of bodies moving are an invitation to the gathering. And I like to pause at the door of the sala and wait for my night vision to allow me to make out the circle of cushions from the last sit the night before and a few blanket-draped humans sitting like mountains. I take my place among them, bow towards the white gleam of the Buddha and close my eyes. There is only my breath and the whisper of soft steps in the room as everyone finds a place. Perhaps a muffled cough, the shush of blankets and then when the abbott enters, a gentle flurry as we bow together again and settle into shared silence.

Anyone who is part of a spiritual community will fill in this picture with their own nostalgic memories. In my childhood, it was the smell of polished pews in our little church, the stiff rustle of hymn books and women's skirts. The whispers of mothers hushing children. The first notes of the piano. There is a great comfort and a subliminal energy in sharing a spiritual practice with others. In having companions of the heart on the path to which one's heart has been drawn.

For a couple of decades now, this path for me has been the Eightfold Path taught by the Buddha. And following that path has meant a devotion to silence and meditation on a daily basis. So, at the monastery, or on retreats in other places, I sit with those who have a similar commitment. At home, physically, I sit alone. But I have developed a practice of imagining my sangha circle. *Sangha* is a Pali word that properly refers to the disciples that followed the Buddha over 2500 years ago. But most practitioners use the term more loosely in reference to the community of practitioners. And so my sangha is made up of those all over the country and the world who are also following this practice. For me then, in the early dark mornings or in the sparkling sunshine, I feel the presence of friends known and potential who are faithful to this discipline. I allow myself to see a circle of remembered faces, to send them loving-kindness and encouragement and to feel how it flows back to me. These few moments each morning are a simple habitual part of my personal practice.

One of the delusions to which human beings are subject, one of the causal fragments that leads us deeper into suffering, is that we are alone. As a species we wish for and dread the discovery of others in the universe. And as individuals, we can feel locked inside our private experience; we can feel that every emotional pain, every intellectual struggle is personal and unique. And yet, the sharing of this very perspective is evidence that the human mind, the human heart, is bigger than that. We spill into each other. We gather and shed bits like snow balls rolling down a hill as we tumble through life.

When I find my breath as I settle on my bench in my small room, the breathing of others, not even present physically, supports me. The Buddha stressed the significance of like-minded friends in spiritual life. Our own experience verifies this wisdom. I am grateful for my community, present in our shared intentions through the seasons of the year, through the seasons of life.

## Closings

Closing of this distance retreat. Each of us in our homes trying to work with a prescribed schedule over the last few days. Fitting the agreed-upon periods of study and writing and sitting and walking, as much as we can, around and within whatever is normal in our days, and checking in at the end of each day. The gift of cyber-connections. So today, our last, I'm thinking of "closings".

Closing a book. Closing a chapter. Closing a door. Closing a letter. It means somehow to complete and finish yet mostly what is closed can be re-opened. A book may be revisited and, upon return, we may find things we missed on the journey before. A chapter may be rewritten. A door re-opened. For another look. A peek backwards. Or even to re-enter. Letters may be mailed or not. Returned unopened. Sequels written. We speak of closing as if it is to end but the amazing thing about impermanence is that endings lead into new beginnings.

My attraction to Buddhism began in part because of my fear of ending, of my attempts to make sense of a world devoid of the old man God in heaven I was taught to believe in. A vague sense of something less humanoid in form and habit. My own explanations were pseudo-science. A belief in a recycling and harmony and connectedness that meant no part of me was truly separate. Every action of mine radiated out into the world. Every action of my ancestors carried forward to me. And in my "chosen" family, my spouse and children, students with on-going connections, life-long friendships, this netting grew and grew. This was simple sense to me. Observable. And when I died my body would feed the earth and so I could not help but feel that that energy and spirit which were also part of me would not be gone either.

I read a book, *Soul Search: A Scientist Explores the Afterlife*, and was left with a visual impression of a conscious universe…pulsing with life so that individual beings were only spots at the bottom of funnels from this source. Some of the funnels were wide, so a tree, a caterpillar, a blade of grass might not have a sense of a separate self at all. But as the funnels narrowed to the finest of openings we came to human kind who lives in an illusion of separateness and with the delusion of a self that stands alone, with a beginning and an ending. Because of this, we are the most lost. We suffer the most because we look back through an opening so tiny we are unaware of the vast source at the head of the funnel.

When I eventually discovered Buddhism's description of the cause of our suffering, the concept of *anatta* (no self) this matched my unarticulated felt understanding. So the closing of a chapter of painful seeking led to an opening in understanding.

Closing this retreat I reflect on how yesterday did not go at all as I had planned. The power went out. My husband was called into work and was there until midnight. I was left alone with a full kennel, my own sons and a visiting child, and too many things to do, to do this "right". So I simply did what needed doing. This and then this. And now, today has been a gift. This morning's meditation opening doors. Not a closing at all.

# 23 Complaining

When you hear yourself complaining (out loud or in the privacy of your mind) add the phrase "And I am very blessed". This is a simple, uplifting way to move the mind in a more positive direction.

**Hymns to the Moment**

*Gathas* are short "hymns", verses or poems that bring us to the moment, applying mindfulness practice where it is fruitful in our lives. Mostly I know them through the wonderful writing of the late Zen master and poet, Robert Aitken, whose book *The Dragon Who Never Sleeps* contains many such verses. Inspired years ago upon reading this book, I began the practice of composing gathas of my own. Most often I took pen in hand when faced with moments that brought me up hard against what I might not wish to acknowledge, but sometimes, like any poetry, they were simply inspired by moments that were suddenly crystal clear.

The gift inherent in these hymns to the moment is that they apply continuously in the round of living, day by day and year by year. One I recite and remember often though it was written nearly a decade ago goes like this:

> Looking up now into the faces of my sons
> Their bodies dwarfing mine
> I breathe and remember
> To be here with this passing of time
> Things are as they are and should be.

It has a flavor of melancholy perhaps, but the reassurance that things are not out of whack. We can feel betrayed by changes – losses or illness or just the inevitable passing of time. But the truth, when we see clearly, is that this is simply the way of things. In the company of my adult children these days I am reminded that while memories are dear, the living is in this moment which will not come again.

This is true too of the fantasies that carry us into the future as an escape from today's pain.

> When the hands of imagination
> Weave some sunnier, better time
> I breathe and remember
> To choose this ragged day
> With its ever-changing weather.

Thumbing through these verses, many written years ago, I find now that while the specific incident that provoked them may be gone from memory, I still know in my bones the feelings they express. This is why mindfulness is an ongoing practice. We do not simply learn to be present and never again fall into the enchantment, the trance of living in an automatic and self-isolated way. Instead we take on the task of coming to the present again and again. Noting how we create our own pain in clinging to what could never be held on to.

> When my eye strays again and again
> To the racing hands of the clock
> I breathe and remember
> To let go – nothing is slipping away.

### Golden Wind Lifts Leaves of Thought

Spinning on quotes from *Golden Wind: Zen Talks* by Eido Shimano Roshi

> Existentially speaking there is no Perfect Way; something is always wrong. But fundamentally speaking, there is no way which is not perfect…. We seek something, somewhere outside. We do not realize that this fundamental Perfect Way and this existential imperfect way exist simultaneously.

Where does my mind go, reflecting on this as I pick up my pen, a slow curl of incense wafting across my vision beneath the desk light? Perfection. Nothing wanting. Is that perfection? Neither too much nor too little of anything. So here is this good moment. But I'm irritated by the stains and doodling my son left on my desk pad and the air is just a bit too cold so my shoulders draw up tight against the chill. Existentially this moment is not perfect, despite the longed-for silence and solitude of this room, the smooth and easy flow of mind to hand to ink on paper. Despite the incense, the pretty jade Buddha, the peace of the night, work done. Nowhere to be. Not required. Yet, fundamentally perfect, Roshi says. I can't help thinking too of how there is always something wrong. "Always" in bold print. If I were to escape to the monastic life I feel drawn to… the hermit life more like. Dwelling in some little place not much bigger than this precious room. Some place of silence…cushions, books, and empty time. Then I would long and yearn for shared laughter, for hugs and sharing hopes and plans and stories. For family chaos. *Always* something wrong. This family began more than two decades ago, a couple at its centre, spiraling out with the boys. A mandala circled by extended family, intimate friends. And it has moments of even existential perfection. True of any family perhaps. So that the blips are jarring…raised voices, injustices, thoughtlessness, withdrawals. Always something. Yet fundamentally perfect. Simultaneously.

> What I do is solely my own work…the virtue of doing difficult work in order to serve others.

My purpose, a numerologist once told me, is to serve. In my twenties then, this rankled. Independent and self-reliant and, yes, egotistical…how could I be meant to serve, to somehow be subservient to others? Mmm. But serving has a different flavor and meaning for me in my fifties, a decade and more into finding my way on a Buddhist practice path. My work. Difficult work. To serve others. To serve in this family as wife, partner, homemaker and mother. Difficult work but mine to do. And what I read here is a reminder that this *is* my practice. Not just these few minutes of reading teisho and writing in a journal. Not just bowing, lighting incense and candles and sitting in the dark of early morning. Doing everything I do mindfully.

The *tensho* (a zen cook) cooks with no waste. Is there a metaphor here? In cleaning, shopping, talking, paying bills, driving…no waste. All is fodder for practice. It's so easy to say so. So difficult to do. With menial tasks, with labor I come closest. Just this. Hand moving. Doing. But disciplining children, thinking about how to broach a difficult subject with my life partner, worrying over some difficulty or phase in growing up and letting go that my boys and I face. These I stumble through. I forget I do not exist. The illusion looks back from the pool of emotion. There I am again. What melts and dissolves on the cushion in zazen, cools and solidifies into some clumsy lump that bumps and rattles off the edges of life again.

## A First World Problem

Returning from a walk the other day with a clear head and a sense of energy, I anticipated settling down at my computer to get some work done. Instead I entered an oddly quiet kitchen. I also noticed that where red glowing digits on the stovetop generally announce the hour, there was only a blank black space - the visual announcement of a power outage. Ah, so that was the pop that had sounded like a dropped bin lid.

A little thing, this temporary power outage. Within an hour the power would be back on and life as I knew it restored. But in the meantime....

Grumbling mind slipped into the space created by a blocked plan of action. Not unexpected. It's sneaky like that and pretty opportunistic. Noted. I shifted around for a positive replacement thought. It isn't winter. Despite our regional disappointment with the slow advent of spring (ah, another grumble) the temperatures are well above zero and the house would stay comfortably warm. The afternoon hours of light are long so no hunkering in darkness or gathering of candles. There are novels to be read and a cushion available to sit. A dog who would welcome a longer walk. A cat happy to snuggle on the step. But mind likes its way and habit's voice kept reminding me of the projects waiting in my office.

I stood at the window awhile, eyes looking outward but attention inside. Then I settled into the idea of a little unstructured time. A gift, really, unexpectedly, in this part of the day.

Some places, as in Mumbai in the slum community where my brother and his wife work, power is a luxury. Even in their apartment in a settled neighborhood, both power and water are intermittent and unreliable.

The brief power outage I experienced is an example of what people call a first world problem. Have you heard the phrase? Applying to concerns about the price of coffee, lack of good service in a restaurant, dandelion infestations on front lawns, a bad haircut. The sort of thing we all find ourselves grumbling about from time to time. The phrase is intended to remind us of our good fortune. Most of us have enough to eat, a roof over our heads and shoes on our feet. The good life is something we've gotten used to.

Unfortunately I think this phrase, rather than moving us toward gratitude, tends to instil guilt in us. Feeling just lucky in some way to have been born in this place and time, when we're reminded of that good fortune, we might experience twinges of guilt or defensiveness. Neither of these negative mind states are skillful. For the one experiencing them there is discomfort that might lead to further negative action. Feeling judged readily spirals into negative self-judgement, ending in toxic brews of inertia, depression or resentment.

First world problems are genuine problems for those who face them because they believe them to be so. Complaining about anything begins with a perception that things should not be this way. For the moment, we wear blinders that prevent us from seeing all the other things in the room. We've got tunnel vision and the dandelions take up the whole visual field. Dialling back to a wider focus brings the green grass into view and we notice that it isn't, after all, on the other side of the fence.

Complaining mind has a demanding tone to it that we can learn to recognize quickly. Let it be the bell that signals a time to count our blessings.

# 24 Intentions

*Create post-its or "flash cards" to use in reminding yourself of intentions. For example: May I be kind to myself and others today.*

### For Just This Moment

Beginnings. There is a hopefulness about them. Things will be different, things will be better. The way ahead looks fresh and new. And, traditionally, the New Year is a beginning marked for many by resolutions. Promises to ourselves, or perhaps more publicly to family and friends, that we are aiming toward something, working on something, putting effort in some direction. As we make such resolutions we are able to hold them as entirely possible. Sure, we know effort and change will be required, but from this side of the fence it all looks like green grass and sunny meadows. All we gotta do is decide.

In a sense, of course, this is correct. Without the determination to change or to work in some particular direction, it's unlikely that we'll put in the effort. But it's where the effort part comes that we catch our toes. Because generally resolutions have to do with climbing out of deeply worn ruts, not just opening the gate of a tidy fence. It's muddy, difficult, uncomfortable work. And faced with such effort, the mind feels a lot of aversion. The default program when we meet aversion is to "make it go away". So if the climb is tough, well, quit climbing.

We've all experienced this. The clichés are so easy to name: quitting smoking, going on a diet, getting organized. Popular psychology says it takes three weeks of a new pattern to break the hold of the old one. And the first few days are crucial because the other mind trick we play on ourselves is to believe we've failed as soon as we misstep once. Slide back an inch? Might as well let go and just slip back to the comfortable rut again. Whenever I hear talk of resolutions I remember the days I was committed to weight training…a regular at the gym. All of us who attended regularly knew that for the first week or two of January we'd have to allot extra time for workouts because of the competition with new comers for equipment. But before the first month of the new year was over, things would settle back to close to "normal" again.

There's nothing wrong with resolving to change. The problem, I think, is that traditions like New Year's Resolutions, make CHANGE look like it's in capital letters, a lot like the Hollywood sign. Big, and one of a kind, a landmark.

But if you're training in mindfulness, you begin to see that change isn't like that at all. It's a moment by moment process. The tiniest of actions taken in the tiniest of openings. That moment when you see the thought or emotion and step out of the feeling or thought itself. When, instead of following the craving, you see the craving. It's deciding moment by moment to make a skillful decision. For just this moment, I'll leave unsaid the hurtful words rushing to my tongue. For just this moment, I'll choose not to have the drink that makes me unheedful of my speech and actions. For this moment, I'll choose to breathe and wait patiently for the child who is moving slowly, noticing how my mind wants to make this a problem.

Inherent in such training is recognizing that moment to moment mindfulness *is* a training. It's not a resolution, a sweeping one-time change. You don't run a marathon the day you plan to get in shape. You know it's a process.

The gift of mindfulness is that when you begin the process, when you commit to the training, you begin to chip steps into that wall that leads up and out of the current habit rut you're in. I'm sorry I don't recall the writer or source but at the very outset of my journey on this path I once read a quote that stuck with me…it said something like this: If one of the things you beat yourself up about is being overweight, and you work at mindfulness, moment by moment, a year from now you'll find you're either thinner or not, but you will be happier with who you are.

We all have a self-critical voice. The topics it chooses to harp on may be specific to you, but the harm it does is something that you share with other human beings. It's part of the suffering we all endure. New Year's resolutions, it seems to me, pay homage to those voices, by handing a megaphone to the one by which we feel most abused. In the face of the shouting, we're bound to lose our grip, lose our will to try. Mindfulness, on the other hand, whenever we are able to maintain it, softens those critical voices. It's a way of finding peace with the way things are now, and yet working moment by moment to make clear-headed choices for greater well-being.

Not for this year to come then, but for just this moment, breathe and choose wisely.

## Considering Karma

I've been thinking about karma, or kamma as it is written in Pali. My teacher is specific in explaining that kamma is action, and action is tied to intention. What we do/say/think intentionally. The consequences of volitional or intentional action have another name altogether in Pali (*vipaka*). Actions may be relatively straightforward but consequences are complicated. Complicated because there is so much more than my own intention and action at play. The intentions and actions of everyone involved, the conditions and context that surround intentions and actions. Here's where it spins out into the 10,000 things that contribute to any one event that takes place – 10,000 being just a place holder for very, very many! I think of the gatha by Robert Aitken:

> Watching a spider at work
> I vow with all beings
> to cherish the web of the universe
> touch one point and everything moves.

The web of the universe is vast. The number of beings who touch it uncountable. This web is vibrating with input from intentional action at all times. The important point for me to remember is that I am one of the beings within that web. My own actions contribute to the vibration. It is important that in this small sphere that is within my control, I make skillful and positive choices. Especially because kamma itself is morphing all the time. I may have acted unwisely or selfishly or with ill will in the past and the consequences of that action are out there, in the web of the universe. However, if I determine to do better and begin to act with wisdom, generosity and good will, I am contributing something else to the kammic web. The message I get from this consideration is that it is never too late to clean up my act on any level. It puts the responsibility on my shoulders to see clearly how my behavior has impact on the world and to make that impact positive, so far as I am able. And never to stop making that effort.

In the teachings of the Buddha there are many references to kamma that make such a point:

> Whatever I do, for good or for evil, to that will I fall heir. To the extent that there are beings – past and future, passing away and re-arising – all beings are the owner of their actions, heir to their actions, born of their actions, related through their actions, and live dependent on their actions. Whatever they do, for good or for evil, to that will they fall heir. (AN5.57)

But this is not a teaching exclusive to the Buddha. Indeed it seems that all spiritual teachings recognize this truth about life in some version of the "Golden Rule".

Just exploring this a little, from the Christian Bible, I found in Galatians 6:7 " A man reaps what he sows." and Proverbs 22:8a "Whoever sows injustice reaps calamity." with its mirror image in Proverbs 11:18b "The one who sows righteousness reaps a sure reward."

Islam takes a similar view. In the Quran passage known as The Star (53:39-40) it reads "a man will have nothing except that for which he has endeavored [to achieve] and that his endeavor will eventually be seen." And in The Event (56.63) "Have you considered what you sow?"

My reflections make it clear to me, however, that responsibility is not a burden but a key to freedom. In the choices I make, and the intentions I form, however small, I contribute to the world. It is beyond my capacity to control everything, but I am not helpless in this scenario…not a fly on the web, caught, but more like the amazing spider making its way on careful feet, contributing, if I choose, to the world's beauty.

### How Am I With This?

"How am I with this?" A new question for a card by my altar. A reminder. I know I've heard it before, read it, but it didn't stick. This time as the suggestion is made to use this question in living the moment, it resonates with me. So as I watch, observe everything happening in the moment, I focus not on the external events and things but rather on my own responses, my relationship with the actions, words, objects around me. How am I with this? In doing so I see the aversion or desire that arise. My body tells the truth.

When I see the internal responses, turn to practice with tolerating, allowing the passing of what is pleasant, the experience of what is not pleasant. Last night reading Ajahn Chah. "Can you endure it?" he asks when someone brings him a tale of woe. This is key to practice. Not gritted teeth but allowing, opening, patient endurance. I think, given the truth of impermanence in this human life, this is the finest, best way to live. To find that place of allowing. To fully love what one loves but not to fall apart when it passes. To not curl up and whimper in the face of pain or sorrow but to allow the emotion its space and know its passing too.

When the boys were small and I'd hold their fat, sturdy baby bodies close and smell them and feel such waves of love beyond any I had ever known, more than I imagined possible, still that love would be flavored with fear for the passing of time, the brevity of the moment. I could not enter the joy fully being so fearful. And when I mourned the passing of my parents, I felt the zest for life dull so that I imagined I'd never be happy again. The joys of life were lost awhile in this place of resistance and anger towards what is. Old age, sickness and death. The practice over time, like the slow wearing away of mountains, changes my habits of mind. It has taken time to find joy again. And now I acknowledge both its pleasure and its brevity. Contentment with what is is the prize. This is the steady balance I move toward in increments I do not see as they pass, yet feel when experience tests me.

How am I with this? With impermanence. With the way it is to be human and mortal. Lately I have had a bizarre and surprising new thought lurking. For so long I agreed with the fearful many who wished for death to come in their sleep. And now, I think, I want to be alert and present for this transition. For life and for death…just a two-sided door.

As the day continues, I make conscious bad decisions at lunch time, stubborn and seeking pleasure. That's how I am with this right now. Later I sit with my round Buddha-belly rumbling with discomfort. These are the consequences I thought I knew about and could endure. Much smiling, despite discomfort, as I sat with noisy and difficult digestion, and no problem attending to the body. It had my attention.

Group discussion later with the retreat leader. Everyone so pleased and then I take the opportunity going round the circle to share my surprise at feeling my own irritation with the schedule. I am the only whiner. This is momentarily embarrassing. How am I with this? Letting go of "me" feeling I've complained inappropriately. Feeling self-conscious. As we come round the group again, talking about expectations and conditions, the leader stresses that we have permission to ignore the bells and sit beyond the scheduled times. I watch my emotions up and down over the course of this. The question that burns: Have I offended? How am I with this? Niggling unease. Then in the observance, acceptance. A friend's suggestion to "surf the moment", comes to mind. Not diving, skimming. Sometimes the diving means too much story telling. Rather I listen to the body and mind and wait.

# 25 Negative Thoughts

When you notice your mind stuck in a cycle of angry or fearful thoughts, ask yourself: how is this helping? Try to replace the negative thoughts with something joyful and real. Remember a moment of kindness, your own or someone else's, and replay that scene in detail.

**Zen Retreat**

I want to catch some impressions and reflections…not quite halfway into this amazing pause in my life. I think of a physics book on time I'm working through at home with no little difficulty. The world not existing in linear time as we're accustomed to seeing it, but as single "nows". I feel that I've stepped into a "now" so different from those I live in…I've moved for a short while into a parallel life.

Six women living together in a silent community in this house-temple. A rhythm of sitting, studying, writing, eating, working. Personal bundles of bowl and mug and knife, fork, spoon, wrapped in a cloth napkin, used for each meal and washed and re-bundled by the user. Perhaps things go so well because of the silence. No chatter, no music in the background. My hips and knees and ankles are already stiff and sore but I walk out what I can in *kinhin* (walking meditation) and stretch in the short intervals of free time.

The open-eyes of Zazen are new to me. The teacher explains this as training. Not retreating behind closed eyes but maintaining mindfulness as we gaze at the world…though the world is just the empty carpet in front of us. Once my body is settled, it is happy. It is moving again after a long time that brings sharp awareness of pressure points and strain. Sometimes touching the breath is easy. Watching thoughts. Letting them go. Sometimes it is very difficult. A spiritual itch begging for escape. Sometimes I am drowsy and that is hardest of all.

"What am I doing here?" I've thought this surprisingly little. I miss home. I have trouble at night, just before sleep, thinking especially of my youngest child, his still-little-boy scent and voice calling for his bedtime song. Yet, I sleep well. Odd. I never do sleep well away from home, from my place and my bed. Ah…maybe that's it. This, too, is my place. I'm here because this is where I want to be. No. This is where I felt I had to be.

"What am I doing?" I am sitting on the floor. Legs stretched after so much cushion sitting. Trying to keep the pen moving. But not hurrying. Not hurrying. How much of life is lost in hurry? How many stubbed toes, fingers closed in gates, snarled hair brushes and lost keys? Yet, the flow of the brain seems to push for hurry. Thoughts in a steady stream, doubled up and riding tandem. Like preserve jars on basement shelves. What's behind those dust-free new ones up front? What's in the moldy, leaky jars at the back, the ones forgotten, where the writing has faded on the labels and the year is smudged and the contents questionable. Yes, that's what I'm doing. Trying to peer that deep, nudge the front jars aside, the bright and shiny new preserves, the ones I serve the company. And find what's back there where the spiders live.

"Fear," this teacher says. That could be my koan. What I need to seek and face. "Lean into the spears," says Pema Chodron, in a book I dipped into last night. Lean in. Peer through the dark. Risk reaching to the back of the self. Lip curled. A bit disgusted. And, yes, afraid. I want to touch it only with my finger tip. I need more grip than that to bring it to the light. OK. What's there? Fear of losing? Fear of loneliness. Fear of harming or being harmed. Fear of mistakes. Some bell rings in the back of my mind. I like to leave doors open. Room for escape. Just touching the jar means I can withdraw if I like. But once it's in my grasp then I'd have to drop it. That's messy.

Fear. What does it look like? Like biological specimens more than preserves. Something faceless and formless floating in the jar. Yet I must look closely. Do I also need to eat my fear? To take it in. Digest it. Understand it.

Fears? Here's one: How, outside of this cocoon of retreat, can I maintain this? Be who I am. This being that feels more me than any I've been. But that's my task. Not to change others. But to maintain this. Knowing that alone will bring change around me. And it is frightening not to know what this will mean. How will it alter the familiar? I am afraid of losing this. I am afraid of losing that. I create the fear as an image in my head to haunt me. A tiger I paint on the wall, one proverb says, then crouch afraid of what I've made.

I wish I knew where this was all taking me. I wish for peace. For peace more than love or anything. For peace and contentment. Kindness, more dear than love, for too often we are unkind even to those we love the most. I wish I could carry this space with me inside. This centered feeling of being balanced and whole amidst the chaos of life.

### Our Way of Looking at Things

> ...our minds, our attitudes, our preferences, and our ways of looking at the outside world can be changed. Effort, introspection and clarity, applied with the breath, do change our way of looking at things.
> from *Golden Wind, Zen Talks* by Eido Shimano Roshi

Reading an obscure and puzzling *teisho* talk of several pages, my mind holds onto a few lines that are straight forward, instructive, reassuring. Until I begin to ponder them.

I know my way of looking at things has changed mightily but it is like surgery, perhaps more painful in the short term. So that the material, the trivial, the escapes and sensory pleasures begin to worry at me and lead me to despair. So too time and its passing. The forgetfulness of our society, of each of us, living "as if" we were in control and time a commodity we can somehow conjure more of. It's not like love. Boundless and bottomless. You cannot give away enough love to find yourself with none remaining. But time? You can fritter it away in front of computer screens and tv's. You can set it loose and squander it in self-absorbed or even destructive patterns. The measure before you is ever less. And yet teachers remind me of the eternity in this moment, this breath, this now.

Why is despair so easy for me to touch these days? And joy is like a rainbow I glimpse and lose even as I am looking. The despair instead like the ground beneath my feet. So solid and real. I have toyed now and then with the idea of seeking counsel or even medication and reject both ideas before they are fully formed. I could not relate in counsel with anyone not sharing this world view of mine. I am become a minority. Interesting. Revealing. It leads to new empathy and compassion for whole segments of our culture...immigrants, first nations. A shared ground is needed for this work. And medication would distance me from what I need to let arise and to let go. For what I need to see and know. Indeed, the pleasures, distractions and technologies of today are medications in their own right. A part, a large part, of the problem. People do not stop, be still and listen....

"Effort, introspection and clarity applied with the breath." I think of another teacher who advises we feel the breath, not watch it. And sitting I let this be like the wave of the ocean. The breathing of the earth, the world. Fleetingly I feel the breath of each individual...faces and postures flitting through. The grouse who hit the window yesterday and rested in the snow, breathing and recuperating. My sons breathing in this house. Those in hospitals connected to machines. Breathing, being. Sitting in the awful Australian heat, breathing. The homeless here in Whitecourt, hunched over fires in tents in the woods, a news article says, breathing through winter. Our cat watching the grouse, alert and cautious, breathing lightly. The tiny moth who flew low skimming the dinner table last night, resting near my glass.

Yesterday, weary, struggling with tired limbs through air heavy as sand, I thought, "Is this what it's for? Doing? Accumulating? Busyness? Training our children to repeat the pattern?" It can't be. So what is it for then? To help. To laugh. To love. To really see. Mary Oliver, poet, says our only job is to pay attention. Paying attention I see my conditioning. It's woven strongly. A hood over my eyes. I lift the edges, pick at the weaving. "Our way of looking at things" can change.

**Three Teachers: Aging, Illness and Death**

In the paper recently I read that aches and pains are not a normal part of aging and this little bit of someone's wisdom took root in my brain where it's a full-fledged weed now. I hurt. All of the time really. Most severely early in the morning. My left side is the worst...shoulder and neck. My back is so stiff I grunt or gasp when I move sometimes. Even after my morning stretch routine and working awhile, I'll bend to pick up something or twist to reach and there it is.

Then leg cramps and foot cramps. When these wake me in the night, the terror is worse than the pain. The helplessness, the immobility, the sneakiness of these muscle spasms frightens me. So is none of this a normal part of aging? I come back to the chronic ailments I battle, the surgical modifications. Searching for a way of understanding. It comes down to learning to live with a sometimes unpredictable illness and all its manifestations.

But what I want to write about is not the illness or the pain, it's the odd tango my thoughts dance...fear of all this, of some really bad news behind some or all of it. I am so easily sucked into fear. My bones are made of collapsible matter and when fear draws a breath I fold and yield.

Fear's partner is disbelief. I cannot really imagine my own death or even a terminal diagnosis. This is a human failing. Despite the reality training of Buddhist meditation, despite the messages of my aging and ill body, despite the tragic news contemporary society feels we all need with our breakfast (though I avoid this when possible), I feel immortal. I know this is not my personal immortality I feel, but the universal one. Life goes on. Still, it feels personal.

If I prayed, it would be to live to see my children settled in happy adult lives. When I wish, this is what I wish for. But it's more than one wish. For my longevity, for their safety and happiness and right choices. For good karma for all. Nothing unusual here. The wishes and hopes of every mother, of every human being, of every being.

They say a coward dies a thousand deaths, the brave man but once. In a reflex of self-defense, I have believed instead that those without fears are also those without imagination. Whatever the case, I find myself here, living through the fears.

I lived much of my healthy, younger life in a slow simmer of anger, resentment and aversion, teeth metaphorically clenched. What I had was objectively fine. But as so many of us do, perhaps more so when we're young, I wanted "different". And like having a tire caught in a rut, spinning, I could not break free of the mindset that was hurting me. Then snick. I just did. In the midst of middle age and more precarious health, even a more problematic life, I broke free of that particular rut. Meditation teachings. Time. Insight. Some kind of readiness. I turned the wheel the right way or some hand on mine did. And I'm here. I'm seeing the sweetness in the moments. I'm feeling my blessings. I'm able to breathe and mean "if this is all, then this is enough." The ruts, and ice and suck of mud under my tires disappearing. There is a breeze in my face again, a freshness. A brightness to ordinary days.

Yet fears of this illness are growing roots, giving rise to a new crop of pain, more weeds of aversion. I need to dig deep and work hard. I can do this when I am here and now and not distracted by longing or useless questions. This is my life and it is good. And it is good to know this.

# 26 Generosity

When a generous impulse arises, act on it: give the compliment, make the offer to help, make a donation you can afford. Then watch the joy that arises, what you gain from such a choice.

**Following My Feet**

The opening of the heart makes some things seem even more complicated than they were before. Or maybe it's adapting to this process of opening the heart. I think maybe the reason it all seems more complicated is that I still too often move into planning mind and analytical mind, rather than letting my toes guide me. They have pretty good communication with my heart.

For instance, all of us who are affluent in this society (and we are many), we members of the comfortable middle class, have more than we need. OK, so some are struggling to pay a mortgage, others still paying for last year's new car or the family holiday in Hawaii. But that's my point, isn't it? If we think we need more, it's because we keep driving toward desires, thinking that getting there is the key to happiness. But, if we accept first the idea that we have enough, and then accept our interdependence with all beings, there is another need there. That need is to give back in some way. One way is through money.

It's never been easy for me to say no. And the result is a constant bombardment of "charity" requests for money. These arrive by mail, by phone, at my door and by e-mail. And I generally give a little here and a little there, recognizing the legitimacy of the needs these charities represent and also feeling that by giving I honor my own connection to all of this. The poverty, the environmental issues, the diseases, the social ills. I have a share in their creation and so a share in their easement. And I have wondered so often as I give these piddling amounts, like a prince sprinkling nickels among his starving people, just what does this achieve? And if I were a celebrity, one of those who throw their name and weight behind a particular cause, what would that cause be? How do these people choose? Is there a measuring stick? For their involvement makes a significant difference. They aren't just throwing nickels. And so I become confused.

I've started research projects to try to select some one charity so that I could give a significant amount that might have real impact. And I've abandoned these searches more troubled than ever by the setting of such criteria. It isn't, after all, a matter of a checklist and logic.

I think what I need to do is learn to follow my feet. They know what kind of path beckons them. They know their own capacity. What I mean is that we each have gifts and skills. We each have experiences that pull and shape us. And so each finds the direction of giving most suited to his/her capacities. This means not only how much money and how much time to give. But where to give it. And I do not need to find some ultimate "best" place to aim my efforts. The web of being connects all of us. The myriad needs, the multitude of skills and the masses of funds that are available all fit somewhere in this network. And when I follow my feet, whatever strand I follow, the gentle vibrations of these movements will impact the whole. Thus, if I am mindful and it is my open heart that guides those steps, I need only walk on.

**Christmas Giving**

When I was a child, growing up in pretty traditional home, Christmas was a time of magic. It meant good things to eat, Santa Claus, and time with cousins and extended family that I saw too little of over the year. It meant decorations and sparkles and snow. But it also meant the story of the baby Jesus. Sometimes we went to a special service at our church. And always both my mom and dad sang a lot as they worked. So the story of Christmas was mixed with melody for me: "Silent Night", "Away in the Manger", "Angels We Have Heard on High".

What do I make of Christmas these days? We still put up our traditional tree, though I think of it as our "enlightenment tree", cross-pollinating traditions. One of my sons has played piano in the Christmas Eve service of a local church for several years now, so the rest of us go to that service and enjoy the message, the music, the candles and the fellowship. And throughout the season traditional Christmas music is very much present. Playing on the stereo. Being hummed as I bake. Or at the concerts and gatherings we attend.

The story of Christmas is a beautiful and inspiring one. The message of Jesus is a beautiful and inspiring one. Love others as yourself. Christmas carries a message of peace and joy and generosity.

The Buddha, who lived hundreds of years before Jesus, taught such things in his own words and ways. One of the most beautiful of these teachings is the

*Metta Sutta* or *Discourse on Loving-kindness*. A part of this lengthy teaching that I love dearly goes like this:

> Even as a mother protects with her life, her child, her only child,
> So should one with a boundless heart cherish all living beings,
> Radiating loving-kindness over all the earth,
> Upwards to the skies and downwards to the depths,
> Outwards and unbounded.

So Christmas for me means that there is still a time officially marked in the year when we are reminded, more frequently than in the regular course of our days, to think of others. The inescapable nature of the calendar means that even a Scrooge has to give this a passing thought. How we mark this is a matter of individual choice: gifts to family and friends, to people who have been part of our lives over the previous year; donations to food banks and soup kitchens; funds to non-profits aiming to help those in third world countries, those in dire circumstances of one kind or another. And, perhaps, we'll remember that giving extends beyond the material to listening, caring for, taking time and making effort. For a moment, the buzz of "acquiring" may be balanced with the more gentle hum of "generosity".

Our affluent society has made it more difficult to hear that hum. The message of love has been sublimated by the call to buy, supporting the illusion that "things" will bring happiness. So it is also not a surprise to me to read statistics that mention Christmas as a time of deep depression for many people. Our imaginings outstrip reality. And even the reality lasts only a brief time. The turkey is eaten, the gifts opened, the fire goes out, the guests go home, the laughter ends. A regular ho-hum Monday morning comes again. Christmas, like a holiday in the tropics, doesn't fix our problems. And we may be tempted to treat this special time as merely an escape. A respite. A dream. Then it's over.

The practice of mindfulness has the potential to turn this around. When we really look at our experience, when we don't turn away, we know that material things, even the company of those we hold dear, cannot guarantee a lasting peace and happiness.

For me, happiness arrives when I do. When I let myself arrive here and now, I find I was holding it all the time in my heart. When I quit longing and give up regret, when I feel my breath and remember the gift of life. When I look around and remember that each and every being is like this. Struggling to be happy. Sometimes skillfully, sometimes not. When I forgive myself and others for the mistakes we make. Then I remember that no matter what the advertisements may say to the contrary, loving-kindness is the gift we give ourselves and a gift suitable for everyone on our Christmas list.

## Ode to Hugs

Why are hugs better than kisses? Because when they're real they involve your whole body. I like the strength of hugs. Shared body heat. Encircling a loved-one, beng encircled. The pulling together. The feel of muscles moving, working. Breath shared. I cannot feel blue in the midst of a hug. Even wounded, crying, hurt, I am pulled in and healed.

Some of the best hugs I get are from my young son. He throws himself at me. It can hurt. He's heavy and rough and intense. He doesn't check to see if I'm ready, my feet balanced, my head raised enough to avoid collision. He just crashes into me and crushes me in close and usually he giggles. And all that energy and intensity and love penetrates me, body and soul, and I feel joyous. It lingers. That feeling of joy. He breaks through my solitude somehow. I am reminded of connection, of what is good in me and the world.

I know this is love of a "particular". It comes with the trailing strings of entangled attachment. His love for me and mine for him. But the physical generosity of it is also liberating. It opens for me into metta, a love that expands and includes the world. How is there room for ill will in a heart so brimming with joy and love?

This is another of the gifts of innocence…what children and animals offer as teachings in our lives. The Dhamma of ordinary life. To love without reserve in this way. Not to be wary and judgmental or seeking acceptance. Just to give and give and give.

I hear in my son's giggle and see in the sparkle in his eyes that his generous expression of love in these enthusiastic physical hugs is wholesome and good for him too. No giving then without also receiving. When I laugh in surprise and wrap my arms around him, sometimes lifting him off his feet. When we bump heads and groan between our sputtering chuckles, we share something wholesome and good and larger than us.

We learn from what we experience. "Wet" is what it's like to stand in the rain or dive in a lake. "Sad" is what I feel when my best friend moves away, or when I lose the "lucky stone" I've been carrying around in my pocket. "Love" is what it feels like to be hugged hard and long, or to share laughter in a moment of connection. When something is felt this way at a visceral level, it becomes real and alive, more than a dry concept. Moving toward the realization of an intention of metta is only possible when we begin from what is known.

Teachers tell us to access this personal feeling or experience as we begin to put effort in the wholesome direction of the skillful development of metta, loving-kindness directed to all living beings. The physical memory of these hugs shared with my ten-year-old child are seeds for the universal love I intend to cultivate.

# 27 Forgiveness

When you find yourself indulging in negative self-talk, stop. Imagine you are sitting across the table from someone who loves you. Take on their voice in your mind, and let that voice tell you about all the reasons why you are loved, all that person sees in you as good and worthwhile.

**Self-forgiveness**

Recently I woke in the morning aware of a dream lingering, leaving its flavor in my mind. I tried to recall what the content of the dream had been, but only smoke and mirrors remained. No actions, no characters, no setting. The flavor left behind was real enough though. I knew I had been angry in the dream. And now, the anger was only a tang under the bitter taste of guilt. I was feeling guilty for having been angry in a dream.

Saying this to myself didn't help. Not being able to get hold of the story didn't help. Knowing the foolishness of this state of mind didn't make it go away. I could wish it were smoke and mirrors like the rest of the dream, but the feeling was in my body...no waking to rested ease, but to this muddy sense of self-judgment. Ouch.

How much more intense is guilt when it happens in waking life. When we feel we've acted in a way of which we're not proud or with which we're not pleased. When we've been in the wrong. Guilt is not a skilful emotion. Rather than allowing the clear seeing and resolve that will help us to make positive choices in the future, it causes us to see ourselves darkly. We create a cartoon goblin self who deserves punishment or at least whatever negative consequences follow from the actions taken. We cast ourselves as the "bad guy". One of the problems with this is that it can become a habit. "That's the way I am. I always screw up. I hurt people. I do the wrong thing." But what's the alternative? How not to go there. How to go towards clear seeing.

We do this better, often, when we're dealing with others. We know it instinctively, whether we can do it or not. We need to forgive. When someone hurts us, or treats us poorly, we can hold onto that too, of course, create a goblin-self for them and pretend we're wearing white, maybe even haloes. But if you've tried it, you know: forgiving eases your own pain, whether the other person makes reconciliation or not. And forgiving lets everyone drop the costumes and be who they are, larger than any one action, more than any one mistake.

So it is the same with guilt. Guilt is a form of self-harm. When we can forgive ourselves for the action, the anger maybe, or whatever caused it this time, we begin to be able to see things more clearly. In the Buddhist tradition there is a tricky concept of *anatta*, usually translated as no-self or non-self. While people can tie themselves in knots trying to make sense of this, the understanding I have reached is that it is the concept of self as stagnant, fixed, thing-like, that no-self is denying. We are processes, moving through time. And not only are we capable of change, we have to change. It's in our natures. It's in the nature of everything, and we are part of that. Creating a goblin-self then is like taking a picture and saying "this is me", it's just a representation in a single moment. The picture isn't me. The moment captured is not me. To feel this in watching the mind's maneuvers in meditation is to begin to see the world differently.

I keep favorite quotes on index cards so that the glimmering insights they bring can be revisited when memory has faded. One such quote from a monastic teacher whose name, alas, I didn't note, is this: "Do not have expectations of others. Only treat them with kindness." Our private expectations are what allow us to think we are in the right. So I would carry this further. You may set resolutions or determinations, but don't warp these with expectations of yourself. Only treat yourself with kindness. Be ready to forgive.

On the morning I woke feeling muddy with self-judgment, I eventually closed my eyes and rested, letting the hectoring voices fade. I let the taste of guilt linger and watched it break apart. I took time to breathe and to see. To be kind to myself. But most important, I remembered: Though I might have said "I am lying in my bed", that "I" is no more solid and fixed than the dream self who had acted unskillfully.

## Doubt

A labyrinth is an apt symbol for this mindful journey that leads in and into a blossoming in the centre. The habits of doubt and desire are strong and it is so difficult to let them go. Thus, there are still days when I cannot help but look constantly around to see how far I have come. And then, doing this, I feel both despair at my apparent lack of progress and doubt in my own capacity to make any difference in my own life or in the world.

It is such a day today. I see that I have once again taken on too many commitments and that I'm feeling harried and worried about meeting them. That I do not seem to change the patterns in my life. Our household still produces too much garbage. My children still yearn for too many "things" as if these will make them happy. My cupboards are still too full of unused dishes and my fridge overflowing with every variety of condiment, fruit and vegetable we crave. We seem to be living still the prescribed western life of middle-class affluence. And yet this is not in harmony with what I believe.

When friends tell me they see repeating destructive patterns in their lives, or my children mourn about mistakes they keep making over and over, or someone comments that even though we know we're destroying the environment, human beings don't seem to be changing, I like to use an analogy: How long does it take to stop an eighteen wheel semi truck? Even if the driver is desperate to do so? There's a lot of momentum there. And what if the road itself is slippery? No, this isn't an easy thing to do. And it may not happen as quickly as the driver wishes.

Awareness and contemplation precede the right intention and eventually, the right actions. With big changes, both stopping and turning around are cumbersome. Patience is required.

When I sit for awhile and follow my breath and then watch the thoughts that arise and pass, I see what is real. That I am causing my own suffering now by desiring the stop-and-turn to be immediate rather than letting this process be, moment by moment. Right thought, right action. This moment and then this. Change not only will come but is inevitable. It is what mortal life entails. My task is only to stay mindful and let the rest follow.

So I sit and watch the clouds of doubt and desire move through. I keep my grasping hands in my lap, softly open, and do not reach for the clouds as I have been doing, pulling them over my head, cringing in the rain they bring. Breathe, let them pass and smile. The middle way is not a shortcut and not a quick fix. It's a way of being.

**Seeking Comfort**

I am clutching a pile of fresh clothes in my arms, along with soap and towel and other assorted items. When I come into the large room, the bathtub is full of strange things. Large things. Broken things. Unidentifiable things. Grubby things. Some sort of project. "I'm not going to be able to have my bath, am I?" I say despondently and my husband gives me a look that says "Isn't it obvious?", while only answering "No."

I head out the door into a corridor and take an elevator up to a prettily appointed spa. A woman I don't know is standing at the mirror, toweling wet hair. She gives me a pitying look and says "Sorry, the water just went off."

I don't even answer, just back out the door and continue my quest. There are several other disappointing stops. It's amazing how many tubs are theoretically available without walking far really, but then that's the way dreams are.

When I wake from the dream I am feeling sad, lonely and confused. In need of comfort. That's the emotional flavor that lingers. No surprise. That's the mood I was in as I struggled with my monkey mind before finding sleep the night before. And baths, well, what's more comforting than a long soak in a tub, away from all those who may have misunderstood and not appreciated me? Melting away body tension and stress. The symbolism doesn't escape me as I swing my feet over the side of the bed.

The evening before I had a very ordinary and undramatic experience. A disappointment. Expecting a certain kind of experience in a social gathering and finding something else instead. Feeling isolated. Feeling unconnected. Contracting into a self that felt misunderstood and alone. And despite all my understanding that I was doing myself no good, I allowed this experience to remain in my head. I climbed into bed replaying the emotions, reinforcing them. I fell into thought patterns around "home" and "belonging" and "friendship"...all theoretical and analytical and completely useless except in so far as they served to wind the spool of thinking tighter and tighter. Pretty uncomfortable. Not sure when I finally fell asleep.

This morning, in the aftermath of my dream, I see clearly the small self with all its stuff seeking comfort. I see the story-telling, the projecting and the wall-building. The blaming directed outward and the pity directed inward. My body still holds the results.

Breathing and feeling now, no longer caught in thinking, I go through my morning routine. Open my gratitude journal and pick up my pen. Begin to move my thoughts toward what is lovely, what is nourishing in my life. I write briefly about only a few. Then I move to the floor, dream mood receding, and go through my yin routine. I move my contracted and stiff body into favorite asanas and breathe there, surrendering into the earth and letting resistance to "what is" melt away. By the time I move to my altar, light candles and incense, make my bows and take my seat to meditate, I am feeling soft. Still a little sad maybe but more open and larger somehow. Not the little stooped being huddled protectively over what is mine and scurrying around looking for an escape. That mood is gone. Impermanent. I find my breath and the beating of my heart and send love to myself. This is what it is to be human and to be led by momentary emotions into painful places that can seem so real, both waking and sleeping. Places that have no substance, that dissolve when I look closely.

This is sadness. This is loneliness. Patches of fog that dissipate in the heat and light of loving acceptance.

All of this, or some of it, I might have done last night when wisdom eluded me. Still, this morning, awake and alert, if not awakened yet, I'm back on track, beginning again.

# 28  Breathe

Today each time you go through a doorway, breathe and be there in this new space and time.

**Now**

It's like this. Like I stepped into a pool of color, the end of the rainbow. Or turned in the midst of walking down a long dark hallway and found a sudden shaft of golden light, or came up from dark, cold water into light and air. The past couple of days happiness is easy. And I don't know if it's something I'm doing or just accident. Have these shifting, troublesome menopausal hormones taken another turn? Settled? In the external world not much is different. Summer is still cool and slow to make itself known though the kids are in "holiday" mode. The kennel is busier than ever. I haven't had a chance to talk to my sister in days and I miss her. Yet, I'm still light and bouyant.

If I'm doing something, it's this: I am seeing suddenly how easy happiness can be. I am not analyzing or interpreting or de-constructing. I am floating in some bubble of "now". Underneath is a wee wave of fear that I'll "forget" how to do this. That I'll let the bubble settle to the ground and it will burst in a flood of "whys" and "hows" and "what ifs" and "used to be's" and "if only's". These are too much for its fragile nature...sharp stones of regret, worry and desire. I feel that this way of being has been available to me but I have not been able to step into the color because I was working so hard with my eyes shut. Concentrating and trying to find it inside. I misunderstood the instructions. I don't need to build happiness, I need to be it. And finding it inside does not mean my eyes are squeezed shut. It does not mean working so hard. When I heard myself say outloud: "When did happiness become such hard work?", it shocked me into stillness inside. Give up the memorizing of techniques, the policing, the effort. I have the teachings and I'm on the path. Now relax. Open my eyes. Breathe. Be. And after a dreadful day of world weariness and exhaustion, I just lifted up and found ease. It was as if I'd been clawing to hold onto something that only held me down and when I grew too tired and sad to try anymore, I floated up into the color, the light and the air that was always there.

Given my nature, the habit of working, struggling to completely understand, I wonder if I can maintain this. But for now it feels so good. On the cushion, be alert. Breathe. In each moment, see and be. And when I feel myself reaching for a grip again, closing down to "think", stop! I am beginning to recognize the triggers. The jagged edges that lift up toward me…moments of irritation, revulsion, despair. They have a taste and a shadow about them. But if I open up, I somehow move past and through without losing this lightness… this serenity. Interesting it is not by pulling in, by closing up, by fighting the threat. Here the teachings are now instinctive. Why so suddenly? See. Note. Ah! Breathe and welcome but don't dwell and I simply move through it. The threats are phantoms after all, delusion.

## Struggling

The Buddha described five hindrances that interfere with mindfulness and I've been taking up the practice of noticing these, loosening their grip in this way, letting them go.

Usually before sitting I spend time in some Buddhist readings. This is supposed to help me to focus, and I do learn more, and explore questions important to me on this path. But generally this activity means I am filled too much with a longing (grasping) for peace and wisdom, to be further along, to be better at daily mindfulness. I recognize this as grasping and when I begin to sit I name this and return to listening to the room around me and then to mind. I return to the breath. Usually the beginning of meditation and several times along the way this "grasping" arises. I make a mental note and return.

Upon reflection I find this hard to distinguish from doubt, as doubt in my "ability" and my "success" follows upon the yearning. Lately, doubt has taken a new shape as I worry about the changes in me, the impact on my marriage in the long term. Doubt arises sometimes in the guise of "Am I on the right path?" "Can this be right action, if it harms my family?" "Is it harming my family?" "What do I mean by harm?" Change, after all, is inevitable. None of the people in any family can remain forever the same. I am not obligated to stay the same, to shape my "self" to the expectations of others. But this is all uncomfortable. When I meditate, I note and let go of these doubts but in daily mindfulness they are more difficult.

Aversion, today, took the simple form of annoyance at the sound of the clothes drier. I finally made the sound my focus and just followed the rhythm.

Sleepiness can creep up on me unnoticed when I am tired to begin with. (Today is one such day.) I often miss the arising and just "come to awareness" as my head droops or I seem to "wake up" and notice I've been drifting in a sort of dream-thought state who knows for how long.

Restlessness is most often dependent on my state of mind as I sit. A feeling of time constraints or "I should be..." will invade then. I have found it easiest to acknowledge and deal with this if I allow myself to plan before I sit and begin with listening and a wide perceiving of all sensory input, not trying to center on the breath too soon.

It is quite easy for me to accept sleepiness or restlessness, as they seem involuntary to me and so don't lead to judgment. More difficult to surround aversion, grasping or doubt with acceptance as there is evaluation, and I do not like to acknowledge these "weaknesses" in myself. I'm finding that the work I'm doing with the hindrances is very much the work of changing my view. It is so true that grasping/yearning makes for suffering in not attaining what one desires and aversion makes for suffering in the moment itself when there is no escape and in the judgment that follows so closely on its heels. Even so, doubt is suffering for it prevents me from following a path, from taking action, and leaves me trapped in some state of no commitment. That leaves room only for yearning and aversion.

Interesting that this brings to mind for me a conversation with my sons about anger...trying to help them to recognize how their own anger hurts them and how actions follow from thoughts. If they can get in touch with what they are thinking and feeling then they can choose more appropriate actions. Anger, I told them, arises from a sense of helplessness (which is very much a state of suffering). My 11-year-old has an interesting "macho" interpretation of this... staying calm gives you power, shows you are strong. Hmmm.

When I set an intention to "work" with the hindrances in meditation, I don't feel like I'm waiting for them to arise, I feel instead that I conjure them. At any rate, when I relax and breathe into this "control", worry subsides.

Desire for me seems most often to arise as companion to aversion and both are related to control. Fearing disorder and needing to plan, carry through. Fear and helplessness about ongoing concerns which no plan or action seems to remedy. To look at the ego's struggle honestly and then let go of these thoughts is the strategy most helpful to concentration.

Away from home awhile ago, helping my mom move, I battled restlessness constantly in trying to continue my meditation. So much to do. So many balls to juggle. And a feeling of urgency...need to complete and get back home. I tried to just acknowledge all this, then back to the breath. And I persisted. I believe the brief periods of sitting once or twice a day helped keep me calm through this time. This time I did not have a Crohn's flare-up, which I often do in times of stress. Also, happily, less exasperation with my meek mom!

The solution to each hindrance, I think, is the same. See what I'm creating. See what this leads to. Relax into the breath. Quit analyzing, judging, worrying, hoping. Acknowledge and release. Breathe.

**Home**

A verse in the *Flower Ornament Scriptures* says "…the nature of *home* is empty" and expresses the wish that "all beings…should escape its pressures." Home is one of those ideas for me that is like a delicious donut filled with a sweet cream of emotion. Appealing, heavy and more than a little sticky.

There is a line in a Billy Joel song exclaiming his love is his home. Home represents longing, somehow. When I think of home I still conjure up memories of childhood. The smell of horses and hay. Our treehouse and the dappled sunlight. Mom in the kitchen. Dad's gardens. Home is still reserved in its first meaning in my heart-dictionary as that place and those people. Where it began.

Home has been more mobile as I grew and there is no house I've felt so rooted in. This piece of land here is enscribed as another meaning of this word for me though. I love the woods, and the squirrels and birds. The paths I walk every day with the dogs. The poor sorrowing May Day tree in the backyard. The one I fought to save when it would have been cut down to move the shop. The one that fights its own battle now against a black fungus the greenhouse woman tells us is carried on birds' feet. The tree I lift my eyes to now as I write. It is the marker of the seasons for me, right now beginning to open in tender green shoots.

The nature of home is empty this prayer says. And the nature (of people) abhors a vacuum. So we fill and fill. With memories, expectation, stuff and ornaments. And it all pushes at the walls of this place, a place only in our minds. The pressure can be painful if we are not able to open up and let it go.

The May Day tree beyond my window may lose its fight, my parents are gone, the neglected treehouse is falling apart, and the gardens and hay and horses of my childhood had been replaced by a storage yard of parked yellow taxis the last time I drove by my childhood home. Because all things are subject to change, to age, their natures are empty of anything constant. Not so much a cream-filled donut then, as one of the more common kind with a hole in the centre.

But home can have a meaning that is not tied to a place or a memory or to a yearning. It is a sense of belonging and refuge and balance. The poet, Robert Frost said "Home is the place where, when you have to go there, they have to take you in." When the haven I seek in a storm is within my own heart-mind,

I live inside it, no matter where my physical body may be. The steady accumulation of practice, of serenity and peace that meditation brings, of faith in the path I'm following as I see its positive influence on my life, is the building of such a home. A place where I am always enfolded, always taken in. And because it is carried in my own heart, it is steady and accessible always. I realize that I've turned the old adage inside out. A magician's bag. Empty? Maybe. But then something beautiful and surprising emerges. Once I believed that home is where the heart is. Now, this open heart is where my home is.

# 29 Silence

## Turn the tunes off in your vehicle and drive in silence.

**Minus the Music**

In the yoga classes at the studio where I teach, there is always music playing. Often, when the classes are slower and more yin-like, or during svasana or in the time of gathering before a class begins, the music playing is gentle and comforting. The kind of music that invites one's heartbeat and breath to slow, invites the body to loosen and let go, invites the mind to follow.

There are many CD's available and on-line guided meditations that also use this kind of music. Chanting perhaps or gentle instrumentals, sounds of nature over flute or piano.

In the meditation classes I lead there is no music. When we sit or walk in meditation, there are only the rhythms of the breath, the soft or not-so-soft on and off cycles of the furnace, the creaking of doors or floors, the shuffle of feet and bodies, the whistle of a train nearby, the filtered sounds of traffic, voices, tunes and laughter from beyond the door. And sometimes someone asks me why.

My short answer is that this is the way I was taught. This is the tradition of Theravada meditation, to sit in silence. And sometimes I may say a little more about the portability of the breath, the importance of not being reliant on an outside "something" in order to access calm and to become centered when life does some sort of spin without warning.

In the yoga classes, music, along with the low light, the supportive and welcoming demeanor of the teachers, and the enveloping sense of community, create a cradle that makes dropping into this time and place easier to do. And this can be a very good thing. At the end of a busy day, in a state of mind that is harried or anxious, all of these supports to coming to the present are valuable. The resulting peace is a thing to be grateful for.

But there is also a place for silence. When you come to yoga class and lie down on your mat and are invited to relax, this may indeed be the first time in your day that you have given yourself permission to do this. And in our yang lifestyles, as we are often reminded in these classes, there is a drive to do and move quickly, to multi-task and to get a lot done. Even our leisure time is generally scheduled by the clock, requiring that we make ourselves get going out the door, whether it be for our child's swimming class, a coffee date with a friend, a movie night or a yoga class. So coming to stillness is healing. Remembering that safe place without an agenda, without a ticking clock.

It is also the case that in our yang lifestyles, our senses are generally on overload. I once read an article that said there are virtually no places on earth anymore where the sounds of human beings do not invade. Our phones are ringing, music is playing, television screens are mounted on the walls even in public venues, advertising signs blink and jitter and spin with slogans and pictures.

When we sit in silence and close our eyes we are letting ourselves rest and retreat from such overload. We close out, voluntarily, for awhile, the dominant sensory gates. And in so doing we more easily fall inward. To the sounds of the breath and our heart. To the chatter of our minds. Without the distraction of an external soundtrack it is that much more obvious how noisy the mind can be, how demanding and how persistent. We see then the thoughts that recur. The thoughts that lead us into narratives that cause anxiety or anger or grief. Music soothes, but what it also does is provide another distraction to cling to. In following the music, we forget for a little while the worries and the plans, but we do not see them. We may not learn to look and so to learn their ephemeral nature. We don't so easily see them drift through and disappear. We may simply tuck them behind the tunes, still believing perhaps in their solidity. Sitting in silence pares away the great bulk of external distractions and this can be challenging because it is so unfamiliar. There is nowhere for unwelcome thoughts to hide. And because of this, when we watch, we also see their dissolution.

Peace, when one can find it through gentle music or movement, through soft lighting and stillness, is a positive and healing thing. And it is skillful to seek this out in a busy world. But it is the learning to look inward, to see the source of our unease in the patterns of our thinking that makes peace more readily accessible in our ordinary lives. Silence supports this.

**Kitchen Dreams**

All the world, this morning, is enclosed in my kitchen. I live in this world sometimes. A place I love, especially in the mornings. Our big bright kitchen. I'm sick of white, says my son, thinking, no doubt, of his aunts' houses with their explosions of color: greens and blues and golds and purple. So much bold, bold color. They laugh at me, my sister and sister-in-law, fondly, their homes so different from mine. I like it all to be simple. All white walls in our home and the carpet that kind that wears well because I hate to redecorate/renovate. It's just squares in shades of beige and floors in white and off-white and all bright. While out the windows everything is green. The trees and grass and private space. I treasure our home. This piece of the world entrusted to our care for a time. The wildness of the woods and weather outside our walls and inside, sunlight in my kitchen and sunbeams across our oak table, our only piece of "new" furniture with its soft golden color.

    I like to sit here in the empty early mornings and watch the birds or if there are none in the winter, then turn to watch the fish in the big aquarium that takes up much of one wall. This is my world where I sit, sipping coffee in the quiet and reading or writing, pondering and letting myself think. Listening to the "discursive flies" buzzing in my head. This is the antidote and companion piece to the silent sitting meditation I've done a little while before in another favorite space in my basement where little light enters, but the walls are still white. Incense has soaked into them so when you go down the hall and pass that door it comes through the door to greet you. My sister slept in there on her last visit and mentioned how the scent was soothing and decorated her dreams. That's the space where I sit everyday alone and imagine my scattered sangha, still figures ranged around the white walls, sitting with me.

    The buzzing flies this morning are weaving a story about my wildest dream. No longer so wild, my dreams, in terms of big or threatening or dangerous or crazy. It is, I think, to live in the temple within my heart. To forgive myself the missteps and backsliding as I move toward this dream, and to just keep moving in that direction. To live in this place wherever I am. Solitude that enfolds me like a bubble in a crowd. Silence that stands between me and the distractions of the world. Love and compassion that keep me still when reactivity twitches. Patience that keeps me rooted in the face of a desire to run.

    Sometimes I think of a physical place. A place by the ocean with its steady breathing in my ear. Brave New World where anger and competition and materialism don't exist.

    But really, the place I want to dwell is with me, in this temple in my heart. Peace I can feel. Not the world peace Miss Universes through the decades have wished for, an external peace that mankind doesn't seem ready to arrange, but peace that is carried in the face of what the world offers. Not a numbing shield around me but joyous energy moving through me, the ease that sitting often brings, anchored and accessible in my heart.

# What Will Happen?

Reflections on a Zen teaching from *Golden Wind*:

> What will happen when thoughts, ideas, opinions, emotional reactions, psychological problems, attachments, expectations, life, death, sickness and old age all fall away and our minds become bare?

What will happen? Deeper than sleep. Different from sleep. Once I would have thought of this as extinction. Death. Undesirable. But even death falls away, this says.

This seems restful. A promise. To move outside of these clamoring difficulties. Like removing a scratchy sweater, tight shoes. Like shaving your head. Like dropping naked into warm, clear water. Fearless. Limp. Relaxed. No agenda.

Sometimes sitting, for what seems in the timeless silence to be the merest of moments, I'm able to ignore the chattering till it recedes and fades, and then, when my body finds its balance…and the twitches and itches and aches are also outside the spotlight of attention, I'll find a place that tastes of this. Not enlightenment but enveloping serenity. A comfortable place to be. But not the golden wind. Yet this is the closest I have to an answer from experience to the question he sets: "What will happen?"

I imagine that, unlike me, the enlightened one would be able to maintain this serenity steadily, and function in the world too. Feeling this golden wind Ummon describes and yet doing what needs doing. There's the real mystery. For sitting, when I find this place with the flavor of being "bare", it's like holding a soap bubble in my hand. Fragile and short lived. It can be broken often by the tone of my clock when sitting time ends or sometimes earlier by an invasive thought or sensation. So that serenity and "here" do not seem able to co-exist for long. No *ideal with the actual*\* here. One or the other. This is what makes it clear that pleasant as this experience may be, it's just another fleeting experience. Like the pain in my knees or the list of things to do replaying in my brain, or the chill running up my back.

The initial impulse drawing us towards sitting may be this idea of escaping and separating. We're making a mistake that we'll see in time. Ummon talks somewhere of the life of the hermit as appearing to be one that escapes responsibilities. I think of myself as more hermit than monk or nun in the core, at the center of my being. But mine is the all too ordinary escape fantasy. Away from, outside of. Less psychological pain when the human elements are set aside. Walden. A hut by a lake in the woods. Some variation of this fantasy must exist in every human mind. Stepping away. Physically or psychologically. Aren't some mental illnesses manifestations of this? The schizophrenic who moves to a new persona. The sociopath who detaches from compassion, morality. The addict who slips into a world less sharp and painful.

I see the golden wind as a different kind of leaving behind. Just shedding superficial, illusory preoccupations. No longer itchy and scratchy and bothered. In that realm one lives inside the actual and ideal together. *Like the box all with its lid.*\* In the midst of the muck and the mire, living mindfully, with clear vision. A kind of Superman x-ray vision seeing through to the pure center of everything…the all and one, the emptiness and the form. Not skimming the surface the way we do, worrying over spilt milk and stubbed toes. Everything so intensely personal. But deeply involved. Immersed. Such that there is no self to trip and fall or be touched by anger and pain and disappointment.

\* words from *The Sandokai, a* poem by 8th century Zen master Sekito Kisen

# 30  Ceremony

*Make preparing your tea or coffee in the morning into a ceremony. Move slowly and pay attention to each action and all the sensory input that arises: scents, temperature, textures, sounds, and finally taste.*

**Of Two Minds**

> Sun on my face
> Firefly spangles behind closed lids
> Is this moment wasted?
> Or fully lived?

It was winter when I wrote the above gatha in a notebook I carried on a woodsy walk. The sun was brilliant. I had no particular place to go. And I let myself sink into the sweet delight of the moment. Cold air, hot sun. Closed eyes, dancing light. But I knew that all around me, within kilometers of where I stood, people were bustling through busy days. They had meetings to get to, children to tend, meals to make and deadlines pending. Clocks on their phones, on their wrists, in their heads. And I was happily doing nothing. Twinges. Two conflicting programs can cause havoc with your computer. Two competing programs can do the same with living. If you believe they are competing that is.

Sometimes I do. When I'm caught in a moment of doing nothing and finding peace, sometimes an old and disapproving overseer shuffles out of some dark closet in my mind, dusts herself off and shakes a finger at me. It's that accusatory finger that causes me to wonder "Is this moment wasted?"

But it's crowded in this mind, the way it is in all minds, and there are a lot of nooks and crannies. Some of them are well maintained these days.

Bright and sunny and open. They have windows and fresh air and I like spending time there. These are the places where I post notes to myself about mindfulness and presence. Where the words of beloved teachers are etched on the walls. Where there are no clocks or schedules and the soft sounds of my breath fill my ears like the ocean. Here I find myself asking "Is this moment fully lived?"

The answer lies somewhere on the middle ground, of course. The Middle Way, as the Buddha taught. No extremes of busy-ness and making life complicated and painful. No extremes of indulgence, avoiding what needs to be done. The "just this" of the moment may include sun on my face and fireflies behind closed eyes, or it may include listening with care at a meeting, speaking my opinion with the intention for clarity and understanding, not confrontation or winning. It may mean eating my breakfast slowly in the dark of a winter kitchen, watching the peach and gold light of sunrise from the window, or it might mean helping a child with homework or packing a lunch for school. It might mean choosing to defrost a frozen pizza on a busy day, or preparing fresh garden vegetables on another, knowing that food is essential to life. It might mean putting in extra hours to meet a commitment, or it might mean an honest discussion changing a deadline that is pending.

And of course, it will mean clocks. If not the ones on phones or wrists or desks or ovens, then the ticking of our hearts and the swing of the sun across the sky, because time, measured in change, does pass.

So mindfulness does not mean doing nothing. It does not necessarily mean slowing down all the time. But it does mean paying attention to what is motivating us, why we're rushing or pausing, what like and dislike buttons we are responding to. Having the intention to live a life that does not contribute to unnecessary pain, my own or that of others. Not accepting every memo in life that seems to come with an "urgent" stamp on its face, and checking this out for ourselves.

So now and then, for me, it means pausing in the winter woods and asking myself what brought me here, remembering my intentions and letting them show me what matters right now.

**Time Capsules**

On the New Year's Eve of the millenium, my family put together a time capsule, as so many people were doing at the time. A colorful cookie tin was filled with things we thought were important and symbolic of who we were right then… capturing the present moment in concrete tokens. When we'd each packed our "stuff" into the tin, it was bound tightly with tape and we put it away until 2025. At the house our family of four lived in then, it resided high on a shelf in the cold room. Here in this smaller home, where only two of us live now, it is tucked into a cupboard of photo albums and other family memorabilia. The New Year's Eve of 2025 is eight years away, but when my fingers found this tin recently as I searched for another item altogether, I was carried back to that evening and found I can already remember only a few of the chosen items... and those in categories rather than detail. Favorite small toys my sons chose. A sketch of the family I'd done from a photo because I was, at that time, revisiting a childhood interest in sketching. I think I remember this because I'm already anticipating the embarrassment I'll feel at the quality of that work almost a decade hence. But more than the content of that particular tin, I am thinking of the concept of time capsules in general. The idea that we can hold on to something fleeting.

Time is a slippery thing. Mostly it is felt by us in terms of change. The movement of the sun across the sky. The budding of trees and gardens and then their bounty and eventual demise. Deer that cross our lawn in shaggy winter coats and then a few months later looking sleek and shiny, with spotted fawns following at their heels.

My own body shows it in the silvery hairs revealed each time I have my hair freshly cut, the veins and spots on my hands that remind me of my mother. And although the scale might say I weigh approximately what I did in my late 20's when I was into running and weight training, the mirror says that weight has been redistributed. Let time and gravity do the work, I tell my yin classes as we hold our postures and relax, gently opening joints and reluctant muscles. Time and gravity do their work in one way or another all the time on these physical bodies. We try to direct that work when we can.

During the holiday season, for a little while, we are four in this house again. But four adults with big boots at the door and an extra vehicle in the drive. For a few days there are three meals a day, because two of us are accustomed to that. There are also remarkably few left overs. All of us tending to hermity natures, sometimes the house is quiet and we're scattered to our corners, breathing companionably, the house holding us as a comfortable unit. And sometimes we gather at the table and the room rings with laughter and talk. Change continues through every moment of the day on one level, through the larger scope of seasons and years on another.

Through the holidays, routines are bumped and stretched and neglected. But taking time for daily meditation and periods of quiet mindful reflection is a habit for me that threads the moments together. This and then this and then this. Mostly I bring awareness to how this feels. This is joy, this is nostalgia, this is anticipation, this is disappointment, this is worry, this is excitement. The naming takes me into my body to remember the physical manifestation of each passing mood and emotion. The reality of change, of uncertainty, of impermanence is sobering, but it also lifts up and supports a stronger presence in the nows as they pass by.

It's nearly the end of 2016. A year that holds both frightening and exciting possibilites is opening and it may feel like something solid, like something in its own right. But the date, the year, are place holders, like the mental labels I use to mark the moments. In truth it is all process and flow. Nothing solid and stable. Nothing replaced by something else, only that gentle morphing of change. My work is to be present to what the moments bring, and to watch the mind's tendency to dive into time capsule tins whether behind or ahead of this moment.

## Six Senses

In Buddhist psychology there are six senses. Seeing, hearing, touching, tasting, smelling, and thinking. The last one is the only surprise if you are accustomed to the ordinary Western ways of looking at things. But this has been life-changing for me.

We see through the eyes. Eyes must see if they are open. In fact, even with our eyelids closed, we see: color, light, maybe shapes and swirls of movement. Our ears hear unless there is damage or we're wearing earplugs or perhaps place our hands over them, muffling sound. Even then it seems they contain the music of the seas inside…an internal cycling, a little like putting your ear to a seashell. Where our skin makes contact with something, we feel. The sense of touch can be numbed perhaps by cold or injury or anesthetic but "touch" is built in. If we haven't damaged the tongue or burned it, if we don't have a headcold that blocks our tastebuds, we taste. And whatever wafts into the nose is smelled. We can hold the nostrils shut or hold our breath. But again, barring damage, we smell via that sense door.

Yet, somehow we think of thought as voluntary and generated. But, like eyes that see, ears that hear, skin that feels, tongues that taste, and noses that smell, the mind thinks. Sleeping, it weaves dreams. Left to its own devices, it follows old paths and flits through fancies. It is a flea market of sensory impressions of what we've seen, heard, touched, tasted and smelled. Including language heard or read. And every sensory impression has come to us with an emotional loading…pleasant, unpleasant or neutral. These too take table space in the mind-market. The mind churns and turns and explores and sorts. It thinks.

When I understand thought in this way, it is less frightening to me to find that shocking or unexpected thoughts flit through. I am not responsible for what I smell walking by a stagnant pond, or what I see if I am witness to a bad accident. I am not responsible for the bit of muck turned up in the churning of the mind. Choice arises to some extent, of course, in what I expose myself to. Images that are disturbing, loud sounds that are uncomfortable, tastes that make me gag. We make choices based on our preferences if we can, although life doesn't always allow this. But if we're wise, we also make an effort to make choices acknowledging this hodgepodge, this flea market nature of the mind: we do not have to let everything in. Still, there will be horrible things that are taken in, because our senses were open and we were present when they took place, or in the name of staying informed, which, it can be strongly argued, is essential. Balance is key in this last case. We know enough not to keep eating the peppers that are scorching our tongues, tearing our eyes and causing turmoil in our bellies. Perhaps this should apply to how many reruns of a disturbing news story we take in as well.

Inspiration arises in the same way. Although artists speak of muses, since being exposed to Buddhist psychology and the notion of six senses, I think of this differently. There are many more sounds and sights out there than I could "invent". There are many more ideas out there than I could "invent". The mind gathers, through the senses, and does its thinking, as the eyes do their seeing. Sometimes wondrous things result and we are amazed at our own "inventions".

When we sit in meditation, beginning meditators often think we have to stop our thoughts. Rather we find that thinking, like breathing, can be attended to and directed. Usually meditation begins by bringing these two things together: directing the thinking mind to the breath. It is like stopping at one table in the flea market. A quiet place where perhaps there is something simple displayed, perhaps just a bowl of water. And we rest there so that the chaos of the rest of the market, the colors and sounds and myriad of odors fades into the background and the mind just sits on the surface of this one object, examining it with infinite curiosity.

As in *Alice through the Looking Glass*, there's a door here out of the flea market entirely. It doesn't open on command, but it can't be found without the curiosity Alice was renowned for.

# 31 Presence

*Resist the urge to multi-task as you fold laundry or do the ironing or chop vegetables for dinner. Be with each movement, scent, sound and texture.*

### Right Now, Right Here

There's an old country song* that has a line something like "Give me forty acres and I'll turn this rig around." The singer is a frustrated truck driver in a bind. Once eighteen wheels and a full load are underway, changing direction, or stopping, can be challenging.

Habits can be like that too. There are those who believe in cold turkey, of course. Just stop smoking. Just quit snacking. Just start that exercise program. Just do it. And quit your whining while you're at it, is often implied. I prefer a more graduated approach.

We're going full bore most of the time in this society. And we're holding our breath. We work and play at such a pace that we're often not enjoying either. And most of us are waiting for the time that we will, that place and time when peace and ease will be available: the vacation next winter, time with friends this weekend, retirement.

What practice has revealed to me is that this is available now.

I sit every day. And these days I sit for an hour most of the time. But I didn't start with an hour and I remember being scared to death when I read once that one should sit for an hour in the morning and an hour in the evening every day. It just doesn't have to be so. What is needed is a commitment to making a space, to being with the breath, to being right here and right now in some sort of consistent way.

Taking a few easy and deliberate breaths upon waking, before jumping up to begin the day. Back in bed at day's end, breathing consciously until sleep descends. That might be enough.

Breathing instead of twitching and counting train cars at the crossing. Breathing at a red light. Breathing as you stand in line. Breathing in a waiting room. Breathing while you wait for the kettle to boil.

It sounds so simple. Of course, I'm breathing. We all are if we're alive. But this is conscious breathing and at first it takes effort to stay present. Only a few breaths. A minute. Two minutes or three. It doesn't have to be long. But what becomes apparent is that moving into the body in this way, stills the mind. The have to do's, the worries, the memories and regrets, the anger, they all stop spinning. Balance returns.

It is absolutely so that when the mind tastes this, it wants more. It's more addictive than "Game of Thrones" or dark chocolate. And just as we'll go back sooner or later, for the next episode, or the next treat, we'll go back to this stillness again.

It has a momentum of its own. No resolutions required. Just the willingness to try it, to see for yourself.

Unlike a vacation or the weekend, as you develop this peace, you find it is accessible any time and anywhere. It's available when bad news comes, when you look in the mirror and know you're growing old, when gas prices go up and income goes down, when there is disappointment and when there is pain. These things will still happen, of course. These are the truths of a mortal life. But right here and right now peace and ease are also available. It doesn't take forty acres and strong arms. Just a willingness to be with this breath. And then the next.

\* "Give Me Forty Acres" by Earl Green and John Green

## This Is Joy

Stepping out of the garage, my arms were full and my eyes on my feet. The cat pressed up against my legs and set my priorities straight. Transferring the load to one arm, I stooped to scoop him up with the empty arm. An inch or two off the ground, he took matters into his own four paws and scrambled, fairly gracefully, to my shoulder, settling inside the collar of my half open jacket, a horseshoe of fur around my neck. Despite the itching, sneezing and puffy lips and eyes that I knew would soon follow, for the moment his cool, silky coat against my bare neck was nothing short of delightful! That this fur collar was purring and vibrating was even better. My own massage cat. No electricity needed. I smiled and cooperated in the snuggle by tilting my head back against him and raising my empty hand to his solid flank to keep him from sliding.

The sky was a revelation. One of those clear and magnificent Alberta nights. Every star burning away in a black velvet bowl. I remembered how the stars disappear in the city and felt the blessing of this country life. This, I told myself, pausing to breathe the icy air, is joy.

Moments come like that. Not when we're looking for them, planning them, seeking them. Just in the ordinary course of living. So many moments flying by and each with its emotional tone. Sometimes more than one feeling is in the mix of a nano second, but occasionally an emotion shoots through with humbling purity. Like this one. Joy! For that moment, nothing else claimed mental or heart space.

Following the advice of many teachers, I breathed again, took a moment to name this, and while allowing it to sweep through and away, as it inevitably would, I set it to memory.

We may think sometimes from the instructions to let go, that memories are "bad" in some way. But letting go also means letting go of this kind of judgment. What tends to be complicated about memory is that we sweep into its narrative, the movie; we move away from now. If I'd been caught in a memory-story as I'd stepped out of the garage, I would have brushed by the cat and kept my head down. I would have missed that true and beautiful moment, fleeting as it was. So it's more about being alert and skillful as I observe the path my mind is choosing. Noting whether it leads towards peace or away.

Is the memory a reaching back with mourning or anger? Is there a sense of loss or despair or aversion? If I were looking down a toboggan hill and saw a cliff ahead, I'd turn or brake if I could. So it is with mindful effort. I notice what my thoughts are doing to my present state of mind. What's up ahead? Do I need to reset the direction?

Similarly, if the toboggan is rushing unimpeded through lovely greenery over friendly terrain, I take note. Not grabbing at a branch to slow the momentum, but being with the exhilarating journey. When I notice I am in one of these pure and simple moments of positive emotion, I try to bring strong attention to memorizing not the story of the moment but the emotional tone that rushes through my body. This gives me material for the cultivation of joy and more skillful mind states more often. These body memories of joy, of love, of peace, are models. This is not a holding on that yearns for that particular moment again, not pinning it down or wrapping it up to keep. Rather it is being there with it, naming it fully, on the fly. The difference between admiring the butterfly in the meadow and mounting it on a board for a museum collection.

How is this useful in meditation and daily life? In meditation, it can be useful to have clear rememberings of what the positive emotions, like joy and love and compassion, feel like in the body. As the body and mind settle into stillness and tranquility opens the hand of the mind, I can open doors for these positive guests. My teacher speaks of this as induction. Putting skillful effort into the stirring up of mind states that lift the heart. Allowing them to inhabit mind, heart and body.

We don't need a photo album for this, or a scrapbook of keepsakes. What we need is to be open to the treasures each day offers. They will be there if we don't miss them. Even tired, at the end of a drive, in the midst of winter, weighed down with luggage and boxes, stepping out into a cold night on possibly treacherous ice. Even then. The touch of a warm and furry body. The audible and tangible breathing of another being pressed against my skin. The sky open and endless. In that moment I knew the presence of joy. And my body remembers.

## Scrapbook

Given the ease with which the human heart-mind hangs onto the negative and forgets the positive, my teacher suggests creating a *metta* (loving-kindness) scrapbook. This project may be a physical book, full of clippings and photos, a shoebox collection like those you had full of precious things when you were child, a file on your computer or mobile phone, or just a clear memory file that you keep current and active. The idea is that sometimes the world gives us plenty to smile about and our cup runneth over. But other times, the clouds move in and it can be tough work getting the metta-machine running. Those are the days we don't want to get out of bed, or we feel grumpy with the world, gazing out through grime covered glasses. We lose our balance and we need something to hold us steady again. These joy seeds, and love sprouts are already planted. We only need to remember to nurture them.

Though such a "scrapbook" might be unique in many ways to the individual, there will also be universals. So here are a few randomly chosen from mine that might speak to you or trigger your own that you thought you'd forgotten:

- the laughter of babies
- watching clumsy animal babies doing almost anything
- a hundred or more spring robins gathered on a snow-dusted lawn
- sleeping children
- Alberta skies in the country on a clear night alive with stars
- purring
- singing or hearing James Keelaghan's song "Dance as You Go"
- fiddle music
- candlelight
- chanting
- holding hands with a beloved other

- drinking cold water on a hot day
- baby held in the arms and gazing into the eyes of a grandparent
- the crazy faces my dad would make to entertain the grandkids
- my mother's big smile
- birdsong
- the ocean, rough or calm
- warm, light rain
- the first snow of the season
- the stone garden Buddha I carried home on a plane from Vancouver Island, like a baby on my lap
- the smell of horses
- the weight of my sons carried on my hip when they were small
- my brother's smile so like my mom's
- laughing or crying with my sister
- my dad singing while he worked
- sucking sweet pulp and juice from a mango seed
- watching our dog and cat snuggle or romp like siblings
- hard outdoor work shared and then the limp and righteous exhaustion that follows
- cold drinks from hot mugs
- soft, friendly clothes
- sweet spaces of silence and solitude
- Mary Oliver's poetry
- Leonard Cohen's voice

Bringing these things to mind lightens my mood and my heart making way for contentment.

# 32 Walking

## Take a walk without a destination and leave your mobile phone at home.

### The Four Elements

The calendar says it's spring. Some days the air is warm and earthy scents are heady. Other days the wind is blustery and cold and snow makes a reappearance. This is the way spring manifests here in the Great White North.

I've lived in Alberta all my life and still I grumble each spring. The winter feels long. The yearning for tulips, for color, for warmth can be strong. And the aversion to what the moment holds is habitual.

When I'm hunched against the wind, stepping gingerly around patches of ice, wishing for the warmth of summer as I feel the chill in my bones, I can't help but remember the Buddha's teachings on the four elements. What I love at this stage in my practice is that teachings I've heard so many times have worn pathways in my memory. I may not have set out to memorize them, but repetition does its subtle work. I just have to catch myself humming an advertising jingle to become aware of that. But while the ad jingle may be unhelpful, the teachings I've absorbed can be like a personal mindfulness bell for me when they arise at the right moment.

The cold hand of the wind pulls the rope and the bell chimes. I am elements moving through elements. I am one with all that is. My bones are hard and stable like the earth beneath my feet, made of the same stuff. The blood that flows in my veins, the tears the wind coaxes from my eyes, the damp drops collecting at the tip of my nose are the same as the water caught in the frozen puddles, the snowflakes that land on my gloved hands. The wind itself is the breath of the earth. I feel the bellows of my own lungs expanding and contracting. I breathe with all of life. And snuggling my chin in tight to my collar I feel the heat and energy of my own body, my own sun, my own fire.

The elements are mighty here in Alberta. And living in a "rural" community I am not as cut off from them as I might be in the city. I feel the breezes on my skin every day, the earth frozen or soft beneath my feet. In that, I am blessed.

Reflecting on the four elements is a way of bringing myself into the present moment. When I am contemplating this connection with all that is, I am not lost, off on some train of thought to past or future. A mind immersed in temperature and texture and movement, is present in this body here and now. This is what is real, not the replay of this morning's argument, not fantasies about a winter holiday, not anxiety over an appointment later today.

Most often walking, whether for a distance, or brief transitions between vehicles and buildings is a way of getting to somewhere else. Or as my son puts it, "walking is transportation, Mom, not entertainment". But treating it as the gift it is, when I'm able, makes it a meditation. This enriches my life and amazingly even helps me catch the reactivity of grumbling. Being able to smile in the midst of the throes of an Alberta spring is indeed a gift of mindfulness.

**Walking Meditation**

Everyone has likely had the experience of walking somewhere, perhaps alone, and feeling at peace. It may be a day of sparkling sunshine, or enveloping mist. It could be a day when the heat bounced from your shoulders, almost palpable, or it could be one of those cold, crackling sort of days when the snow crunches under your feet. I've had this happen walking in sand near lakes or oceans, walking in the woods near my home, or even walking some quiet residential street, shaded by the spreading branches of trees planted generations before my own. The point is, it doesn't seem to matter a lot where you are or what the weather. The coming together of natural easy movement, relative quiet and time to see and feel those things your body is experiencing right now, all this is enough to bring this momentary peace.

So, I was mildly surprised to find how difficult the practice of walking meditation was for me. In walking meditation, whether indoors or out, the task, as in sitting, is to slow down. Rather than cultivating stillness and turning to the breath, in walking meditation the student must learn to break down the process of walking and to focus, carefully, on each step. Lifting the foot. Moving it forward. Placing the foot, shifting the weight. It reminds me of the kind of surrealistic movement of slow motion photography or of deep sea divers in those cumbersome astronaut-like suits.

I learned walking meditation on my own, with the help of books, tapes and a distance instructor to answer questions via e-mail. And I found it very, very hard. In walking meditation, I found myself again and again in planning mind. "I will go to the end of the hall and then turn", "I will walk until my toes touch that shadow before I turn." And when I tried to practice outdoors, as was suggested, the changing terrain kicked off this fore-planning to a greater degree, and the impatient dances of our family dog and his confused whining at my odd behavior wasn't conducive to concentration either.

But then I walked a labyrinth. And the beauty of this practice was allowed to unfold for me. Given over to the looping of the path, I had no need of planning and the movements of my body, the lift and place and shift of each step melded with my breath, and slowing down was simple and inevitable. I walked the labyrinth most often with others and yet the shuffle of footsteps was no more a distraction than the breeze or some days the rain on my face, or the sounds of the surrounding village.

Standing in the petalled centre I would feel both grounded in this physical body and soaring in spirit and no contradiction in this. At home, practicing on my own, I still most often prefer to sit, but the lesson of the labyrinth lingers so that in walking anywhere I more often allow myself to relax into my body and find there serenity of mind.

**Dog Walking Meditation**

I spend hours every day walking dogs. Sometimes I'm distracted and lost in thought. But when I like it best, when I love my job, is when I'm there with each dog. Every walk then is different even though the woodsy loop we walk is the same. And each canine companion is my teacher. Here are a few lessons from today:

Tuff is my energy buddy. When I open to his world view everything is interesting and exciting. Tuff is a big black Lab who likes to jump up and give hugs. He's so eager when we come out the gate I have to talk to him first and get his attention. He's big enough to pull me off my feet if he just took off when I wasn't ready. We chat awhile first. He still lurches out the gate but if I keep talking he checks himself and waits while I close it. It's icy on the first little hill that starts our loop and I talk to Tuff and make sure he pays attention. This slows him down so I can get my feet into the slushy snow at the edge of the path and don't slide down the hill. He's doesn't slow on the little wooden bridge, but once we're past that, he circles off into the deep snow when he has to do his business and rolls his eyes at me as if to say "Don't look now. This is private." When squirrels cross our path, Tuff has trouble remembering there's a human at the end of his leash. He lunges and jumps at the trees, just playing really. He knows the squirrel is out of reach and when it goes too high, he just moves on. He knows which shelf his treats are on and points his nose that way when we get back to the kennel as if the box were another squirrel up a tree.

Timber is Tuff's partner but they're too big and excitable for me to walk them together. Timber is a Rottweiler. He's as tall as Tuff but broader. He likes to wrestle Tuff in the outside run, wrapping his big paws around Tuff's neck. But he doesn't bark. When it's Timber's turn to walk he dances on his front legs and stares through the gate, waiting. He wants to listen about staying while I close the gate but he's all aquiver and sometimes he forgets. I can't keep Timber's attention going down the slippery little hill, so I jog to cross to the snow quickly and keep jogging till we get to the bridge. He usually slows down there to watch his footing on the boards. When Timber needs to go he squats suddenly wherever he is on the path and gets it done with in a hurry. He doesn't pay much attention to the trees but keeps his nose down sniffing and he's quick to roll in "stinky" stuff if I don't give him a tug and a scolding to keep him moving. He wants his treat too when we get back but he puts it down at his feet and waits till the pats and leave-taking love talk is done. Then he picks it up and goes back to his blanket to lie down. Timber knows about contentment with each moment his day brings.

I think Smitty should be a circus dog. He can jump straight up almost my height. He's an American Eskimo Dog whose black eyes are always sparkling in his white face. When Smitty knows walks are on the agenda he begins bouncing at the gate of his kennel like a jack-in-the-box, barking madly the whole time. He keeps this up until I'm inside then sits and quivers, barking like crazy while I drop his little chain collar over his head. That is like hitting a switch. He stops so abruptly in mid-bark, he makes a sort of "bmf!" sound that always makes me laugh. Then he points his nose where the gate will open. Smitty has a long retractable leash and he likes to explore, keeping it full out most of the time though he's pretty smart about the trees. I stop when he runs off the path into the bush and when he's had a look he comes back to me the same way and doesn't get wound up. There's a big tin on the table when we come into the kennel and Smitty knows he gets a dog cookie from that when we get back. He isn't barking now, just watching for me to get one, then he dashes to his kennel. He knows the routine and doesn't want more than his share.

Cuddles is the baby in his family. His kennel is as crowded as a nursery with his bed and little Winnie-the-Pooh chair, blankets and toys. His dish has his name on it. He's a Cocker Spaniel Bichon cross and our smallest border right now. He likes to lay spreadeagled so he looks like a frog and despite all the furniture and blankets, he usually sprawls on the cement floor at the front of his pen, with his nose through the chain-link waiting for his walk turn. He is the picture of patience. He has lots of energy though and trots fast on his walk, sniffing here and there, wandering into deep snow and rolling in it sometimes. His family brings homemade peanut butter doggy treats in the shapes of cats and bones and he loves 'em. Spoiling hasn't spoiled him.

Ali and Ana are huge, fierce-looking Rotties. They're lambs really and when I go in to them they lean hard on me and compete for hugs. Ana raises her paws and tries to hold my arm but she's in such ecstasy at the rubbing that she loses her balance and topples over. Ali's chest is so wide I couldn't get an arm around him all the way. His head is as big as a beach ball. They have soft black eyes and when they're lonely, sometimes they howl but never bark. They have fierce sounding play growls when they wrestle each other, but their stubbed tails wag when they sniff the little dogs through the fences and they're quiet then. This morning our goofy cat rubbed back and forth on Ali's head when he met us on the trail and Ali just sniffed him with lazy interest. Ali walks just ahead most of the time but never pulls and checks for me sometimes. He'll circle back and roll his head into me for pats and love talk from time to time. Ana barely leaves my side. She presses in so close it's kind of a stumble walk a lot of the time because she's so big and heavy. She looks up a lot instead of at the world around, just begging for a word and a pat or scratch. The language their family uses with them is German and though I know only a few commands taught to me when I first met them, they listen with great respect and immediate response. I like to save their walk for last because they are so loving and easy. Like big bears with hearts so huge they gather me in. With Ali and Ana I am just with Ali and Ana. We breathe together and different languages, different species don't matter.

# 33  Autopilot

Interrupt automatic pilot: take a different route to work, brush your teeth or hair with your non-dominant hand, walk to the laundry room or kitchen in your home backwards!

**Awake**

A friend recently drew my attention, with a chuckle, to the little webnode icon that marks my website when you bookmark it: a cartoony set of wide open eyes. "Not exactly calm," were her words, I believe, and I laughed and agreed, explaining that not going for my own domain, I didn't set an icon of my own. But since that conversation I've been thinking. And I've come to the realization that those wide open eyes are the perfect representation of mindfulness. After all, tradition says that when the Buddha was asked what he was, he answered, "I am awake."

That is why I meditate. That is why I work to carry my practice into my daily life. I want to be here, awake. I thought at the beginning that I was after serenity. That lovely sense of peace that can arise staying with the breath in sitting is certainly a welcome state. As are all pleasant states, whether related to meditation or not. But like all pleasant states, it's fleeting. I can't hold on to it. I can only be with it while it lasts.

The point of mindfulness is to be with whatever is there. To see clearly. To have the eyes, and all the senses, wide open. To drink it all in and investigate. Looking not just outward but inward. Watching the mind. "Believe nothing, no matter where you read it, or who said it, no matter if I have said it," the Buddha instructed, "unless it agrees with your own reason and your own common sense." Look, in other words, at your own experience.

So when I really look, when I keep my eyes open, what do I see? I see that I am not separate. That my actions have consequences not just for me but for others. What I say and how I say it. What I do and how I do it. What I buy and where I buy it. What I strive for and what I do in that striving. What I choose to act on and to ignore. Who I disregard and who I revere. Karma is a big and complicated thing. And you do not have to believe in a karma that stretches into another life to understand that. We only need to see that each thing that happens is part of a chain in this life, part of a web. And it is my responsibility, then, to be as awake as I can be in choosing my contributions to that.

I see, too, that all the things I love and value will not last. That acting as if there are endless tomorrows to make things right is acting foolishly. That acting as if I can create the conditions for a perfect life and keep them that way is a mistake. That like every other human being who lives or has lived, I will grow old and I will die. And that if my happiness depends on changing that, on avoiding death, then it is unachievable.

Wide open eyes also allow me to see the poignant beauty that comes with all change and all impermanence. If human beings were immortal, how would that change who we are? It is our hearts, our loving and our caring in the midst of both joy and sorrow, that makes us human. And it is our heart-mind that makes it possible for us to choose wisely and well, if we begin with open eyes.

Yes, the more I let myself reflect on this accidental icon, the more I found myself smiling. I could do a lot worse in choosing deliberately. I want to live my life mindfully. Seeing what is. Being accountable for what I do. Trying to choose skillfully. Investigating my experience and my motivations. Knowing that I will fall short of perfect, and being OK with that. Accepting that that too is what is, right now. But doing the best I can. And that means seeing that I get overwhelmed, and that sometimes I choose to turn away from something I should look at more closely. But if I see the turning, not letting it happen on automatic pilot, then perhaps, eventually, I will also be able to turn back and look again.

### Ordinary Objects of Meditation

A few weeks ago we made the decision to give up the housekeeping service we had begun the first time I was so sick with Crohn's. That was nearly five years ago now. So, it has been some time since I took on the daily tasks of household cleaning, tasks I have never much liked. And I find there is something interesting that has changed.

Since I began mindfulness practice and formal meditation, I have found that cooking and baking are more enjoyable to me than ever. These have always been pleasant duties for me, but when I use the process as a meditation, this is enhanced. So the smells of the ingredients, the sounds of chopping, the repetitive motions of stirring, the textures of vegetables or flour in my hands…all are entered into as objects of meditation in the way that I focus on my breath when I sit. To the point that when a guest recently asked whether she could help with preparation, I said "no thanks, I enjoy it" and found myself meaning "I need this." The household is busy with small children and guests, and my head is foggy with not-enough-sleep. I need this refuge. When it is oh-so-difficult to find the time to sit for 20 or 40 minutes, it is always possible to find this refuge in preparing meals.

But here comes a more recent surprise.

While cooking and baking have always been pleasures, I have never liked the routines of cleaning…vacuuming, dusting, scrubbing toilets, washing floors. But having accumulated more experience in my practice, these days I work to undertake such household chores mindfully, and find them transformed. The repetitive motions, the sounds, the scents of cleaners, the glint of light on wood or porcelain, all make for meditative objects. So that, like cooking, these menial tasks are elevated to the sacred. For the sacred is this moment.

During the years that we had housekeepers, I would often notice the uncomfortable itch of irritation about small things: the basket not put back on the floor, the books shuffled into a single pile, items moved about on the kitchen counters. At the time I learned something about myself, and the way my mind reacted with aversion to these trivial things. But now as I take the tasks on again myself, and reflect, I see something more about activity as a human being. When we do something "simple" day after day, and maybe something we don't enjoy or that we view as a somewhat unpleasant necessity we lose immediacy. We "go through the motions", while our minds are miles away. And so we all lose the beauty and intensity of this moment, every day. Thus it is possible to pass through a traffic light and then wonder if it was green. To go to the basement for an item and forget what was needed. To scrub a floor and forget to complete the task by replacing items moved during the process. This is the stuff of life and this is what we discount, choosing instead to live in anticipation, in planning, in judging.

I've learned a small but invaluable lesson as I go back to cleaning my own toilets and scrubbing my own floors. Breathe, smile and be here. Slow down to just this, and this and this. Dwell in this moment. It is not simply about being with the unpleasant, knowing it will pass, but that being here may change the very nature of the experience.

**Wearing Mittens**

I don't remember hearing the term "The Experience Economy" before, so guess I'm a little behind the times. What caught my attention in an article I ran across on this phenomenon, was the simple claim that contemporary consumers are "clearly chasing moments".* The author went on to describe some pretty elaborate scenarios.

In its most familiar form, as I understand it, the "experience economy" makes itself known in the difference between grabbing a cup of coffee in the food court at West Ed and sipping a tall Americano in Starbucks while perusing possible purchases from Chapters. It's not essential that there be any qualitative difference in the coffee itself. It's the ambiance of the bookstore/cafe, the relative seclusion from jostling crowds, and even the laptops on tables vs. McDonalds bags, the urban professionals instead of frazzled families that share the space.

The article, however, describes something far more extreme: Diners bundled in winter gear, fumbling with forks and wine glasses in mittened hands, during a six-course dinner served in a hay-bale-enclosed area in a farmer's winter field near Viking, Alberta. Chasing moments, indeed.

OK. As someone committed to living mindfully, I have to ask what's really going on here. Something odd, strange, unexpected, yes. Not good or bad in any obvious way. Who cares, really, where someone eats her dinner or what conditions make that pleasant for her? But is this pleasant? I couldn't help imagining tongues frozen to the prongs of forks, and gravy solidifying in gelatinous, chilled pools. A general spattering of tablecloths and clothing as cutlery and food bits are dropped from numbed, bare hands. Or fuzzy bits of woolen mittens consumed with bread.

Thinking about this a little further, I was reminded of a silly game once played (does this still happen?) at baby showers attended by female family and friends of the mom to-be. Diapering dolls, in the days of cloth and pins, while wearing oven mitts. Good for a few laughs. Camaraderie. But no one was paying big bucks for the "experience".

What's happening, I wonder, that we need to dress up moments in this way? Sated by plenty, with expectations driven by movies and games. It seems there's a kind of desperation here. We can't be with ourselves in ordinary moments. Can't stay there long enough to find the texture and the depth. Instead, we strive to make life into a kind of roller-coaster ride, with sudden dips and hairpin turns, and shrieks of fear and laughter.

But this artificial intensification is unnecessary. Life is already like that. The flux of pleasant and unpleasant, the ride of aversion and craving that we see when we look closely, is a crazy ride. Nothing lingers long. When we don't see this it's because we're not really here. We might be off exploring memories, the making of which is one of the functions of the experience economy. Memories with bright crayon colors and not too much nuance or ambivalence. Or we might be planning and yearning for the next moment we're chasing, whether it's a dinner in a farmer's frozen field or the beach vacation a month away.

Maybe the problem is that we're already wearing mittens, we're muffled up in layers of insulation that separate us from our experience of the moment. Inattentiveness allows this to happen. Until the only way to have an experience that catches us, that engages our senses, is to go for overload.

It's just me speculating. But the mental pictures I had of these diners went quickly from amusing to melancholy. Count the moments of a life. Then think how many are wasted, unnoticed because they are lost beneath the muffling of habit.

* "Three Ring Meal" by Jennifer Cockrall-King in *Eighteen Bridges*, Winter 2015

# 34  Immersion

The next time you are alone and unworried about appearances as you eat a tiny treat (a chocolate, a wedge of cheese, a piece of apple) make it last as long as possible. Take the smallest of nibbles, close your eyes, observe the textures, the tastes, the variety of sensations in the various areas of your mouth.

**The Mind on Vacation**

I don't take vacations very often. Overall, my "getaways" are to meditation retreats or for work-related training. Sometimes trips might center on visiting family or spending time with someone not often seen. But for me it can be years between the kind of vacations that many people plan as annual or semi-annual events. There are a lot of reasons for this, none of them of very much interest to anyone but me. But what is interesting, I think, is what happens when someone committed to watching the mind's natural inclination toward clinging and distraction, takes a vacation, because a vacation is the very definition of distraction. It is an immersion into all that the mind clings to: good food, lazy days, interesting new experiences, following whims and impulses, indulging desire. When we plan a vacation we want it to be of the five star variety. The horror stories people tell are usually of poor service, unacceptable accommodation, flight delays, bad weather, accidents and disruptions in the easy flow of pleasure. In short, we expect a lot of a vacation. We're holding it responsible for fixing whatever is not going well right now, we want it to be an escape from a reality that is sometimes too much. And, big surprise, few vacations can meet our expectations fully, because even if they do, even if they are perfect while they're underway, they have to end, and we return to the unmade bed and the things we didn't put in the suitcase.

So the kind of vacation we planned recently to celebrate a significant anniversary was something I anticipated with an unusual state of mind. I wanted to enjoy this time. Why not? Sensory pleasure is one of the gifts of being embodied. But I also was carefully watching my anticipation. What did it feel like when I was drawn out of the moment in the weeks before, looking toward what was to come? Mostly, I worked to keep my pre-vacation mind excursions centered on the details of tickets, reservations, and packing, not the building of fantasies. I was trying to leave the vacationing for the vacationing.

This centering in the task at hand I also hoped to maintain through the vacation itself, and to my surprise, this vacation reinforced a very simple learning: whether at home or in some exotic locale, being present in this moment is central to happiness. Keep the attention here and let craving and aversion mumble in the background and dissipate as they will do when unattended. This, right here and now, is the way it is: organizing passports and travel insurance, doing laundry, or walking along the Mississippi on a sultry New Orlean's evening. Whether listening to street musicians and watching the moon reflected in the water or scrunching my nose as I wound around garbage cans simmering in the heat, the mind was on the move, and my determination to watch this moving towards and moving away was my practice. Being here allows me to live what I'm living, not miss the moment as it flies by. But it also allows me to see that the mind leans…it yearns toward the magnolia blossoms, the saxophone's song, the colorful parades in the street. It leans away from the bodies curled on cardboard in doorways, sleeping; the too hot thump of the sun on the top of my head; the clanging of garbage trucks and the revelry of partiers interrupting sleep in the wee hours of the morning. Yet, all of these are part of what a visit to New Orleans entails. Sitting in the damp grass listening to a gospel choir, I let the music flow over and through me, or closing my eyes to savor the aromas and flavor of eggplant and crab cakes in crawfish sauce, I examined the textures and sensory detail with sweet delight. The tiny voices that wanted it to go on and on remained murmurs in the background of the current experience as it arose, lingered and passed away. And when the vacation ended and the moments held a cramped airplane seat for long hours, a prewrapped sandwich on the run between flights, and a long drive at the end of the day, presence undermined the "poor me", resistant mind of aversion, that wants things to be otherwise.

The mind likes what it likes and doesn't like what it doesn't like. If we hand over the controls to this "blind driver" as I recently heard one teacher call it, we're going to have a crazy ride. The mind thinks that everything it doesn't like can be avoided, and everything it wants, should be attained. It heads toward the sunshine and avoids the clouds, heedless of the shifting ground and sheer cliffs along the way. Then when things go from bad to worse, it's given to sulks and tantrums. It blames: others, myself, all of the above. When we train in mindfulness, we give the controls to the watcher, that which knows that the weather will change on its own. There'll be some of each, sunshine and rain. That's the nature of the journey. The watcher keeps to the moment, savours the pleasant and patiently endures the unpleasant.

This path, if we stay the course, means not being reliant on conditions for our happiness. It means no more horror stories…not about vacations gone wrong, nor about the woes of life that make us seek vacations as distractions and escapes.

### Food

Like many people in this society, perhaps women especially, I have had a lifetime of conflicted and complex relationships with food. Choice is part of the problem. So are the variety of messages about indulgence versus self-restraint. We have busy lives. We eat out a lot. We fall into the fast food, unhealthy eating trap. We want a bargain. We fall for the super-sizing strategy and make-it-a-meal deal that seems to offer more for our money.

Add familial messages about food as comfort and love, and then contrast that with magazine covers of super-fit, super-thin models, countable ribs, rippling abs, and diet tips on the front covers of nine out of ten magazines in the supermarket cashier line.

Then, in my case, throw in dietary restrictions related to health conditions. My restrictions might be personal, but it seems to me that large numbers of the population deal with some form of this last complexity: digestive difficulties, health conditions, allergies, food intolerances.

We need fuel to live, so eating isn't like drinking (alcohol) or television or gambling or any of the myriad distractions and diversions in our life that may lead us into a morass of remorse and self-judgment. We have to be able to handle it skillfully, not simply give it up. Most of us waffle. (Pun intended.) We try this diet, then this new restaurant, another diet and then visit a resort with a gourmet menu.

Some of us pay tribute to the overlap between food choices and ethical considerations that have weight for us. Arguments about the taking of sentient life. Arguments about food production and acreage requirements for some "products". And so some people shut down particular avenues by becoming vegetarian or vegan or pesco-pollo-vegetarians. That would be me…the label itself is a mouthful. You can play with this last category as well. (Fish=pesco, poultry =pollo) Of course, though vegetarian is in the description for me, that doesn't mean much. My vegetable intake is limited by my digestive tract modifications.

It's a bit of a mess. And the complexity leads to a lot of over thinking. Which leads to more voices in a crowded head. And less space for hearing the quiet wisdom of the body and heart.

I've been going on meditation retreats for a couple of decades. Fewer meals are usually offered at these retreats. One or two meals a day instead of three. And often the menu is vegetarian. So, being personally restricted in vegetable intake, I eat a lot of rice. Surprisingly, I still like it. But what is most telling in these retreats is the time given to a meal blessing. Somewhere, no matter what version of the blessing is used, there will be a line or two like this:

> Mindfully reflecting, I take this food
> Not for fun, not for sporting, not for beautification…
> Relieving feelings of hunger
> And not inducing new feelings of discomfort from overeating.

A bit different from "God is great/God is good/Let us thank Him for our food", the blessing I learned as a child. Gratitude is important, but it is not helpful in clear thinking around my own consumption.

A few weeks back I had the sudden inspiration (OK, I'm a slow learner) to make the lines in the retreat blessing a part of my daily meal routine. I've done this only sporadically before. And here's the interesting thing. When I begin to consistently recognize the voices that urge me to eat for fun, to eat for sporting, to eat for beauty, and when I watch my thoughts enough to know when hunger is present and when it's sated, the problem around food dissolves. If I purchase a grilled chicken burger because life is busy, but then, bite by bite, notice when I've had enough, there is no problem with this choice. If I prepare a meal, and then take my own servings, listening to my body's needs and not "Desire" bellowing in my head, or "Self Pity" shouting her down, I choose according to what this body can digest in comfort, what makes me feel well and not guilty or ill afterward.

In my home, the division of duties means that I'm the one who buys the groceries and prepares most of the meals. So thinking about food goes beyond the moment that I put a bite into my mouth. This is true for most women still, I think. I am grateful for the abundance on the supermarket shelves, for the good life that we lead in a country of affluence, even with the economic downturn. I am also intent on being mindful in the choices this good life affords me.

## Unplugged

Many years ago I bought a book of intricate mandalas for coloring. At the time it was a rare find. Now, adult coloring books abound in the aisles of any supermarket. What's the appeal? Examining my own use of my original book over the years, I know this kind of activity is calming: repetitive small movements of arm and hand, simple choices of color and slowing down to focus on the small, intricate spaces in the design as I fill it in. Then there is the surprise of the beauty as the infusion of color brings the line drawing to life. I have worked on these pages at my kitchen table, in partnership with my sister when we visit back and forth, and in quiet hotel or residence rooms when away from home.

The profusion of coloring books for adults is a fad, but a fad that indicates a common need. Too many of the activities we engage in still the body, on office chairs, car seats, and couches, without giving the mind any peace. We are constantly diverting the mind, adding to its frenetic activity with TV shows, You Tube, online gaming, texting, and many forms of social media. A plug adapter that permits you to plug six or more cords into a single outlet is a great visual metaphor for what we do to the mind, not just in our working hours, but too often in what we label recreation.

Health care professionals have urged us to get up and moving. Running, playing baseball and tennis, doing yoga and walking the dog. All these things are good for body and mind. But so is a bit of companionable stillness involving both body and mind. Of course, I'm an advocate of meditation but meditation is a practice that not everyone feels ready to take on.

In meditation classes I have suggested to people new to the practice that they already know what tranquility feels like. Most of us have sat around a campfire on a long summer evening, empty of words, mesmerized by the dance of the flames. Many of us have watched a sunset or sunrise, or stood by the ocean or at the side of a burbling creek, completely immersed in the sight or the sound that makes up the experience, unaware perhaps that a great part of the joy that is infusing our hearts comes from the stillness of the mind during such immersion. When we learn to meditate, we learn not to be dependent on the external "accidents" or occasional moments that trigger this experience. We learn how to induce it, here and now.

While the serene mind that is accessed in viewing a sunset may be welcome, it also feels like a fleeting gift. It can leave in its wake, a few minutes or hours or days later, a greater sense of agitation and unease because of the longing to return to an experience that we believe was tied to a certain event or object. Home from the beach-side holiday, there seems to be nothing to do but count the days until the next one or maybe peruse the photos and conjure some weak memory of the real thing.

In her new book *Birds, Art, Life*, Kyo Maclear, an urbanite, living in Toronto, shares her discovery of the joys of bird watching...within the city. Many of her captivating descriptions, lifted out of context, would sound like descriptions of meditation. Maclear is lyrical in describing the stillness of waiting for the appearance of the birds. I've heard similar descriptions of sitting on the bank of a river or lake with a fishing rod. Maybe this is also like the focus of doing embroidery that follows a pattern or building tiny intricate models. Painting by number. I'm not thinking of unique art here but instead of allowing the mind to settle in the same way mind comes to settle in the body during svasana at the end of a yoga class. Trusting there is nothing really to do here but to wait, watch, be open and still.

Coloring books may disappear from the shelves again, replaced by some new fad, yet our human need for this kind of deep immersion in stillness will remain. It's worth exploring hobbies, interests and pastimes that bring this balance to our days, unplugged and recharging.

# 35  Pause

## When your phone rings, pause and breathe before answering.

### Distracted Driving

Not everyone agrees with the details of the distracted driving law, but if we examine our own behavior behind the wheel we have to admit that given the power of the machine we're operating and its potential for damage, it's a good idea to pay attention. For me, as a long-time mindfulness/meditation practitioner, it's also a great metaphor for life.

Most of us live too much of the time on a kind of autopilot. Sometimes a mistake that is especially silly or painful reminds us to slow down and pay attention, but once we've navigated beyond that problem, we fall readily into our old patterns of habit again. It's human. And often it's efficient. But it's dangerous when we trust to this process completely. It's sort of like having a running chainsaw in one hand while you try to comb your hair. We can be lethal to ourselves and others.

One of the Buddha's central instructions is to look at your own experience, to test out his teachings for yourself. What happens when you don't pay attention? What happens when you don't check in with body, mind and feelings throughout your day? When you act, speak, choose from pure reactive impulse?

When you tune into your body and realize you are feeling queasy after a conversation, what replays itself in your mind? Did you unintentionally hurt someone with a tone of impatience? Did you agree to something you don't feel comfortable about now? Are you worried about the consequences of what you said? Are you wondering if you understood correctly what someone might have meant? These kinds of mistakes often happen because we don't see the window that opens between thought and speech. We let ourselves be tugged by our moods and the conditions of the moment. We speak and then we think. And as we all know it's much more difficult to undo the tangle after the fact than to avoid it in the first place.

Who hasn't hurt themselves in embarrassing ways because they were guilty of distracted driving in this body, never mind an automobile. Closing a gate on your own fingers. Forgetting to step up at a doorway ledge. Reaching into an oven without an oven mitt. Over-pouring into a glass or cup because someone called or the phone rang during the process. And annoying inconveniences are even more commonly the result of such inattention. Lost keys, misplaced glasses, the milk left on the counter to spoil as you rush out the door after breakfast. I've even heard happy-ending but scary tales of kids forgotten at the babysitter's; or handbags, groceries or even baby seats left on the trunk of a car in a parking lot as the car pulls away; candles left burning that might have caused a fire.

These are the neon lights that remind us we're inattentive. The visible embarrassments or physical injuries, the churning belly or headache or bout of insomnia. But these are equivalent to the fender benders and accidents distracted drivers may be involved in. What about the near-misses we aren't aware of. In the car, this may be because someone else swerved in time or there was no one else on the road. In our lives, inattention may leave a trail of mistakes we are unaware of that negatively influence our relationships, our work, our health and our happiness.

Laws are often made, rightly or wrongly, to protect us from ourselves. Unfortunately, a lot of our energies may go into seeing how we can circumvent them rather than seeing the benefit. But this is only a metaphor here. We're dangerous to ourselves and others in so many ways when we are unmindful. It would seem common sense that we should pay attention. Yet, this takes effort. New habits can only be formed with practice. The benefits are reaped over time. It starts with noticing whether the way you're operating now is effective. Only you know the answer to that. Check in and check it out.

**Whinefulness**

During a recent family-related crisis where I could feel my world shift a bit on its axis, I made the Freudian slip of saying to my husband I needed a moment to breathe and work on "Whinefulness". This made us both smile. The slip was not intentional but shone a brilliant and immediate light on the crevice into which my mind had slipped. Whinefulness is an apt term for the cycle of "shoulds" and "if only's" and "what if's" that dominates during times of stress. Stress, when you examine it, is always fear based in some way. This might happen. Now this will happen. What if this happens? Story telling uses fear-energy to vault from this actual moment into myriad imaginary others in nano moments.

Being aware of the whining and the vaulting, even if your imaginary feet have already left the ground before you're aware, slows the momentum. Instead of flying, you're floating. As in slow motion film, you have time, perspective and a clear view of where you came from and where you're about to land.

So after our laugh, I used the bubble of humor and lightness, a little like leaning into the controls of a glider, to nudge myself toward a different place. I have to be persistent. The winds of fear and habit can be strong.

The effort I need is a little like the patient hopefulness, the watchfulness our terrier shows as he follows us place to place through the day with his rope toy or favorite ball. He never lets awareness of our actions lapse. Even when we think he's sleeping, chin resting on the woven rope, he leaps instantly to his feet if it looks like there might be an available opportunity for interactive play. So, with my own mindfulness. Knowing the strength of whinefulness, I need to match that with my own persistent effort toward more positive mind states. If the pup didn't stay alert, he'd get very little play as his busy, aging parents follow routines of housework, office time and personal leisure. But he knows to intervene. So it is that my mind runs on habit energy and when something sets off the familiar human reactions of fear, negativity and worry, it'll keep going that way, unless I intervene with this playful and persistent energy modeled by my terrier. Over here. Come here to this moment where there is just this.

Here in this moment certain things are true. The fears I'm being drawn in by are fantasies, ephemeral. Yet, if I leave them free rein they'll bring me down, body and mind, for a hard landing. Headaches, tight muscles. Bad dreams. FEAR is an acronym that appears in positive thinking posters for "False Evidence Appearing Real". Remembering this can be very helpful when Whinefulness seems to be winning the day. Come back to now, to what you know for sure. Be with that in the body. Loosen tight shoulder muscles; flex the tight jaw; smooth the forehead; open slitted, heavy eyes. Nourish the body with cool breath. Warm the body with a loving heart. Be kind to this suffering self and anyone else involved in the situation.

In the current situation, as I nudge and adjust my state of mind, deliberately moving toward the positive and the skillful, a cartoon animation of "Whinefulness" appears in my mind: the "W" flips and rights itself to become an "M". The little chair of the "h" I'd been settling into, folds up and fades away. And the tiny cramped "e" rocks onto its back, opens in a full circle and stretches its curled tail up to become a "d" again. "Mindfulness" enables the effort that dissolves stress, making me alert to the work I need to do.

The crisis here is playing itself out moment by moment, but now I'm soft enough to be with the ride as it happens.

# Recorded Live

"Out of the mouths of babes." It's an old adage. Mostly, I think, it's supposed to imply honesty and wisdom, from a source unexpected. But out of the mouths of babes, often, we hear echoes of ourselves.

The little girl in the video clip posted on Facebook is maybe three or four years old. She has huge dark eyes. Adorable child. Both shy and bold as she tells her story to the camera. She was in line, you see, behind someone who was "soooo slooooowww", in line waiting for a treat. At the end of the story she asserts that "I have things to do," and then reminds the audience "don't be slow!"

Where'd she get this message? This little love who showed up in my Facebook feed had me seeing double. Superimposed on her dark-eyed features were the huge round glasses on the baby face of my own son at the same age roughly, urging his mother as we put on our shoes, "Hurry, hurry!" I knew it was my own voice I was hearing parroted back to me, but it's only over time that I've been properly chagrined at the memory.

We might worry about the cameras and spyware and records of our private information gathered everywhere in this technological age, but the fact is, if we're parents, our kids are recording our actions and words in their memories, with consequences that are arguably much more sweeping. It's a bit unnerving. Well, maybe a lot unnerving. I'm not talking here only about slips of the tongue, what they overhear that we don't intend. What I'm referring to is the general recording of our attitudes and values.

Recently I watched a segment on bees learning new string-pulling behavior from a single bee who had retrieved a candy in this way. We're all familiar with the documentaries of a monkey or bird who learns a new food gathering strategy and eventually passes it on to his whole extended family simply through using the technique as they observe. Even so, human societies perpetuate behaviors through mimicry. Our kids are great mimics. Hopefully that gives us pause, as parents, because pausing is what I'm talking about.

There are many larger philosophical and social points that might be made from this, but I'm after something quite simple. Kids can be our greatest teachers. My young son taught me to walk slowly through puddles and notice just where the water was too deep to go further without filling our boots. He taught me to look carefully on the first frosty mornings of winter for the crackly ice that made such delightful sounds under our feet. To dawdle over breakfast and take time to sing. To read a book more than once and study the pictures. To look up and down when walking and to take detours.

But along the way, too often, I taught him that he needed to hurry. That getting somewhere else was more important than being here.

That was the regret that surfaced for me as the little one on Facebook spelled out her Lesson to not be slow. My chuckle at her serious and articulate story was shot through with a thread of sorrow. Give preference to this moment being "recorded live", because there's no rewind for what gets missed. Build in the happy, conscious pauses now and avoid the uncomfortable ones later.

# 36  Listening

*When someone tells you a story from his/her life today, an anecdote or incident, listen with all your heart, not thinking instead of a story of your own to share.*

### Mindful Parenting

Parenting is, without a doubt, the most difficult role I've taken on in my life. And mindful parenting is both indescribably difficult and indescribably rewarding. To be present in those wonderful moments my children bring each and every day, not to lose those moments in the haste to be on with the next task, in distraction with some difficulty or worry, in planning for something else I wanted to do or share with this child, is a gift to myself. It does not mean that I have found a way to make these moments linger…as I still often want to do. But I am in them more fully when I am mindful. And what is more, the children feel this and respond. The story my little one tells me at the end of his school day meanders off when I am distracted. It grows and he glows when I am there for him, attending to his words. It seems so simple. But like many simple things in life, it is hard to do.

So too has mindfulness taught me to walk over the toys on the floor and to rein in my tone of voice and to let my children do some task imperfectly but unaided when it is needed. But in no other case have I found this so consistently difficult either. When a child speaks with disrespect it is difficult to hear the unspoken message instead of the tone. Is he hurt? Is he tired? Is he frustrated? It is difficult, when those little egos are working so hard to shape themselves in this world, not to respond from one's own small self. To breathe and be and listen. And difficult to know that even if I am successful in keeping this mindfulness in my response, this will not bring a magical end to the confrontation. If my adult friend speaks irritably to me and I respond with mindful concern…her irritation may vanish and I may well receive mindful communication in return so that a breach may be healed. Not so with a child. My calmness and compassion may be met again and again with anger. He is just learning to be him and not willing yet to give this up to something as amorphous as "us" and "we".

What I try to remember is that this is as it should be. A child is newly risen from the ocean of being. A small wave gathering momentum on the way to its crest. His task is to grow and to become. Somewhere in the climb, at the peak, as the wave curls, he too will begin to see the water from which he came and so to curb the ego. For the small child, guidance and protection are needed, but as a parent, I must also see that each child is travelling on his own path towards the shore. And he may test out his growing powers against whatever rocks he encounters. But a parent should be a wave too, traveling beside him, not a rock to break his growth prematurely. This is what mindful parenting means to me.

### A Door to Compassion

For a few months now I have been concentrating a lot of daily meditation effort, on and off the cushion, on what traditional teachings call the *Brahma Viharas*, the Divine Abidings. Of these teachings, loving-kindness is the most familiar. Compassion, the second in the list of four, is also familiar, and neither, of course, is exclusive to Buddhist teaching.

My "formal" work with these teachings includes a number of chants, and recitations as well as some free-form prayer: wishing for my heart to open in certain ways. I am very specific about this in these private prayers, mentioning particular people and particular situations that are challenging, expressing my heartfelt desire to look clearly at my part in the picture and to let go of my preferences and judgements that are causing difficulties. And I spend time in meditative contemplation of what I discover, in the calm and tranquil times that permit clear seeing.

Not surprisingly, this intention to open my heart continues to have impact on daily life. And I do not mean only on direct interactions. As a lifetime reader, I am discovering anew the deep gifts of fiction.

A superficial take on fiction is to see it as entertainment and the lesser cousin of serious non-fiction writing. But fiction allows what is seen from the outside in non-fiction to be lived from the inside. My personal bias is that books do this much more effectively than film. We are inevitably viewers of films. Books take up residence in our bodies and minds. When I read a good novel I am temporarily re-embodied. I take on the life, the views and the emotions of some other being. This is the door into compassion, and into sympathetic joy, understanding and sharing the joys of others without envy or judgement, the third of the Brahma Viharas.

This aging, white woman, university educated, middle class, and living in an affluent province in a country with diversity and in a time of opportunity and freedom, is sublimated to the character whose story I am living in the pages of the book. This character may be male or female or even transgender, younger or older than me, of any class or religion, of any race and ethnic heritage, in a country and time period beyond my experience. Thus, I am drawn into a new way of living in the world.

Recently most of the books I have read have had female voices. But these voices have ranged from that of a nine year old Afghani girl to a one hundred and fourteen year old Japanese Buddhist nun. I have lived vicariously within cultures in France, India, Afghanistan, Trinidad, and less exotically in Toronto and San Franciso, to name only those that come immediately to mind. I have moved from the 1500's to medieval times, to the WWI era to contemporary times. Inside the minds and hearts and lives of these differing beings I have learned about a range of hope and loss far beyond my personal experience. I have been inside points of view that fit comfortably and view points that were fraught with dis-ease. Yet for the time I lived inside of them, I was able to see more clearly the ten thousand things that make a being. Familiar furniture to the being for whom they are home, these are the things we so often trip over and bump into in our understanding of others.

These have always been the possibilities of fiction and even when reading purely for the pleasure of story, I have been exposed to them. However, the intention I have formed to open my heart has meant an opening on a new level, that surprisingly applies not just to those born and not-yet-born, as traditional chants say, but to those never-born in the sense we usually mean. The characters in these stories borrow this mind and heart awhile to become "real" and this mind and heart is made more spacious in that union.

### The Way It Is

At first it seemed to me that it was simplistic to think that much of human suffering is self-inflicted, being the result of what Buddhist teaching calls desire and aversion. But it takes only a little while of practiced mindfulness to see the truth in this. Perhaps it is the word suffering that obscures that truth at first. For suffering seems such a large thing. We suffer when we are severely injured, critically ill, lose a loved one. This is easily acknowledged. But the word seems too great for the smaller woes that make up our lives. The stubbed toe, the lack of communication with a teenaged child, sleeping in on a morning when we have an important appointment, being over-charged for a necessary service. These are merely irritations, aren't they? How can we label the emotions they provoke as suffering? But we can. They are. We suffer in these cases, whether the triggers be significant or trivial because we wish, we desire, for things to be different. We want the doctor to take back the terrifying diagnosis. We want our child to tell us what is wrong. We don't want to face the explanations at the meeting we'll be late for. We don't want to pay the outrageous fees. What we want or desire, what we push away or feel aversion for, these are the causes of our suffering.

Mindfulness, at least for me in these early days on this life path, does not erase suffering from my life. But it does put me in a placid place, a place of stillness and ease from which I have some choice. When my young child, in a fit of helpless anger at having his own desires thwarted, tells me he hates me, the pang in my breast is softened. I do not feel an immediate surge of indignant anger at this injustice. Instead, I see clearly this moment. His desire for the way he wanted things to be. His suffering. And his unskillful response. I see too that his acts do not make his suffering less. When I choose to accept this moment, and not to spend it wishing for him to be reasonable, pushing away the unpleasant nature of this encounter, it passes and we move on.

I do not live in a TV scripted family of the 50's where everything runs smoothly, in a too-perfect world. None of us do. But the key is not to desire this, not to wish for it. And when the trials come, as they must, do not push them away and wish it to be different. And so, I am learning to let each moment be, and let each moment go. I cannot make my child's anger disappear by wishing it so; I cannot make his warm bedtime hugs last forever either. The baby smell of his skin is already only memory and so too will each moment be…whether pleasant or unpleasant. But I am more alive when I am here for the living of each one.

# 37  Frequent Action

Choose some daily action that occurs frequently for you (ie. typing in a password at your computer, taking off shoes, getting into your car, turning on water, etc.) and mark it as a mindfulness bell of your own, bringing you to the moment, consciously breathing and checking in with your thoughts and feelings.

**Ocean of Bounty**

"The ocean of bounty, forever and pure." A snippet from *The Flower Ornament Sutra*, scriptures in the Zen tradition. I think of dropping below the surface. Into what is. Forgetting what has been and what will be.

While I cannot drop into the real ocean like this, the metaphor moves me. Dropped into even the warm waters of the Caribbean, I can't let go. I fight the waves. I struggle. I dislike the salt in my mouth and eyes. Too often this is how I live my life. Struggling when surrender would serve me better. But, I've found that if I walk in, slowly, mindfully crossing the sand and letting the water lick ankles, then shins, finding my way one step at a time, I can appreciate the wildness that welcomes me.

So with life then, the changes come moment by moment, day to day. Move along with the push and pull of what is. "As green leaves turn in the wind," Robert Aitken says in one of his gathas. Shifting and moving. This is what happens in life. I'm getting old. I see it in the mirror now. My mother's hands, my mother's face. The eyes may be the blue of my dad's, but I see my mother when I look into my face.

These days I know in my bones that life is exceedingly brief. A wink. A flicker. Moving now into the second half of a century of living, I think of my grandmother who lived till 101. And how I imagined her changed inside as she had changed outside over time. Yet both these things are true: I am still the me I was and I am not. There is no age for whatever morphs moment to moment. There is nothing but change.

Is age only a decaying? Physical only. Asking this, it is easy to see where the idea of "soul" comes from. Something different and apart from this exterior. This aging body that makes me what I seem to be in this moment and then this, is ephemeral and fleeting. But the "I" I struggle to define is nothing. Only this finger pointing at the moon. "I" is just that pointer. There and then there, without substance.

At this moment I see the age spots on my hands, and the wrinkles at my throat, but hair that hasn't greyed yet, and the birthmark I've had all my life. This body I know so well. How it moves. Responds. What it can do. What it resists. How it reacts. Stomach lurches in elevators. Cringing from loud noises and jarring music. How it moves toward water, stills in a breeze. How it sinks into blankets when it shivers.

I can close my eyes and look into this well-known mind. The familiar rivers of thought, the landscapes of memory, the storms that move through, the constellations of bright insights that arise from time to time.

And meditation has helped me to discover the open near-emptiness of awareness. "The ocean of bounty, forever and pure." The undulations of the mind, the trials of the body, are surface waves. The deep, mostly unknown waters stretch wide, all undisturbed beneath a frothy surface. Touching that then. Submerging into that. Letting this be where I dwell. A small and integral drop in the ocean.

These glimpses, whether on my cushion or moving through the world, give me perspective when small bumps in life seem like mountains, when winds of fear or sorrow seem to have such strength. A breath away, the ocean of bounty is accessible.

**Morning Meditation**

This summer my son works the "morning shifts" in the kennel every second morning, and on these days my husband and I alternate taking a "sleep in morning". I do sleep in, for me. Instead of 5:15, I rise at 6:30. I splash water on my face, pull on yoga pants and a tunic top and step slowly into the day as I would into the shocking pleasure of a hot tub. I avoid anyone still in the house, savoring the serenity of solitude. It is such a fragile thing. A tone of voice or a mumble, even from a distance, sends me tumbling into that complicated world of relationships...interpreting moods, worrying and reacting. I want to stay muffled in the silence where my ears are tuned to the birds and the fall of water and my heart beats in an easy rhythm I can follow with all my attention if I choose.

My nighthawk family shake their heads at this rising early when I don't need to. They'd choose to sleep. But that, to me, is like throwing an unwrapped gift into the trash having only admired the ribbons and pretty paper. I'm a morning soul; given the chance I'd live to this inner clock. But that doesn't mean I have a wish to dash out the door. I like to linger, to prepare.

This morning I pad across the hall to my meditation cushion, light candle and incense and do refuge bows, settle in blankets to meditate. Rising and falling. I see how long the out-breath is and the long-long pause before a shorter in-breath. And I see planning mind...what is left over in the fridge, what to serve for lunch, if I bake today what will I use of the fruit on hand ripening too quickly. Then an inward smile and back to the breath. A voice, then another in the kitchen down the hall. I hear abruptness and begin to analyze mood. Stop! Breathe. A thought pattern arises about how I create suffering in this analytical mind...ah, so I analyze that! Smile. Stop. Breathe.

And so the time of no time passes. My little bell calls to me. I unwrap the blankets, do homage bows. Blow out the candle. The incense is ash now in the bowl of rice. My breathing is smooth and easy. My heart is rested and open. I take a moment to remember my intention to remember this. One of my teachers calls it, "re-minding", this coming back to how the mind is over the course of the day, remembering this intention to pay attention.

My day won't be quiet. It will be filled with barking and doggy kisses, customers coming and going, family needs and activities. It will be filled with pleasure and with irritation, maybe even pain. But whatever fills the day will be absorbed with more grace and ease by a quiet heart and mind.

**Past, Present, Future**

From *The Flower Ornament Sutra*:

> The worlds of past, present and future have no distinction in
> the succession of instants....

This moment then and the moment my father died and the moment I first held my firstborn son, and the moment my first marriage ended, and the moment I chose to leave Calgary, and the moment in the future when I will die, all these in the instant. No distinction. Or am I reading into this because I have this fascination with the idea of the end of time? Of time as a human construct. Once I read something, an explanation of omniscience in Christian theology and it was the first explanation that made sense to me. Not God as some gypsy seer who foretells the future, God inside time. But God outside time. In the grandstand, so to speak, and the whole of time spread out on the playing field so that his gaze merely swings from here to there. Having an interest in physics, I've also read of "nows" as a grid-work in which consciousness moves. Consciousness, the stuff of the universe, of all universes. And we lowly creatures are only capable of seeing the bit we take part in so that we make up a linear story of past, present and future because that's what we see and know. Tiny bits of time. The way I can't imagine how the world looks to an eagle. Or a fly. Or a jellyfish. We're stuck inside this perception and that gives us the parameters for our explanations. Sometime ago in an article in *Discover* magazine, I came across a discussion of parallel universes, a metaphor of sheets on a line moving in the wind. Separate but so close and touching now and then. I struggled to explain this theory to my young son, to make sense of parallel worlds in *The Golden Compass*, the fantasy novel we're reading together. Time again as a human construct, its existence in our imaginations. The author of *Zen and the Art of Motorcycle Maintenance* (I'm reading this now) would say it all is. All laws of nature.

We make up a linear story of past, present and future and in so doing we make up cause and effect too. I look back and ask "how'd I get here?" and identify certain junctures and certain decisions or accidents. I see the turning points. I think of how now, at 51, I feel such complete disassociation from former selves. I tried to explain the sometimes bizarre actions of adolescent girls to my confused older son the other day. He feels carried along on the current of his girlfriend's changing moods. And she says to him she can't explain it herself. But being his mother, and once an adolescent girl myself, I see I behaved in remarkably similar ways. So I try to explain. But even as I did I felt like some kind of interloper. Who was I to say I had been there? Because I feel no more identification with that young girl I was then than I do with the young girl I'm trying to explain to him. Me and she, both "I", seem so far apart. Indeed, are. Thirty-five years or more. And a gazillion decisions and incidents later.

So, I've been thinking, how can a writer write anything but autobiography? At 30, how to write about 50, at 50, about 70? Or across gender or culture? Yet they do. Good writers. Because there is a human unity underlying it all. We are not just this single puzzle piece. We are in the big picture too. Can we soar above, outside, to view it all? Is that what we do, what we're striving for, in meditation? To move out of our place in the picture…the edges, the story, the context that make the I, and gain a broader perspective? Or to delve into what underlies it all? Do the directional metaphors of diving in or soaring above even make sense here?

When I follow the breath and release the past and the future, even this present I. When "I" dissolves in the sensation, the experience, there is something that also dissolves the questions. A sweet relief from theory, analysis, intellectual understanding. The felt sense of "just this" that has no perspective at all.

# 38  Morning Intention

When you wake in the morning set the intention to be present today. Placing your feet on the floor as you stand, place one foot and say mentally "be", place the other foot and repeat mentally "here". You may want to continue this walking meditation as you move through the first steps of your day.

**Making Room for a Sneeze**

It's difficult to imagine being happier than I am this morning. This is the kind of serene and contented calm that speaks clearly in my mind: "This is perfect as it is." It is easy for me to begin the stories that explain it in terms of the externals: a wonderful night's sleep, no aching in the body beyond a pleasant "echo" of yesterday's long hours of sitting, a cool and delicious breeze coming in at the tiny window beside me while the air in my room is warm and cozy. I have a huge mug of English Breakfast tea and nearly an hour of solitude before first sit this morning. Pen and paper. A soft blanket spread on the floor for yoga when I finish this writing and the possibility of a walk in the birdsong, wet grass and morning mist. Indeed, I think this blissful state is so pleasureable that conditioned mind has always attributed it to conditions: retreat=happiness.

This morning it is ridiculously easy, suddenly, to see this mistake. Mind is still. Here, in this clear and natural state is the freedom from *dukkha* (suffering) I seek. On retreat I sink into it. Retreat gives me space but it is not the immediate cause of the deep happiness I find. That, I carry with me. On retreat I am able to clear away the debris that masks it.

A favorite book I'd read to the boys when they were small was called *No Room for a Sneeze* and it comes to mind for me now. The harried farmer and his wife who take in their animals, parents, and all manner of beings and things till their home is cluttered and full and uncomfortable and everyone irritable and anxious and they blame it all on this tiny home where there is "no room for a sneeze". Of course, as they clear it out and the space emerges, their smiles and good humor return and the little hut is perfect and spacious. Like our minds, our life.

All the clutter of cares, opinions, possessions and plans, the gotta-do lists and schedules. And the mind is soon an irritable and anxious mess. On retreat we clear this out. Ahhhh! I think this morning. Not the externals but the internals. And I knew this. I knew this intellectually. I've had other "eureka-style" glimpses over the years.

This morning the insight is in my bones. All things are impermanent, I laugh to myself. Don't hold this tight. Don't make it another "possession". Let it rest in that open space the mind has become this morning. Look into that clear, cool pool while it is still and don't try to stop the waves that will come. Inevitably. Only enjoy this and know it fully. Be here. The neural pathway is there now. It will be easier to clear it and walk it next time.

**Being Present For My Life**

I'm not sure at what point on the journey I realized that meditation and the path I was on had to do with being present for my own life. At the very beginning, I think I even wished that it meant exactly the opposite: that is, escaping from those things in my own life that were too painful. Disappointments, physical pain, anger, loss, grief, yearning. All those universally human experiences that we'd easily classify as undesirable. And meditation, it seemed to me, would be a way to enter a place where all this receded into the distance, and for awhile, at least, I could rest in a warm and peaceful place. I thought, that with enough practice, over time, I'd be able to maintain this. Keep the kind of bubble around myself that I'd like to keep around my children. A place that is warm, safe and good.

Indeed, at the beginning of the journey, just touching such a place was a great blessing. Like a massage, a vacation, a good book, an invigorating workout, it was a place where the world, and life didn't enter for awhile. And this had/has its benefits. But eventually, the bell rings, whatever time has been set aside for meditation ends, and the rest of life is waiting like an eager and sizable puppy who has been neglected. It'll bowl you over if you aren't prepared. If your feet aren't solidly on the ground and your eyes open, ready to deal with the onslaught.

With persistence, and as my practice deepened, I came to realize that the point of all this was to develop a place of balance and clarity that would allow me to face that onslaught and stay on my feet. To deal with the puppy in a kindly manner. Whether it represented too many things on the do list, an illness or injury, a conflict, a sorrow, a decision I didn't want to make.

I keep index cards near the cushion where I sit daily. And on these I like to copy teachings, often cryptic, that have moved me, have brought a sharp and silvery moment of understanding. One of these is "Suffering does not go away; the one who suffers goes away." I would not have been comforted by this as someone new to meditation, but when I encountered it a few years ago, it brought one of those "ah!" moments that define insight.

After nearly two decades of practice, my life still holds disappointments, physical pain, anger, loss, grief and yearning. I still have to get off the cushion and deal with a busy list of to-do's; a chronic illness; daily sorrows , both personal and just related to the nature of the world; and decisions that have to be made ready or not. But the self who got tied in knots about this is becoming less and less of a bully. The ego that feels resentment or self-pity or hopelessness or pressure, doesn't hold the reins all the time anymore. There's a struggle sometimes. Internal nudging and poking and pinching that isn't always comfortable. But the vast spaciousness of awareness that meditation practice opens, surprisingly, has much less room for a cranky, hard-edged ego setting itself against the world.

It's in this place of spaciousness that I am able to be present for my life. Not pushed and pulled by the need for escape and the wish for something other, I can rest in this moment whatever it holds. When I'm grounded and present, there is no need or wish to run away.

### Maintaining Practice

Children immediately need to see the consequences of their actions. If you explain that running across the road without looking was very dangerous and they should never do that again, you're likely to be told something like "But I'm OK." There was no negative consequent, other than the lecture you are now providing, and so it is difficult for them to imagine the possibly nasty outcomes you describe. By the same token, an ice cream cone now is better than saving the fifty cents to put towards the new dinosaur playset they've been wanting.

To some degree we never outgrow this. Our ability to pursue longterm goals with no immediate payoff does generally grow with maturity but at least a little of the child who wants things now is always there.

This is why keeping at something that is difficult can be such a monumental task. As adults we are likely to enact some version of the fox and the grapes when the going gets tough. We decide we haven't got enough time, or that something else is more important, or that the goal is not desirable anyway. Often we don't even see the chain of reasoning. Sometimes we do, but manage to shuffle it aside so as not to be embarrassed by its presence.

Sitting meditation is difficult in many ways. Despite the constant words of encouragement to continue, just to begin again, to practice. And despite the warnings of the obstacles that will arise, we're not quite able to conjure up the experience until we're in it. And the unease can be unpleasant. So aversion kicks in and we decide this isn't for us after all.

I've been sitting in meditation practice for a number of years on a pretty much daily basis, times ranging anywhere from 10-15 minutes to an hour. Weekend retreats are the only more intensive practice I've had. This is not a lot when you think about those people who go into retreats for three years where sitting is their prime focus. It's a drop in the bucket compared to the lifetime practice of aged and wise teachers. But in my middle-aged, middle-class life, taking the time to sit each day is a commitment I consider pretty major. Yet, so very often the sitting itself is difficult. The worries and plans of the day intrude, other tasks beckon, household sounds and activities draw my attention and I hear the fox in the back of my head grumble "You're not getting anywhere anyway. Why bother?"

It is the glimpses that lure me. Though they too can be obstacles when I find myself striving to repeat some former experience. The branch never shakes and a grape never falls when I try too hard.

What is difficult is learning just to be. To see the plans, to hear the noises, to acknowledge the tasks to be done, and then to go on sitting and breathing. The ladder I build with each breath puts mindfulness within my reach throughout the day. Sweeter by far than the fleeting taste of the grapes I thought I wanted.

# 39  Naming

Sitting in a waiting room or just alone on your deck in the sunshine, anywhere with a bit of open time, close your eyes and just listen for two minutes. Try to hear without naming what you hear.

### Breaking Free of Concepts

Over the years of my practice, in various ways, teachers have instructed me to be with experience or sensation in the body, just as it is. Not labeling or judging. Not creating a narrative. At first this was incredibly difficult to do. I was accustomed to thinking of thinking as discursive, a kind of talking to myself. I am someone who loves language. I was an early talker; my dad used to like to say it took them less than a year to teach me to talk and all the years since to get me to be quiet! I've been a reader from the time I was old enough to understand that those shapes on the page contained "words". And a writer since elementary school. Sometimes my mind conjures pictures, which some people describe as rich visual thinking. I carry tunes around in my head and like to invent rhymes for fun and as memory aids, but I have musical friends who seem to actually think in music, minus the lyrics. I know I have some tactile memories, so I imagine there are even people who think at least some of the time in ways that could be described as more tactile than verbal. But personally, I've had narrative going on for as long as I can remember. My "self talk" is definitely that. Words, words and more words.

In learning to meditate and to focus on the breath, it was natural for me to use labeling when I began. To say to myself "breath in, breath out", or sometimes just "breath–ing", breaking the word to mark inhalation and exhalation. It took awhile to keep mind with breath without a word to give it "substance".

And it took longer to feel into the experience inside my body without creating a narrative to describe it; adjectives and metaphors were there as soon as I looked, it seemed.

In his wonderful small book *The Sun in My Heart,* Thich Nhat Hanh says "Our mind creates categories – space and time, above and below, inside and outside, myself and others, cause and effect, birth and death, one and many – and puts all physical and psychological phenomena into categories like these before examining them and trying to find their true nature. It is like filling many different shapes and sizes of bottles with water in order to find out the shape and size of water. Truth itself transcends these concepts, so if you want to penetrate it you must break all the conceptual categories you use in normal daily life.... Meditation reveals not a concept of truth, but a direct view of truth itself."

How wonderfully he uses language here to describe something beyond language. This is all we have to communicate with each other: language, music, art. But as each of us fine-tunes mindfulness, training the mind to live with full awareness, we follow the path of personal insight. In examining our own experience, we don't have to translate into anything else. We understand directly through awareness. The truth we touch here is primary.

Years along this path, I see how the internal narrative habit goes hand in hand with one of the categories my mind creates, the category of "I" or "myself". Direct experiencing is subsumed by the experiencer created...the concept of myself as a "thing". The confusing teaching of no-self is only confusing because of our mind's "addiction" to categories. I've poured experience into a container, as Thich Nhat Hanh describes, and then I confuse the container with the experience. I think this "I" is the shape of experience.

I offered here a description of myself as a word-person, but I've been breathing even before I was talking. We all have. We've been feeling the body as body since long before we sorted out an idea of our own fingers and toes. Experience came before any of the concepts we use to pin it down. In meditation and daily mindfulness we return to what is primary. In this disentangling we often taste peace. With patience and persistence, I believe, this way leads to freedom from the suffering we create along with the concepts; this way leads to wisdom.

**Nature Meditation**

Marmots. Squirrels. Chipmunks. These abound around the monastery. Perhaps other "critters", less visible, too? On my hot and sweaty T-shirt walk yesterday, something made a meal of me and I've several big red welts now. Combating the scratch reflex, I opt for antihistamines before breakfast and then find I'm sleepy in the sala in the sit that follows, struggling with "sloth and torpor".

No one seems to be venturing outside with the low dark scoops of clouds and intermittent showers, but I layer up and go. At the door, from the communal basket, I choose an umbrella the color of milky chai. I go up the logging road instead of down today. At first, no rain, and although the ground is wet, it's not puddley. The umbrella is bound and swings in my breeze-chilled hand at my side. Breath. The shuffle of feet on the sandy path. I feel my pulse even and slow in my throat. Still drowsy but also energized by the motion. A lovely trance-like state.

Some ways up I find a huge stone under a little lodge pole pine and veer off the path to sit on its inviting flat bench-like surface. Room for the umbrella, still closed, beside me. Hands tucked between knees to warm. I am elements, among elements. My breath and the breeze. Air. The hard stone beneath me and the dirt under my feet, the long, firm bones of my body. Earth. The heat seeping into my hands and the sun sending its own warming fingers through the clouds. Fire. The rain begins a lighter than light patter. The soft thrum of blood in my veins is marked by the beat of my heart. Water. My eyes are closed and the pleasant energized trance continues. Air, earth, fire and water. This, just this, pleasant abiding.

In awhile the stone's cold penetrates and I rouse myself, open the umbrella and walk on a little before choosing where I'll turn for the walk back.

Just as the members of the rhythm section in an orchestra take turns in leading, the patter of the rain is sometimes so light it is inaudible beneath the shuffle and step of my feet; then it will pick up, a tipping and tapping that envelopes me beneath the blossom of the open umbrella. Birds call, whistle and sing. Melody rising above the rhythm. And then, surprise, the deep thrumming of a grouse that I feel in my body as much as hear in my ears.

So it goes. Listening meditation now. Following sound. Back at the monastery the whole orchestra awakens as rain sings and rings on metal, taps or thunders on wooden ramps, and shushes through spouts and gutters.

I stop under the eave to shake out and fold the umbrella, to breathe in the stirred dust smells and the high scent of green. Then open the door and step back into a deeper silence. There is still a lethargy in my body that is a sign of deep relaxation...like after a sauna or massage. But the choice to move has brought my mind to a clear alertness. Not curled and sleepy now but sitting up and taking in. Being with the moment as it passes.

**Death Meditation**

It is not common for teachers of Buddhism in the west to address the various aspects of death meditation. In truth it seems a little morbid and gruesome when viewed within the context of our culture. Our culture does its best to forget about death, to give it into the hands of "professionals" just as we give the aging and the ill over. As well, despite evidence to the contrary, we tirelessly pursue the idea that youth and life are possible forever if we just keep working at it and trust in science. It's a strange irony that though our daily entertainments contain more graphic violence than the generally unpleasant nightly news, we can't bear to think of the slow descent of illness and aging that is inevitably contained in a mortal birth. I'm a child of this culture, and it took me a long time to appreciate that reflections on death could be helpful to me in learning to live more mindfully and compassionately.

There are some quite graphic forms of death meditation that grew out of the funeral traditions of another culture and time, but they are not the only ones available. It is possible to recognize that this culture and time handles the process differently and yet to bring the process into consciousness as an ordinary thing. I strongly believe that some sort of reflection on the brevity of this life, on the truth of suffering, aging and death, are vital to the development of a worldview that does not become obsessed with material gain, that understands connection to all living things, and that values the moments of this brief and precious life, even moments that are neutral and ordinary.

The simple and clear Five Reflections were my first entry. I began to reflect daily that I was not an exception to the rules of mortal life, but would age and sicken and die, would lose what I held precious and that my actions had consequences in the world. This practice had an impact that was not noticeable in an immediate way but began to warm and inform my practice like an underground spring. In time I found that the gathas I composed from time to time reflected these ideas. And the gathas themselves allowed for a strongly personal take on the passing of time in my life.

Illness and aging are ordinary experiences. When I turn my face toward them, I recognize this so that whatever I am suffering becomes not a solitary and unbearable thing, but the experience of being human. Like the black night behind the stars, these experiences enhance the brilliance of the sparkling individual moments, and throw a wide net which reminds me that all of this is included in what it is to live.

And so I acknowledged, during the difficult years of menopause:

> Weeping in the night over aging and change
> I breathe and remember
> To hear the sighs and sobs of all mortal life
> Nothing unusual here.

Living with the chronic illness I've struggled with for more than two decades:

> When illness reminds me of the vulnerability of this physical self
> I breathe and remember
> That even as I care for this body, it does not mark my boundaries.
> I am one with all that is.

And passing my 60th birthday a couple of years back:

> When my body speaks in aches and twinges
> And aging makes itself known
> I breathe and remember
> To value these intimate teachings
> Words in a universal poem.

Mindfulness is not only about pausing to note the blessings in life, but also about noting the real:

> Catching a glimpse in the mirror
> Of this aging stranger's face
> I breathe and remember
> To smile in recognition and pause
> Not deny our acquaintance and run.

Death meditation does not require us to visit the boneyards of the Far East but rather to listen to the messenger that is our own dear body.

# 40 Joy

Take a few minutes to make a list of things you enjoy doing, activities that help you to re-charge. Post this somewhere you'll see it often and form an intention to find time for at least a couple of these things in each week.

**Clap Your Hands**

When I was a child in Sunday School, we used to often sing a little "joy making" song. I don't recall all the lines but one that still goes through my mind sometimes when life is just undeniably fine is "When you're happy and you know it, clap your hands!" Just remembering this instruction when I'm curled in a comfy chair by the fire, or rubbing the belly of my silly dog or sitting at the table in comfortable conversation with my family as they enjoy a meal I prepared for them, brings a broader smile to my face. Yet, how many fine moments slip by, I can only imagine, when I don't "know it"?

Mindfulness instructions of any type point out that we should be aware of the moment, not missing out on our life. The Buddha's instructions stress that this awareness should be cultivated, training the mind to notice it all, not just the fine and the happy. We train to be aware of body, of the feeling tone of pleasant or unpleasant or neutral that accompanies sensation and thought, of the condition or state of the mind, and of thoughts or the content of mind. We train to "know it" when the mind moves and not simply to be sucked into its vortex like lint on a carpet when the vacuum comes along. When we "know" what is present in this way, we may truly be moved to clap our hands with the joy that can arise. And if the emotion is not happiness, but sorrow, we are able to bear it, and know it for the passing and changeable state it is. We are able to watch it rise and pass away as all things do, not giving it strength through our own resistance but opening our hands to let it run through, run its course.

Sometimes when we watch a child, bouncing with laughter, energy and excitement one moment, then lamenting a minute later over a dropped cookie, hugging a dear friend and then pushing roughly past some other child to be the first to ride on the merry-go-round, we think we are seeing an example of someone who is in the moment. With the complexities of adult reflection and interactions, we may even long for such simplicity of emotion and action, what appears as honest expression of feeling. But a child is lint on the carpet. The great rushes of emotion move him or her this way and that. Pulled in by happiness, by anger, by sorrow, by desire. There is no "knowing" of what is at play. Think of the way we will talk to a child lamenting over the loss of a cookie, for instance. We often try to explain, to reason, to interpret the child's actions, looking into what moments of mind may have triggered the behavior. "It was only a cookie. You're tired. What you really need is a nap." Or we comfort and sooth, "It's alright. Shh." Or we banish the emotion by promising, "There'll be more cookies tomorrow."

As adults, we learn a little about doing this for ourselves. Too often, though, we go for the last gambit…promising ourselves we'll fix this, we'll ultimately get what we want later somehow. We want to rush forward to the time it will be OK again. To the time when things go our way. Training ourselves in mindfulness is a bit like re-parenting our inner child. Yes, the cookie is in the dust. It's lost. Even had we been able to hold it safe, we would have eaten it, it would be gone. Or we would have had enough in a few bites and abandoned it on the picnic table forgotten as we rushed off to join a game of tag. Each moment holds sensory input and a feeling charge, each moment is passing and transforming into the next.

What I like about the old Sunday School song is the reminder to allow joy. To notice it. To pay attention. It's OK to be happy. When it comes to lingering and loitering over the bad stuff, we seem to have a natural aptitude as human beings. "When you're sad and you know it, hang your head. When you're angry and you know it, curse out loud." The problem is that in doing this we get better at it. Creating an easy path for sorrow and anger from thought to action. We've posted direction signs: This way to suffering. We march self-assuredly on toward our own deeper unhappiness. On the other hand, making some noise about the good stuff, celebrating the things we often don't notice at all, begins to clear the brush in another direction entirely. It's a reliable short cut to more joy. So clap your hands!

## I Want to be Happy

Sometimes people get confused about the Buddha's teachings and think that it is somehow "wrong" to want anything. They see desire as a problem. But this is missing a subtlety...the distinction between the desire, the wanting, and the clinging to that wanting. Though you may want good weather for the parade you plan to attend on the weekend, you'll likely have an alternate plan in mind in case it rains. That is, you'll either get out your umbrella, find shelter in a store front alcove, or decide just not to go this year. If you spend the day moping, and won't entertain any suggestions about how to accommodate the weather, or what other activities might be possible for the day, instead opting for complaining and ranting, well then, that's clinging. It's the formula that says "I can't be happy unless...." And, oddly enough, you prove it to yourself by being unhappy for at least the whole day of the parade.

Intentions are entirely different. In the Eightfold Path, Right Intention is the second factor. We set our gaze in a certain direction, make our efforts with a certain aspiration in mind. Ultimately, on the Buddha's practice path, this aspiration is freedom, liberation, *nibbana*. This is lasting happiness, where we are released from the suffering we cause ourselves because of our misguided notions of what is true. Because of greed, hatred and delusion, we flounder about and cause our own suffering, while believing we are pursuing happiness. As we begin to see clearly what happens, we're able to steer our mind and our life in a different direction.

Giving a talk within the "Awakening Joy" course offered by Spirit Rock, personal change coach and author M.J. Ryan, makes an interesting and helpful distinction. Consider, she says, the difference between "I want to be happy", and "I intend to be happy." While the first statement is passive, waiting for "happiness" to materialize in my life, the second is active, indicating a wish I mean to carry out. When we form such intention, we acknowledge our own role in whether or not happiness is experienced. Notice though that desire kicks things off. A desire to be happy, wanting to be happy, precedes the intention to bring it about. We have to be clear here about what happiness feels like. How do we define and measure our own happiness? Through honest and persistent observation. Through daily, ongoing mindfulness.

Coming back to the Buddha's teachings, we discover the role of observing our own mind and our own experience, discerning in this way the difference between skillful and unskillful actions in moving toward "happiness". If I mistakenly equate happiness with a particular thing, I may discover that sometimes, as in the case of the sunny parade day, I cannot make this happen. In the case of some other "things", I may be able to make a plan and get that thing, only to find that happiness doesn't result. This runs counter, I soon notice, to the claims of advertising: this holiday, this car, this brand of clothing equals happiness. Careful observation of my own experience will teach me that this isn't so. Perhaps there will be momentary pleasure, but eventually the holiday ends, a new model of car is released that I like better, or the clothing doesn't look as great on me as it did on the ad model.

Ryan completes her formula with "persistence". Keep the intention in mind and keep working at this, even through failures and disappointments. It takes courage to honestly look at and acknowledge thoughts and feelings, to assess what occurs in your mind and heart along the way, and what actions of your own, internal and external, lead to peace or to turmoil. Patient, persistent effort in watching our own experience teaches us where lasting happiness can be found. It isn't as simple as a car or a week on the beach. It's an attitude, an inclination of mind. "Don't lose your intention", Ryan says. "It is more stable than the day to day flow of emotions and energy will move toward it."

**Nothing Lasts**

I think there's a rock song that has a line "You can't go home again". I can almost hear the tune when I think the words, but that's all that comes to me, no artist or song title. Apologies to the composer.* This line has been running through my head at intervals since a recent trip to my hometown. It was planned as a pilgrimage, a nostalgia trip of a sort, so that it caused this synapses to fire is no surprise, I guess. The whole experience was both lovely and melancholy. That mix that makes a deeply moving poem or ballad turn in the heart like a knife, producing what humans understand as "sweet pain". The kind of perverse impulse that can make me play over and over again a song that reminds me of loss or disappointment, or that finds me flipping through old photos with tears running down my cheeks, companions to a kind of joy in the heart. What is this about?

It's the heart telling us, I think, what the mind tries to deny. The impermanence of all we hold dear. A favorite Dhamma-folk-singer/songwriter of mine, Eve Decker, sings "I ask myself what really matters in this world where nothing lasts." Ah yes. That's the piece we'd rather deny, though the human heart knows the truth. We deny it because we think this somehow undermines the value of what we have, what we do in our lives. Yet, the heart knows this is what gives value to so much. We see the beauty in the sunset, knowing the day is ending; hold our children to our hearts, knowing they'll grow and leave; give our best effort to our work, knowing that the house we build, the book we write, the meal we prepare, the crop we grow, the broken arm we set, the lost person we seek to support, all of it is only a blip in the vast web of being and the great sweep of time. Our efforts, our commitments, are made in the face of this.

When we forget what the heart knows, it seems that we fall into mistakes. We imagine that the product and the process itself is significant in a way that makes us unreasonable. We are angry with delays, greedy for recognition, demanding of others, abrupt or dismissive perhaps of the needs of others. We develop tunnel vision around our needs and desires. That's one kind of mistake. The other is allowing the perception of impermanence to lead to apathy. Why build houses that will crumble? Why write books that will be forgotten? Why care for bodies that will only sicken and age? Why strive to help if our efforts don't seem enough?

On this trip, I visited the graves of my beloved parents, reminded of times that won't return, and of the brevity of the little lives given to us. This recognition makes the time spent now with loved ones still living, all the more precious. Visiting the home where I grew up, I found my father's gardens buried in gravel, the house my parents lovingly maintained, neglected, paint peeling, roof sagging, windows grimey. Some glorious trees remained, circling instead of a green sweep of lawn, a muddy stretch of torn earth where well-used gravel trucks were parked. When I returned to my current home I thought about the angst that goes into every decision we make in caring for what is "ours". The grieving that takes place when we leave a place we've lived in and cared for, placing it in the hands of others. Our wishes that what we've done will be preserved. And how this is simply not possible. We care for what is ours…people, places, and the rest because loving means paying attention, but we recognize that this is only for now. We are stewards only of all that threads its way through our lives, our hands, our hearts. Loving and letting go is a recognition of both value and impermanence, twin truths that are uneasy companions.

* My research discovered many, many songs with this title or line.

# 41 Kindness

## Having a blue day? A deliberate act of kindness directed towards another will inevitably lift your spirits.

### Faking It

"Faking it" sounds like a dishonest act. Pretending to be something that you are not. Yet once at a retreat, someone in the group asked the wise and experienced lay leader "What do you think of the adage 'fake it till you make it'?" and she answered that it was absolutely good advice.

The question came, I'm sure, from that overwhelming feeling we may have as we set out to open our hearts and change our minds, that there is an impossible perfection we're striving for. That even giving it our best shot, we're never going to get there. It comes, I think, from a sense of inadequacy and self-judgment. Only a saint could measure up.

I've given the teacher's answer a lot of thought since then. I've watched its impact on my own practice. And I've sat with it in meditations centering on loving-kindness, on equanimity and on compassion. And its wisdom, I'm convinced, runs deep.

Body, breath, mind and heart are intimately connected. When we are full of fear, our breathing changes, our heart rate quickens. When we are anxious, our stomach clenches, we have trouble sleeping, and we may suffer from headaches. When we relax in the warmth of a steam room or under the hands of a massage therapist, our minds unclench and our thoughts soften. Cycles of anxious mind-chatter quieten awhile. Breathe long and deep and you'll begin to relax. Deliberately make your breaths quick and short and you'll feel not just energy but, after a moment or two, the seeds of panic. Our thoughts influence our world, our bodies. And the postures and actions, the behavior of our bodies, influence the quality and content of our thoughts.

Thich Nhat Hanh says that while joy may be the cause of our smile, it is also possible for a smile to be the cause of our joy. His meditation instructions include curving the lips upward in a smile. Try it and you'll find a lifting of the heart, a lightening of the mind, is inevitable. Is this smile false? Is this faking joy? I think the question of which came first is one of those that mysteriously disappears, a kind of Zen magic trick. But there is a caution here. There are two kinds of "faking": the distinction arises at the level of intention.

We often think that to pretend, to fake it, indicates duplicity. And this can be the case. When faking it is motivated by the intention to deceive, then it is a dangerous thing. Not dangerous just for the victim who may be taken in, but for the heart of the deceiver who is engaging in unskillful thought and action. If you put on smiles and kindness in order to convince your aunt to loan you money for a new car, this is duplicity. The intention is to take advantage, to harm another in seeking selfish ends.

How different is this from the mother who, tired and wanting only to rest at the end of the day, pretends to be excited about the sledding outing she has promised her child. Who, intending to please the child, intending to bring something good into the day, fakes her excitement. What often happens in this case, is that what began as a case of "pretend" gives rise to real joy for both mother and child.

Ajahn Sucitto suggests that the measure of what he calls the "great intention" is whether it is "for my welfare, for the welfare of others and leading to peace." In choosing to smile when we sit to meditate, whether we feel like smiling or not right then, whether we feel like meditating or not right then, we choose what benefits ourselves and others, we choose what leads to peace. The skillfulness arises in knowing that when I am aiming not at perfection, but at harmony and non-harm in this moment, though I may need to "fake" the current action, I am working change on my own heart and mind.

Our impulses do not change in an instant. But as we learn to see them, we learn that we do not need to follow them. I can snap at the person who interrupted me, or I can take a deep breath and fake it, by responding with patience. Chances are that if I do the latter, I will notice the irritation evaporating.

If our deepest intention is real, faking it becomes making it, one action at a time.

**Immersion in the Moment**

I'm thinking about practice. How it threads through my days. Not just the formal stuff…the sitting, the chanting, the sutta studies and Dhamma talks. But mostly how this ongoing journey on the Eightfold path informs every encounter, activity and moment of my day, like wearing sunglasses that tint everything a certain shade. This is my world view.

I notice when the glasses slip or the lenses smudge. These are the moments when I forget where I put down the keys. Or open the fridge instead of the cupboard and then wonder what I'm doing, what I'm looking for. There was a time when this sort of forgetfulness was frequent, just something I accepted in a too busy world, and a life with too much multi-tasking. Aging may impact memory and these days I might encounter someone I used to see often and find I can't recall their name. But the loss of the moment as it passes is less frequent then it was in my 20's. That's something.

Throughout the day the flow of body and mind is threaded together. Moving here, lifting this, closing this, stirring this, opening this, kneeling here. And out of this presence arises a sense of contentment and peace. A central characteristic of unhappiness, perhaps, is the lack of presence. Or is it that lack of presence is marked by unhappiness in some form?

When you are feeling blue next time, notice whether you are in touch with this moment, with body and mind. Perhaps you explore the "weather" of the mind and find it stormy. But if you move below this and into the body, to the tension, the aching of the heart, then something shifts. And as you make contact with pure sensation, a lighter mood emerges. That's the way it seems to me.

My teacher explains that "moods" feed on themselves, and a little investigation shows this to be true. Feeling sad, you conjure sad memories and sorrowful visions of the future and sadness grows. Feeling happy, the sky is a brighter blue, even the rain smells delicious and makes the world new, what you anticipate is promising, what you remember makes you smile. But you don't have to be a helpless victim of "mood".

Practice teaches us to notice and interrupt the negative. To dig into the closet, throw open the shutters, empty the bins and find something that sparkles, something to start from. For me, most often, this something is in the body. In the smooth and involuntary movement of the breath. In the touch of the earth. In the feel of the air. In a drink of cool water. In the sound of silence. Not escape from this moment but immersion in it.

Living this practice means to be devoted to the ongoing cultivation of gratitude, appreciation and joy. It means keeping my eyes open when things are bleak, and looking closely. Then stepping back for the wider view that shows this moment for what it is…a single pixel in the big picture.

### Rough Ride

There's a joke we used to pass around in our family during the years that kids were small and there seemed to constantly be turmoil of one kind or another.

The joke was that when things were feeling overwhelming, and it seemed they couldn't get worse, it was a good idea to phone someone in the family who had their own problems. At the time, the guilty chuckle we'd give as we said this was because this seemed to imply that our problems looked smaller in contrast and we could hang up the phone feeling better. But practice soon taught me there was another dimension to this.

When we listen to a friend whose life is going badly, who is dealing with illness or financial worries or relationship problems, or parenting issues, the kind of difficulties that plague us all at one time or another, our heart may be encouraged to open. When we listen mindfully, with our full attention, our response will not be a spiteful and selfish "Thank goodness that's not me", but rather a compassionate recognition of the universal. All of us suffer. Things don't go the way we wish. So, when we're immersed deeply in our own tales of woe, it can be wise to open our ears and hearts to the woes of others.

Strapped into the seat that carries us on the ride we're taking through our own difficulties, the view seems to be going by in a fast and dizzying way and it is difficult to imagine what to do about some of the problems. We can just end up closing our eyes, hunkering down and trying to get through the scary parts. But if we know we're sharing the ride, we might find we hold each other's hands, or speak kindly and cheerfully as we try to help our companion through. Sharing difficulties can be like that. We're encouraged to open our eyes and our hearts, to be there for someone else and perhaps to be less immersed in the "me" who is having a rough ride.

When we grumbled about our troubles as kids, my mom used to quote the old adage: "I cried because I had no shoes till I met a man who had no feet." There will be troubles bigger and smaller going on for others through any trouble we meet on our own journey. Finding actions or words intended to ease the pain of another may be easier than self talk about our own pain. The lovely surprise is that doing something to ease the pain of others is exactly what will ease our own pain.

This doesn't have to be monumental. I don't have to make huge monetary donations to global charities, or provide meals for every person who is homeless in my town. But I do need to be aware, through my own suffering, that others suffer too. And then be open to what I can do to help a little.

Offering a ride to the friend whose car breaks down, babysitting for an evening for the couple who need time to re-connect and talk, picking up a medication or even just cough-drops for a shut-in friend. Whenever we lift our head, look around and acknowledge we are not alone, this means noticing that our actions count in the lives of others, as theirs do in ours. A single act of kindness can bring a better moment into the lives of others and our own. This is where the future begins. This is where a turning is possible.

# 42 Continuity

## Change the passwords for sites you frequent often. Choose words or phrases that remind you to pause or breathe.

### Why Meditate?

Why do I meditate? Closer to the truth...why do I want this to be part of my life? No, integral to my life? I think of my friend Kuya's short story. The woman who longed for monastic life, continually pulled by family needs to roles elsewhere. Knocking at the gates of the temple finally, an old woman now, but moving into the world that called her.

The story spoke to me. To my need for, love for, solitude and silence. And yet, being honest I know I need and love my family with the same intensity and also that the variety of my life is important to me. Yet, there is undeniably a kernel of my being that is and always has been drawn to the spiritual life, asking the "big" questions.

This has been my spiritual quest. The experimentation with this and that path when I was a kid. The reading of sacred books from multiple traditions. Even my choice to study philosophy and the hollowness that I first felt when the God-space inside me was emptied. And now, in these years, to find a path that echoes explanations I had tried to articulate for myself.

Why meditate? Because it is important. Because of all the busy things I do in my day, two seem most significant in the world. First, to love. And then, to be still and to see, to breathe. When I love well...when I am there for family, friends, animal or stranger, I know I have touched what is real. And when I am still, when I feel my breath and know the connection with past and future and all beings, I feel this truth too. Then, the busyness of shopping, cooking, eating, cleaning, remembering events, paying bills and entertaining others and myself...all this falls away. Sometimes I feel the pain that my life is slipping away...

at 50, half of it is gone, maybe two-thirds, and yet I keep stepping back into the "busy" stream of traffic, not able to stay quietly at the side often enough.

Exhaustion is my biggest enemy of late. Love your enemy. Enfold him. Too often rest is my greatest desire. Just to collapse and sleep. And so I settle for oblivion, sleep over that alert and knowing stillness. Not the same at all. I need both kinds of nourishment.

I am disgusted sometimes with myself, sad, irritated. Ah! Judging. And yet how do I achieve the discipline to do this if I do not first judge and determine to move in the direction I intend? I am still so much the novice when it comes to understanding, to letting go and letting be. I try to remember there is no secret, better place to be behind the monastery gates. To remember that this life is my practice. Can I be still in the midst of it?

## A Seasonal Practice

Today we scrambled through age-softened cardboard boxes and set up our Christmas tree, our Enlightenment tree. Roughly calculating, we figure we've had this one for two decades. It sheds a few nylon needles every year but, to our eyes, looks just as rich and magical as ever by the time we've twisted the little branches into place, strung it with lights and settled each decoration in a carefully chosen place. It's a ritual I love. Ornaments made by my children or with them. Ornaments that were gifts from friends or family. Ornaments we purchased on vacations or chose particularly to represent a special event in the year coming to an end. And in my mindfulness practice, this has another dimension. It is a reminder of impermanence, a reminder of change.

The Buddha taught us to reflect on death. To be aware of the precious brevity of this life. And to understand the suffering that comes from denying this truth. My teacher has suggested that reflecting on death does not necessarily mean imagining yourself dead, imagining your life ending, but rather reflecting on your human fear of the unknown. How often in our lives do we stay with things as they are because of a fear of change? And how often do we try to deny change even when we see it happening?

Unpacking my Christmas decorations every year, I lift into my hands one reminder after another of impermanence and change. The crushed paper angel. The pets no longer with us, represented in photos and caricatures on ceramic snowflakes. The baby faces of my now-grown boys framed in laminated stars. And the years printed in "permanent" marker. Decades and decades gone by.

As two of us decorate the tree, I am reminded of the years when there were four. When stools were required and glass bulbs were broken and teddy bear or reindeer ornaments ended up in bedrooms instead of on the tree. I am reminded as I stand back to admire our work that not many people will see this little bit of glory. We no longer have house-fulls of family arriving to share dinner. The generation before us has dwindled. This generation and the next are more scattered than ever. Work, weather, financial restraint in economic bad times. They all rein in plans and travel.

This sounds like an ode of longing, but it's not. Every year represented by an ornament on our tree held wonderful times, and every year held disappointments and pain. This is the stuff life is made of. And the shifting flow of change is the one steady thing that runs through. I have changed. The people in my life have changed. The landscape of my home. The circumstances of the world. And this will continue to happen. The "good old days" were never fixed, like the home-movie memories we re-run in our minds.

Mindfulness teaches us to be here in this moment. To appreciate this breath, this place. To face what is good and also what is not so good. And to cling to neither, push neither away. But it also teaches us to put forth effort towards release from our own homegrown suffering. To see that fragile distinction between a thought train that brings joy and one that brings pain. Between a thought train that leads to positive words and actions, and one that will carry us in a direction that might mean words or actions we'll later regret. When we see this clearly, we open up a moment of choice, the possibility of behaving inwardly and outwardly in a more skillful way.

Today, setting up our family tree marked the beginning of the holiday season in a personal way for me. *Sati*, the Pali word for mindfulness, literally means "remembrance". I remember my lost loved ones with joy, I vow to love well those still here for me to love, and I remember great beings, great teachers, who have set examples of a better way to live. Such remembering opens the heart and puts fears to rest.

### Held in Compassion

Some years ago I heard a teacher describe how our capacity for mindfulness, the ability to stay with discomfort especially, grows with time and consistent practice. Patience is key. So we gradually find we are able to stay with the slight discomfort of waiting in line, of a long-held yin pose, listening to the long monologue of someone we disagree with without interrupting. That sort of thing and maybe much more difficult experiences. Losing a job. The end of a marriage. An illness. But for all of us there will be surprises. Things that arise in our life that are outside the scope of that skill we've been cultivating. And when this happens, the second surprise is to find that the newer habits we've been consciously developing may be less stable than we imagined.

Recently in my life such a crisis arose. My first responses were careful and reflective. Although I could not change the circumstances or the event, I felt that I caught my own reactivity quite swiftly. I settled in to ride through one of the ordinary sorrows life offers, shored up by practices of mindfulness and the clear seeing of the way things are. It was in the night that I discovered that my feet were sliding, slipping into older, less skillful pathways. Dreams were troubled. Sleep intermittent. Body restless. I understand Right Effort and I continued to come to the breath each time I woke, to scan and relax this aching and weary body, to soften and relax the hand of the mind as it twitched, reaching for a place for blame and fear to take hold. It was a long night.

In the morning, I watched my breath and moved through a gentle yin practice and spent some time in *paramita* chanting. These chants are reminders of the truths I have seen for myself in my practice. This moment is the only one I live in. Past and future are ephemeral creations of the mind. I knew I was painting tigers and then cowering in fear of them, as an old teaching story goes. I sat with the breath, beginning again and again. And then, later in the morning, I took my troubles to my Dhamma community.

When the Buddha's cousin, Ananda, said to the Buddha that friends were half the holy life, the Buddha answered him that no, they were the whole of the holy life. The Buddha knew the value of support on this practice path. Each of us struggles with the human perception of being alone in this world of the mind's making. Each of us needs reminders of those with us on the journey, the connections we share, the universality of our expereinces. Everyone knows the comfort of spilling worries into the ear of a friend. But often our friends may inadvertently increase our burden by pitying us, by being shocked, by trying to fix a situation, because they wish for our happiness again. They too are uncomfortable with our suffering. What I found among my Upasika sisters and brothers, instead, was a depth of love and a reminder of what I already knew. They did not climb into the river of emotion with me so that we were all swept away. They did not turn away. They pointed in a steadfast way at the shoreline within my reach, the solid ground beneath my foolishly scrambling feet.

And that next night I slept. I pulled back to the moment and found the ground again. I am not saying that without them I would have been lost, for I've been on this path a long time. The toolbelt I carry would surely have weighed me down to the ground again once I wearied of the struggle. But it was a welcome reminder of why this community, the *catuparisa*, the fourfold community of monks, nuns, lay practitioners both women and men, is valuable on this journey.

The strong and solitary, the rugged individual, is a dear myth of the west. Perhaps if we look closer, however, we'll see that the lone figure is an illusion of perspective. When we broaden our view, we see many such individuals, the strength of each possible because of the support and love and goodwill of the others.

# 43  Blessings

Designate a clear vase or bowl as a container and place in it plain white stones as you count your blessings. Make adding a few stones a daily or weekly ritual. This is a wonderful visual reminder of blessings.

**Ocean Wave**

I have a tattered photocopy on my office door of a woodblock print from a famous series of Mt. Fuji by the 19th century Japanese artist, Hokusai. The picture has a curling ocean wave in the foreground. The spray from the wave and a flock of passing birds meld one into another. Mt. Fuji itself is small and comparatively insignificant in this picture.

   I like this picture for the range of associations and symbols it brings to mind. For the reminder it presents in such a beautiful form. The wave is a common Buddhist explanation of the nature of the self. Each of us but a wave on the ocean of being, rising out of a single ground of being, moving along for awhile, and then bowing down again to join the water of which it is made. The stuff of each wave is both unique and not. What is the wave but the water? The wave is not something solid and substantial and separate. It is one with everything. The artist has rendered the spray of the waves and the passing birds in such a way that the division is not as clear as the unity. Flight, not uncommonly, is associated with freedom. And here the stuff of the wave itself and the freedom of flight are one and the same. To me this is a reminder that nothing of individual freedom is lost in understanding the unity of all. Instead, freedom is gained in this realization.

   The solid bulk of Mt. Fuji comes closer to the western concept of the separate self, the stolid individual. Yet this enduring mountain is dwarfed by the powerful kinetic wave image. Yes, the illusion of self as separate is strong. And it has its place in the way the world works. Yet it is the ocean one sees in this picture, a reminder of what is seen during careful observation of experience and thought, during mindfulness and meditation. Not a solid Mt. Fuji self, but the flux of thought and senses arising and falling so that even in this body I am reborn with each breath.

The ocean print on my study door is one of those physical reminders of mindfulness that I have chosen to keep around me. I see following the Buddhist path as a way of living, not a belief system. The emphasis is on practice, on the personal experience of the clarity and truth that mindfulness and meditation bring. Yet I do not live in a Sangha community, or a monastery. My days are not centered on rituals designed to support this mindfulness…as the days of a hermit, a monk or even a lay teacher at a meditation centre might be. I am a middle class, middle-aged woman following the Buddha's Middle Way. I have children to get off to school and to take to various practices and activities. I have shopping and errands to do, cooking and laundry and cleaning. And because I work at home as well, I have students to respond to and to contact, marking piling up, contracts to be honored. Yet, when I slow down to live my days as mindfully as possible, I find the sacred in everything and that happiness is here now…not waiting for the weekend or next year's vacation.

But because I choose to strive to live mindfully in the context of my life as it is now, without forsaking all this for something other, I have discovered the helpfulness of reminders. Thus the ocean print. And the paper mandalas taped to my computer and my wall, the tiny porcelain dish that sits at my left hand holding tinier stones, shells, even a cherry pit, brought home from retreats. In my kitchen there is a small singing bowl, or mindfulness bell. And I have explained this to the family such that sometimes I am awakened when I become too harried because my youngest son has invited this bell to ring. These and other items scattered around my home serve as visual reminders of my commitment to this path. This parallels the way the ring on my left hand stands for the commitment to my marriage and a locket containing photos of my sons, worn when I am away from them, keeps them near my heart outwardly, as they always are inwardly.

The Middle Way to me means to stay in the world I know but to change the way I live in this world, the way I am in this world. Just a wave changing shape, moving through.

**Retirement**

Retirement. We talk about it likes it's something definite and definable, but really it's just this odd spaciousness that opens up. I've dropped all paid work…

the teaching, the kennel, except for what might come out of my writing, and even that I'm doing in such a whimsical way these days. Gone is the driven pattern of researching markets, seeking contracts and shaping the flow of the days to deadlines.

What does this new space mean? In conversation, in thought and often with a book in my hand these days, I am suddenly aware of so many streams of ideas and possibilities that I stumble. A kind of ADD I don't recall before. Overwhelmed by an onslaught of too much: too many things I want to say, too many reactions and too many notions of all there is that could be done. But then (above? below? behind?) – a current of awareness so strong it moves these worries to a distance, moves self-doubt to such a place it is like a tiny object to examine through binoculars, not quite my own, no matter how hard and real it seems.

Meditation, too, is odd. I struggle with images and thought awhile, unwanted, trivial things: moments from the day or a movie, the melody of a song, some checklist of memories. Then stillness and that lovely indescribable place I move to sometimes where even the breath drops from consciousness and there is only fragile spaciousness, a tiny flutter of something like the concentration when you're holding a needle still to thread it and there is wishing that it hold, that it hold. Later the current of trivia begins again and so the seesaw until the bell.

During the day I spend segments of time at the computer working on the tasks I have for the Dhamma Talk cataloguing for Birken. And time flies. There is great satisfaction in each "victory", in learning skills I thought I could not, feeling confidence grow. Trying to fall asleep at night, the next task, the next hurdle becomes the predominant thoughtstream, delaying sleep. Yet, as I find how I enjoy this and immerse in it, how I feel its tangible value, I am moving back from other volunteer tasks mentally, letting other roles go.

As I pare and focus, the energies and plans for writing squirm and move and tangle and grow like a slow motion film of stems and buds and leaves unfurling. And without writing at all, I find my direction changing. No straight arrow effort towards a goal. But each moment pure and precious in itself. Just this and then this.

Who am I then, as I let go of the work and the roles that have given me direction? Yesterday listening to a Dhamma talk on Right View. From the Pali texts a description likening it to the first pink glow of dawn. When it arises, all else follows on the Eightfold path. Sitting this morning and a moment of clarity came, as can happen sometimes, almost impossible to articulate, yet it is my nature to try! There has always been a sort of melancholy for me in the idea of non-self, particularly around the letting go of attachments…not things, but people and deeply held views. Ah…my sons. And the notion of living in peace and of tolerance. So suddenly this morning I see that in letting go, I lose nothing. Everything is as it was before. But with Right View I see it differently. I see it clearly. Like a fog lifting or the sun rising. No change but in my view.

I think of a friend who said to take only what you need from the world. Keep my attention on the brimming bowl I carry: peace, mindfulness and dawning understanding growing with practice. A gift of retirement, perhaps, is that I use both hands to carry this bowl, and both eyes to watch it. The diversions of life are fewer as I let go of striving to be someone, to get somewhere.

### Ordinary Life

I've been thinking about "ordinary life". We usually use this phrase to mean the humdrum and neutral quality of living. Sorting the socks, driving to work, taking a shower, eating a sandwich at our kitchen table, listening to the weather on the radio, walking the dog. The list is endless when we move beyond our own context to what might be considered "ordinary" by people in different places and times. Drawing water from a well, sleeping in doorways, dodging bullets. If ordinary means what we, as human beings, come to expect in our days, what fills most of the hours, then its content is huge.

Of course, most of the time, I don't think a lot about ordinary life. What's ordinary for me goes by and my work is to be mindful, to pay attention. And to see when reactivity to ordinary things might lead me astray, using the interval of awareness to allow me to choose more skilful responses. When a sock goes missing as I sort the laundry, I see the irritation that itches briefly, before setting it aside and accepting the task of the hunt when it's convenient. When I'm driving and a truck passes spraying sludge on my windshield, I note the tiny flicker that could become anger, and choose to just turn on the wipers and wash fluid and move on. Taking a shower, I allow myself to relax and enjoy the steady and reliable warm and clean water and to notice gratitude, or to plant the seed of gratitude if it doesn't arise on its own. This is ordinary mindfulness for ordinary life.

Then there are the times that life doesn't seem so ordinary. There are extremes of good news or bad news. We win a trip of a lifetime. Or we lose a loved one. We tend to think of this as unusual, as lucky or unlucky maybe, as blessing or as curse. Yet, the truth is that every life holds these events we label as extremes. We know the times of perfect and unexpected joy. And we know the times of devastating and unanticipated tragedy. And so, my thoughts go, if this happens to all of us, in some measure, all the time, why don't we see this as ordinary too?

When life hands us these kinds of extremes, we may lose our equilibrium for awhile. We fly or we dive as the occasion seems to dictate. Yet, just like the missing sock or the spray of mud on the windshield, these are moments in our life when paying attention and using the interval of awareness can make all the difference. These, no less than walking the dog and reading the mail and going to the dentist, are ordinary life.

Ordinary life holds it all. Mindfulness may mean we find more enjoyment in the little things, but it also means we see the movement of the mind that wants to fret and complain, that wants to hold on and push away. It means we can choose other than to go with that flow. We can begin to see the flux and flow of life, the ups and the downs, to live in them and be with them even when they are not to our liking, not becoming bitter by the mistaken view that our lives are cursed, and not becoming caught in the endless restlessness of the adrenalin junky who needs peak experiences all the time. There is happiness here, riding the breath, knowing what is and opening to the vast possibility of ordinary life.

# 44  Right Now

Next time you notice your grumbling mind muttering "now I *have* to do this", change one word and say instead "now I *get* to do this". The smile this brings tells you a lot about how this changes mood and attitude.

**Duties**

Rereading this morning that lovely meditation by the Buddha most often called the *Metta Sutta*. There are many translations of this work. I have one favorite typed up on bright yellow paper and taped to a bookcase in my office. The version I read this morning is a little different; the message always the same. Whenever I read this meditation, some particular part of it speaks to me. This work outlines what it is to be skilled in wholesomeness…which is the goal of mindful living. And the line that called to me today was that someone seeking this should be "unburdened with duties". On my pretty yellow sheet, the version reads "not caught up in too much bustle." Ah! If ever someone spoke to the harried working mother in this early 21$^{st}$ century, it was in this line.

Our duties sometimes seem numberless. To shop, prepare food, keep the house clean, do the laundry, remember birthdays, plan vacations and outings and celebrations for the family, pay the bills, make and keep appointments with doctors and hairstylists and dentists and tutors, taxi children to and from activities. And keep our own work deadlines as well. Look after pets. Do for elderly parents. Be involved in the community. Yes, there's a lot of bustle in every day.

A work colleague I once had used to say "Ten years and an old pair of boots and what's it going to matter". And this ought to be a guideline for measuring the urgency of the many duties that fill our days. Her words used to make me smile and sometimes they succeeded in making me see the insignificance of some trivial thing that had me worried or anxious or even panicked. These days, slowing down is the duty I try to put first. It isn't easy.

I talk to myself in positive affirmations about the way I want my life to be. I ring the bell in my kitchen and pause to breathe. I nap when weariness overcomes me. But still I feel the need to do too much too often. And still I let myself worry over the things I think I neglected or didn't do well. And still after saying no I sometimes think I could have, maybe even should have, said yes.

But when I meditate upon the words of the metta sutta. When I consider deeply the path I have chosen for my life, the journey toward happiness and wholesomeness that I am on, that I wish for each and every being, then I know that the performance of duties alone is hollow. To give without giving from the heart, to listen only with your ears, to say rote words devoid of feeling, to do and do and do, so that there is never time to reflect and be, led me, at one time, to view this line as meaning we should pare down, not take on so much. But I heard a wise monk speak on this once and put the stress on our attitude. To feel burdened is an attitude. And it is skillful to let this attitude go. Do what we do, do our duties, with joy.

So when I attend another meeting today, I will remember the three B's (old boots and burdens and bustle) and perhaps this will help me maintain a healthy perspective. May it be that I act from the heart, giving with love and keeping to the path that in the end serves us all so much better.

### The Buddha's Words on Kindness
*Metta Sutta*

This is what should be done By one who is skilled in goodness, And who knows the path of peace: Let them be able and upright, Straightforward and gentle in speech. Humble and not conceited, Contented and easily satisfied. Unburdened with duties and frugal in their ways. Peaceful and calm, and wise and skillful, Not proud and demanding in nature. Let them not do the slightest thing That the wise would later reprove. Wishing: In gladness and in saftey, May all beings be at ease. Whatever living beings there may be; Whether they are weak or strong, omitting none, The great or the mighty, medium, short or small, The seen and the unseen, Those living near and far away, Those born and to-be-born, May all beings be at ease!

Let none deceive another, Or despise any being in any state. Let none through anger or ill-will Wish harm upon another. Even as a mother protects with her life Her child, her only child, So with a boundless heart Should one cherish all living beings: Radiating kindness over the entire world Spreading upwards to the skies, And downwards to the depths; Outwards and unbounded, Freed from hatred and ill-will. Whether standing or walking, seated or lying down Free from drowsiness, One should sustain this recollection. This is said to be the sublime abiding. By not holding to fixed views, The pure-hearted one, having clarity of vision, Being freed from all sense desires, Is not born again into this world.

**Lenny and Me**

We have a terrier. Although we've both loved dogs and mostly had at least one in our life at a time, a terrier is something new. Well, the fluff ball puppy we brought home is three years old now...new enough. Terriers are high energy creatures, and they tend to have strong wills as well. Not at all like the laid back, please-you labs and retriever crosses we've grown accustomed to. But we knew what we were getting. Or at least we thought we did. This little fella of ours demands that his aging "parents" get play into every day, and rewards us with personality and enthusiasm as well as affection. But he can be a handful.

Because our regular walks are on a country road that runs through an acreage subdivision, it can have quite a bit of local traffic. This is one good reason for leash training for even a "country" dog. We let him have space on a long retractable leash, but he's been taught a few appropriate commands: "By me" means to come in close and heel. "Have fun" means go ahead and use the leash length to explore the ditches or run ahead...maybe even lag behind to sniff something good more thoroughly. But "Keep up" means it's time to move along and remember you're not in charge here.

The restrictions we put on Lenny* insure our peace of mind and his safety. They also make for a more harmonious relationship in this little family. This is the way it is with mindfulness and the peace, happiness and harmony it brings to my own life.

Many teachers use the comparison of a puppy or a monkey or a small child when describing the impulsivity and energy and general lack of discipline of the ordinary human mind. You might think yours is unique in its wild and wide ranging adventures, but believe me, if you talk to anyone out there who has looked inward at all, you'll discover this is the human condition. This can be a good thing. In bounding around we often make new discoveries, write gorgeous poetry, imagine amazing possibilities and go where no man (or woman)

---

* His registered name, which the breeder kindly allowed me to choose, is Skylark's Tribute to Leonard.... Need I say, I am pretty much a lifelong and devoted fan of the late, great Leonard Cohen.

has gone before. So far, so good. But like my beloved terrier, the mind needs to be watched over. We need to know when to say "have fun" and when to say "by me". This distinction is made through the wisdom of seeing where our adventures are taking us.

If my vivid imagination is weaving a tale around the tone of voice that a co-worker or friend used, then I need to rein it in. This kind of unchecked wandering can lead to suffering on my part over some slight that was not intended, or even to speech or an action on my part that harms another, if I decide to confront or get even. If my pocket book is empty, I am not being skillful to incite the desire for expensive and frivolous items by exploring the on-line catalogues of appealing products. If I have an exam next week, I am not being skillful in postponing study yet being anxious about the dire consequences of failing the exam. I need to watch over the mind to understand the tricks it's playing. I need to be gentle but firm. My dog is not a bad dog because he needs to be told to keep up or to stay by me. He's just a dog. And I am not a bad person because a critical thought or resentful thought appeared. It's what I do with that. I call the dog in, I call the mind in. This is part of the effort of being mindful. Not just seeing what arises, but steering the mind in a direction that leads towards its own peace.

No one wants to be unhappy. This may seem like a truism. Yet so often we do not notice that our wish to be happy and our behaviors are out of alignment. It takes persistence to train a terrier. It takes love too or you'd just return the little rascal to the breeder. The same goes for this mind. It's the one I have. I'm working on patiently and lovingly making it a happier place to hang out.

## Right Now

"What are you doing right now?" Searching for perhaps an appropriate wise nudge, I open a book of Dhammapada quotations I keep on a counter I pass many times in a day. It has been a good day over all. Nothing to complain about. But it's fall and things are gearing up and I find my mind moving here and there and little niggles of discontent arising like pebbles dropped in a pool or water-walkers on the surface of a pond, the kind of disturbance that is easy to miss. But missing them means I make way for the torrent of confusion that could follow if I am hit by a wave of worry or anxiety later. The work of practice is to gradually become adept at seeing these first miniscule movements.

So I open the book and find these words "What are you doing right now?" The short passage of Dhamma teaching goes on to invite me to look into the content of the mind. Where am I permitting myself to dwell? What preoccupies or diverts my thoughts?

Instantly I feel my focus sharpen. The indistinct sense of something not quite settled that is the ground of anxiety gives way to a clear view of planning mind. Not just the kind of planning mind that is necessary to live in the world: Checking the calendar, making calls, gathering materials, doing the work. But the kind of planning mind that wants to re-visit the plan time and again, to look for flaws, to anticipate difficulties, to create scenarios where I miss the mark in some way, do not meet the standards I've set when I define the boundaries of who I am. And then I have to smile. For there it is again. The self and its boundaries, the self and its vulnerability, the self and its expectation of being in control of everything, of having nothing go awry, ever!

What am I doing right now? I'm allowing myself to feed this human and habitual pattern. I'm not offering a feast…yet! But I've left a trail of crumbs the hungry ego can follow.

So what's the antidote? Although we believe we are multi-tasking as we go through our day, in fact we are simply moving very quickly from task to task, allowing the attention to move spasmodically or even steering the attention in quick turns and jumps. And in there somewhere, the light landing of the pebble or the water-walker of misgiving takes place. So I begin by noticing this. Acknowledging the unease in my mind and its trails in my body. Then I find a place for the mind to land for a few moments of stability. For me most often this is the breath. One Dhamma-friend I know makes a conscious effort to take three mindful breaths at various points throughout the day. This is her anchor. The place where the mind stills again for a moment and the mad spin is disrupted. For me, the triggers I leave scattered about my home, which is my workplace for most of the day, provide a reminder to come back. In this case the little book of brief teachings. Beside my computer, various stones and crystals that I pick up to hold awhile, dissolving into touch. Above my kitchen sink the row of fat laughing Buddhas (based on the ancient Chinese monk Pu-Tai) who offer a less serious perspective on the day, a reminder of ordinary joy. In the windows, prisms that catch the light and break it into rainbows. Shimmering jewels that invite me to stop and take them in and that being as they are, dependent on the angle of the sun, remind me of causation and uncertainty.

It doesn't matter really what the reminders are, but the world is pulling us out into busyness and activity and the future all the time. We need to arrange for some reminders to come back here, to look inside, to slow down, to feel what we're feeling before it surprises us by giving rise to some unskillful action, some irritated remark, some sleepless night.

What are you doing right now?

# 45  Well Wishes

Begin and end each day taking a few moments for well wishes for yourself, those dear to you and outward to all the world. You might enjoy composing a few lines for this that are meaningful to you and that you recite each day in the same way.

**Abiding in Compassion**

I guess if someone were watching they'd think I was pretty miserable. I'm sitting in the morning darkness in front of a small table on which a candle and incense burn. I'm wrapped in a blanket against the Autumn chill because others in the house are still sleeping and I don't want to bake them out of bed by turning up the heat. My eyes are closed, my back erect and my hands folded in my lap. What is relatively unusual is that tears are running down my face.

The hurt I feel is sweet and all-consuming. The pain of an open and yearning heart. It's akin to the surge of pain cued by listening to Leonard Cohen's *Hallelujah* or his newer song *Going Home*. The pain of loss remembering loved ones no longer living, remembering the milky sweet smell of babies now grown, knowing most of my life is behind me, knowing I can't fix the pain of someone I love.

Why do I say it's sweet? Unlike physical pain which has a bitterness to it, the mental suffering we all endure has a taste to it that invites surrender rather than struggle. When I cut my hand, I flinch away. When a sad memory arises, I pull it close, I let it cover my head like a hood. It is a crazy kind of human addiction.

But we too often think this pain is personal, mine alone, and not the "gift" of being human. It's what allows empathy if we can open to this, "inhabit[ing] simultaneously the first person and the third person", as Alice Major, a renowned Alberta poet, puts it. When we understand that to be human is to feel this, it is a doorway into connection. A way of understanding that we all yearn to be alive, to love and to be happy. We just go about it in ways that tend to be counterproductive to that end. So we all experience this sweet pain of disappointment, loss, and the charade of denial. Neuorscience tells us that if the brain is being monitored, we can see that the same parts light up for the same type of experience, whether it is our experience or that of another that we merely witness. When I see someone weeping, the part of my brain that is active when I weep, mirrors theirs. It would seem to follow then, that when we build defenses and shut off to the pain of our own lives, we shut off to the pain of others.

So what has brought on my tears this morning? It's a bit of a mystery and yet I think I know what I have done. From under the suffocating blanket of personal pain, and disappointments, I have burst out into the world of all human suffering. For a little while I am overwhelmed.

A few weeks ago I began to spend more of my daily meditation time on what traditional Buddhist texts call the Divine Abidings: loving-kindness (*metta*), compassion (*karuna*), empathetic joy (*mudita*) and equanimity (*upekkha*). One of the strategies I employed to enable me to carry this intention throughout the day, was to commit to memory a beautiful passage known as the Discourse on Loving-kindness. This passage outlines the actions and attitudes required of "one who knows the path of peace." This act of memorizing meant that I read the passage multiple times a day. I took it in small meaningful bites and carried it in my head throughout the day. I would fall asleep mentally reciting these bits, and eventually the whole passage. I was busily opening new channels in my brain, new avenues to my heart.

"Whatever you think and ponder upon, that will become the inclination of the mind," the Buddha said. And so my mind was inclined toward these divine universalities. I was amazed to find that falling asleep hearing the words in my head, I'd wake to find them there, the first thing my waking self reached for in finding its place and time again.

This isn't my first tearful sitting. But it is one of a recent series that leaves me not depleted and worn out but feeling renewed, tears watering the seeds of compassion and metta in the heart's garden.

**Family Tree**

Awhile ago an older cousin I haven't seen in decades contacted me by e-mail. She'd found her way to me through the convoluted net of family and was looking for information for a family tree she was building that goes back several generations, and forward beyond my own to the generation of my children, and the generation following that. Wow! A monumental task, this, locating everyone, persuading them to take part, gathering photos and names and organizing all the information. Incredible numbers of hours and dedication.

I did my part, sending off names and birthdates and photos and got back to day-to-day life. Weeks or months later the family tree, pretty much complete for my mother's side and in parts on my father's, since their families were intertwined by more than one union, arrived.

I scanned it casually at first. Interested in the names that re-occurred through generations, the places where relatives had lived or were living. But the impact of this project of hers, for me, took a little time to be felt. When it settled I noticed two overwhelming heart responses.

The first was that seeing this wide net of people on paper, people I could walk by on the street and not recognize, people with shared ancestry, with similar or completely different names, was like examining the beginning of a big bang. This spreading out into the world, this net of relationships goes on and on. It is not just a net of shared blood, for there are step-parents and half siblings, and step children, and adopted children. The nuances any family would include. My cousin had chosen an arbitrary starting place with our great grandparents, but she could have gone back in time indefinitely if she had the information. And she only stopped with the forward momentum because that's where we are at in this point in time in the tracing of this family tree. Presumably, it will continue to shoot out new branches, sprawling into an unknown future.

The Buddha's teaching on rebirth tells us that every being was once our mother, our brother, our child. And this seems to the Western mind perhaps an odd claim to make. But looking at this unwieldy mass of names and places and even faces, where photos were included, made me feel from inside the vast idea of family, instead of just defining it in my head. Family is not just my husband, myself, and our children. Not my parents, myself and my siblings. It is not a thing that I can pin down at all. It is a shared sense of connection. So in what way is this my family tree? Well, oddly, at first it felt like it wasn't. How could these unknown people be my family? Then, reading and re-reading, chanting softly to myself names and places scattered in the world, it all turned like a prism in the sun and I began to feel how if these people were, then all people are, my family. For even without a belief in multiple births, this notion of kinship is ambiguous and malleable. This heart response was joyous.

My second heart response was the flip-side to this, a twinge of melancholy. The effort this project represented, brought to light for me how our attempts to define ourselves and construct a place for ourselves in the world, causes us to be drawn to such things as family trees, boundaries and rules of separation. Our human wish to understand means that we choose the small, manageable bits to take into consideration and leave out what is too vast and amorphous.

Start here, end here. Include only these. Ignore the rest. Not just in the making of family trees, but in deciding who we feel any sort of kinship with. Rather than focusing on names and marriages, we might focus on country of origin, gender, beliefs, eye color, level of education, lifestyle, income, dietary habits. It doesn't matter. Whatever arbitrary lines we draw, we are choosing to overlook other aspects that we share.

I appreciate this family tree and the lessons my cousin's work brought home to me. When I study it now I see the way it extends endlessly beyond the page in all directions. And nestled in there is the being I think of as me. Part of this flow of life.

### Civilizations and Change

*2008*

When civilizations begin to crumble do the people notice? Do they say: "This is the end of this life? I am living at a turning point in history" Or do they just go on, incorporating change as it impacts them, just living? I'm thinking about these things these days as the political and economic upheaval of the world begins to mirror the environmental mess we've created. We live in "garbage" of all kinds. And it's been so a long while.

It is only that BIG EVENTS now bring it to our attention. The first black American president. The great mess of the American economy he comes to after the Wall Street collapse. Our minority government and the political games that the other parties play now with their "alliance" discussions. Terrorism coming to the fore again in relatively stable countries…the recent precision attacks in India. Then there is the economic downturn here. The fall in gasoline and real estate prices after the highest prices ever and a greedy market. The world turns. Weather patterns change. We have winter rain and little snow. Mild day temperatures and treacherous ice. Or is it only that all of this is symptomatic of the changes always happening? And that we only see patterns from our human perspective, our desire to control and understand. What is that saying about history being stories chosen, composed, created in the telling?

*2015*

Running across the entry above in an old journal gave me pause. Seven years later. Another economic downturn. Different acts of terrorism. Different government games and quandaries. Different worrisome world events. Same sense of momentous change and perhaps inevitable disaster. At least media would have us think so. Our own fears making us willing to listen and nod.

This must have been so in the final days of the Roman Empire. In the lives of First Nations people facing new epidemics of physical illness and foreign values. In the lives of peasant farmers driven to the cities in the Industrial Revolution by the slow tide of change. In the lives of those in the Great Depression unable to find work, watching crops fail.

Sometimes changes are momentous and sudden. A bomb. A hurricane. A tsunami. Sometimes they are creeping and insidious. An infection. Climate change. Resources disappearing. Always they are mysterious and frightening and seem to be, with hindsight, avoidable. We tie ourselves in knots trying to undo what has been done. To return to "the way things were".

Yet in the world, still and always, incredible acts of courage and kindness. Not just those that make the news…the rescues, the volunteers, the fund raisers, the interfaith events, the helping hands and willing hearts. In every day there is evidence of kindness and goodwill: A neighbor clearing another's driveway. A clerk taking time to answer questions, smiling and connecting with a customer. The driver who lets someone into a steady flow of traffic. Meals provided for those in need. Food gathered at local shops for the food bank. Accounts opened for families facing loss or illness. The stranger who holds a door open for someone whose arms are full. A young man who stands on a bus to let someone less able sit. A friend taking time to listen to another who is having a bad day. Generous tipping of low wage earners. This list could go for pages.

I have been a writer for many years. And my reflex is to weave a story. To pick and choose and find a plot, a pattern. Yet, life can only be lived in this moment. The stories will be told in some future time of what it was like to live now, how we came to this, the causes and then the new directions that were found. For those of us living now in the midst of it, there is only one useful approach. To do the best we can with each moment as it passes. To add to the goodness and the kindness, not the fear and the destruction. Let us choose in each moment to do no harm.

# 46  Inner Listening

Feeling wound up and anxious? Close your eyes and take a few moments to "listen". Just notice the sounds coming to your ears, not naming them. Notice the sounds inside the body, that ear-against-a-seashell sound that is our inner silence.

### Mind Weather

In this moment I'm sitting in a warm and softly-lit morning kitchen. My hands are wrapped around a favorite mug full of hot tea. And beyond the window the snow has a sugar sparkle under the blue sky. At my feet my curly blonde and beloved dog lies waiting patiently, hoping, no doubt, that I'll share just a bit more of my breakfast banana.

A moment ago my husband turned on the radio, anticipating morning news, and my preferred silence was broken. I've been breathing gently, watching the aversion arise, working not to bother the music, not to reach for the sound, staying with the breath and the peace that is possible here, no matter what the external situation. So far, so good.

Then I'm hooked by the weather forecast and let my attention move out to gather this bit of information. It drops like a small pebble into a still pool. Ah! Today lovely. But later in the week, heavy snow predicted. Later in the week. Later in the week I have scheduled travel to the city.

The external present moment is perfect. But my mind is not here. Spinning into apprehension, amorphous memories of nasty drives, vague anticipation of a nasty future. This moment holds the flavor of tea, the bright day, the warm breath of the dog on my stockinged toes. Nevertheless, my mind holds fear.

But mindfulness is not just about being present with what is pleasant, what is easy to be with. It's about being here with what is, no matter what that is. And I know what's required. Back into the body. This moment in the body, the tea tastes a little different, colored by the metallic bite of anxiety; there's a closed feeling in my throat, just at the soft hollow above the collar bone, and a tiny ripple of tension in my shoulders. What was an easy posture a moment before has changed. This is also the way things are. Never staying the same. Moving like a river. And if I watch these unpleasant feelings now, don't clench my mind around them, they will change too. Just know them, watch them.

There are two things I can do that will give them longer life. I can let the amorphous memories and vague anticipation become the skeleton of a detailed plot; I can spin a story. This will take very little effort. All I have to do is believe the fear, which my mind will willingly do. Believe the fear and hug it close. See it as real and present. The habit of thought will take over, composing stories of disaster and danger. Been there, done that. Or I can deny that I'm feeling fear. Call myself a woose for the momentary shivers, clamp down on the mind, force the images into a box and close the lid. They'll wriggle and bounce around in there and break through periodically for who knows how long. And I'll keep pushing them back and sitting on the lid. These are both ways of losing this moment and many more to come. Ways of adding to the suffering that arose spontaneously when I heard the weather report.

So, what would be skillful? I picture the mind as an open hand. This is almost habitual now when the unpleasant arises. I notice the fear. I understand it is a form of aversion, of not wanting what the future may hold, of moving out of this moment now. Then I let it be. Yes, this is fear. I've had a lot of experience with this particular variety. Who hasn't who knows Alberta winters? But the moment holds more than this fear. It holds the safety that surrounds me right now. My reliable breath. The dog, the tea, the blue sky. It's a mixed bag and in my body I can trace it all. Getting out of my head, I let go of the reactivity that might close up or push away. I get back in touch with what is, and leave alone the mights and maybes. I quit "believing" my thoughts.

I might have to repeat this trip a lot today…head to body, head to body, but the trip to the city will only happen once, when I'm well prepared with winter gear and warm clothes and on the road.

**Worldly Winds**

So there is this thing about being a writer. Most of the work is done in solitude… just me, my computer and the dog by my chair. Sometimes there is a flurry of e-mails or even a phone call with an editor or, if the piece is non-fiction, then with a source or subject. And then the piece is submitted.

Things that are written on spec (that is, not requested, assigned or pre-approved) and are not successful, go in a file and maybe get sent elsewhere or re-configured down the road. Maybe not.

Over the years, a lot of my work has seen print, or, these days, been published in electronic form. Most of my stuff meets with little fuss. Textbooks. Small audience literary or genre magazines. Some glossies with specialized audiences. Maybe newsletters. A few anthologies. I have a lot of practice with "obscurity".

"Obscurity" or "insignificance" is one half of the pair that also contains "fame", one set in the Buddha's list most often called The Eight Worldly Winds. I'm sure you'll have had experience with these yourself. You'll also be acquainted with the other three pairs in this set: loss and gain, praise and blame, joy and sorrow. These pretty much tally up the vagaries of human existence.

But my thoughts today are about the current experience I'm in the midst of. When, now and then, something I've written catches attention among a wider audience of those who know me, beyond my family and closest friends, I get a taste of that partner to going unnoticed...fame. At least local fame.

What we're used to dealing with on the practice path doesn't cause too much stir after a long while. Been there done that, we say. I can deal with being unnoticed. The opinions of others are unimportant really. That's not what I'm in this for. All those things. The mind doesn't have too much fuel for misbehaving or taking off on story-lines. The surprise is when life gives us a taste of the unexpected. It can go either way. From the negative to the positive or the positive to the negative. It's the unusual experience that wakes us up. The hero caught cheating, for instance, might be shocked by rejection. Or Eeyore winning a lottery. What would he do with his woeful attitude?

So I was talking about "fame". Being published in an anthology of writing by Canadian Buddhist Women is exciting to me. It's close to my heart because Dhamma, the Buddhist practice path, is so important to me. It works. But I had to smile when the editor who has asked for each contributor to do what she can to promote the book, also sagely warned me to "watch ego". She's a Buddhist practitioner too, of course. Ego is just a more familiar term for created self. We understand it instinctively unlike the tricky teaching of *anatta* or no-self, that is central to Buddhist philosophy. I am not my accomplishments. I am not someone at all. There is just this stream of experiencing, and if I get tied up in identifying with some description of "me", then I'll create suffering. Back to the hero who felt above it all and is not prepared for the fall. And sad little Eeyore who self-describes as a loser. For someone who expects to lose, winning can be scary. He might deliberately lose his ticket before he cashes it in.

So, watching the ego here means for me that I remember that this current experience is just a moment in the flow that is my life. It is pleasant, mostly, maybe a bit uncomfortable at times; it is gratifying and satisfying. But it comes along with the grocery shopping, walking the dog, sad friends to comfort, and stunning sunrises. It's part of the mundane, the beautiful and the difficult. A wind blowing through.

### Just a Retreat Day

Providence can be a busy place. It's a lovely multi-use facility where I often come to retreats. But today was a day for testing concentration and practice through distracting sounds. In the morning sudden bursts of loud hip-hop dance music…seems someone was testing the P.A. system. This went on at intervals for perhaps 15 minutes and when Bhante (who last night had expressed gratitude for electricity here, not having it in his *kuti*) observed that this is what comes of ready electricity, there were waves of laughter.

A further personal test for me was a tiny woman wearing enormous trousers, who arrived late and has placed her seat next to mine. She was exceedingly restless, moving and pushing papers, blanket and towels and cushions about, slapping down the notebook she scratched into from time to time.

In the afternoon, children crying (thwarted desires) outside the window and a cheerful group of arrivals practicing readings and hymns in the room next to our meditation space. Tonight I recall the words of a Zen teacher shared in a book I read some time ago: "Don't bother the traffic". Keeping the mind here, and letting the sound be there. There are never "perfect conditions".

In a couple of breaks over the day I read about *jhanas*. Test my cynicism like placing a thumb against a blade. But I'm inclined to accept there are states of consciousness available that I've no inkling of. Whether I need to achieve these is a different thing. Back to the breath. Finding tranquil spaces. I am reminded again of being with what is, of the need for the right causes and conditions to come into play and that the hard work of virtue and mindfulness do not require seclusion but patience and practice and determination. This is the foundation I continue to build.

The day has gone quickly, as has the retreat, which ends tomorrow.

There are times when I am dismayed by flights of anxiety arising from horrendous fantasies that my mind is able to weave in a flash. I try not to follow my instinct to turn away but instead to look closely at the physical manifestations and not the story…my pounding heart and great surges of adrenalin, tearing eyes and closing throat. These are nothing new and have plagued me always, but especially as a mother. Most often the stories are in regards to sorrow or pain for my children that I am, of course, powerless to avert. What practice has changed is allowing me to look at the emotions and not the story. Not to ask why I do this, but how am I feeling when these arise. To recognize the unskillfulness of such thoughts. Replacing them with focus on body and breath. As I keep watching and breathing, this passes, as everything does, and in awhile I am calm again.

I think so often of my mom and imagine that what I could see from outside of her lifelong anxiety was the merest tip of the iceberg. How did she manage? And how we made sport of her fears. Sorry mom. I know that prayer and belief in a God who listened and protected us all must have been some solace to her, but when the protection failed, when we suffered, when dad was dying, what did she do? "My rock", I remember dad calling her, watching her from the sunroom window. He was fragile and wispy as a feather then, his voice and body pared to nothing. She was walking back from getting the mail at the gate. Determined, unsmiling, not knowing she was observed. Inside, the rock was crumbling and at his funeral she fell apart.

Will my practice assist me in finding a better way to live with life's losses? Knowing the fact and inescapability of change and loss and decay. Watching it every moment. Living just this. Such that wisdom opens the door to equanimity. What little experience I've had so far gives me confidence to continue on this path.

# 47  Peace

When sleep is elusive, do a simple body scan. Moving from head to foot, place your attention in a particular body part (forehead all the way to toes), breathe with the intention of sending kindness there and consciously relax that place, before moving to the next. Chances are you'll be asleep before you've completed the mental journey.

**The Kind of Work We Do**

During a bad time a number of years ago I remember thinking "Why does it take so much work to be happy?" You see, it felt at the time that I was sliding toward an abyss, a nasty place I didn't dare to look toward. As if I were scaling a rock face and happiness was a waving flag at the top. Just a glimpse of color moving in the wind. It moved in and out of my sight line, but I was so preoccupied with the climb, the difficulty of keeping vigilant, of finding toe and finger holds one after another in this torturous journey, that I never could look up for long. And I couldn't look down for fear of what awaited me if I were to slip up, let go, relax the tremendous effort I was exerting.

Over time I learned, with wise teachings and persistence, that I had the image all upside down. Opening my eyes and looking down I would see, not very far below me, a grassy field. A soft bed of blossoms and scent and natural joy that I could fall back into with perfect trust, if I'd only allow it to happen. The flag I caught sight of now and then as it flapped in the breezes above, was really a red flag of warning. A flag marking out the territory of what I'd claimed as mine, as necessary, as subject to my will. And I was exerting all this unnecessary effort in the belief that somehow I'd be able to find peace with my back against that flagpole. I was trying to work my way to perfect safety, where my life would be secure and comfortable, all that I desired would be available and those I cared for would be safe and happy too. It's a fantasy we all have. And we work hard at the stories that keep the flag waving.

We tell ourselves there are reasons for the anxiety we feel, the anger that eats at us, the guilt we carry. That all this is necessary and justified. If we've screwed up, we need to carry guilt and sorrow. If someone hurt us, the resentment and anger are part of our armor so it won't happen again. Not only have we set ourselves an impossible goal…a flag waving over all that is "ours" in the distance, in the future somewhere, but we've weighed ourselves down with burdens to carry and we've worn our fingers to the bone with the scratching that moves us in what we think is the right direction.

The truth is, we are working hard. We think it's to be happy. But the effort we're exertng is mostly in keeping alive the stories that prevent our happiness. Stories that prevent us from seeing how close at hand peace is.

My teacher talks about realizing, finally, that the world goes on by itself. It is not our undying worry and work that keeps it going. When we sleep, he says, we are not on duty and the world does not fall apart because we dropped our worry, fear and guilt for a time. We are allowed to take a break. To unpack the resentments, put down the anger, let go of the worry wall and fall back into the sweetness of peace. The second Noble Truth the Buddha proclaimed is that there is a cause for our suffering. This cause is the kind of work we do. When happiness seemed so difficult to me, it was because I was driving myself toward some imagined "perfection". These days it is only a breath away when I open to what is reachable here and now.

## Ouch

Today I got my feelings hurt. You know how that happens. A miscommunication when you think you've explained well, but another hears or interprets differently and expectations do not match. So the other speaks in a way that is colored by irritation and blame. And this self pulls the comment in like Golem's ring, wrapping around it and stroking it and examining it from all sides. It hurts. All of us have had a bruise we can't keep from fingering or a scrape that we examine over and over with finger tips and mirrors. Sometimes we do the same thing with words, or even with a look or a sigh or a gesture. We make it real and important with our attention.

So, I've been noticing this. Asking the helpful question: "Why am I suffering?" The answer is pretty clear. It is in how I first described this brief moment.

"I" got my feelings hurt because "the other" spoke in a certain way. The experience was unpleasant and I've owned it, made it mine while pushing away from what I perceive as the cause. Thing is, these instinctive reactions do not protect and soothe me. No matter what I mumble to myself in my inner voice about how I've been wronged or how this was unjust, I don't feel any better. This is unskillful. It's also a human habit.

I once heard a teacher speak of a circle we live within as practitioners of mindfulness. This circle contains all that we are able to deal with skillfully. It starts out a very small and crampy place where we bump our elbows a lot. As we first begin to watch our minds and notice clinging and aversion, the pulling towards and pushing away we human beings habitually engage in, we have no spacious circle around us at all. The world rubs up against us. Things happen. The mind reacts. We speak and act in nearly immediate reaction to what is happening to this "me". Life is a constant and inevitably impossible struggle to have only good experiences. The ordinary mind wants to believe this can be done. But as we begin to develop the capacity to see what happens, we make an amazing discovery. It isn't the slings and arrows of the world that are causing the greatest pain. It's our various maneuverings and whinings against this. So we begin to clear a little space. This is the circle we create.

It's a little like cleaning the attic. We find that once we see what we're doing we can easily give up this fruitless behavior in some instances. It's snowing when we wake up on a travel day and we simply change plans accordingly, not taking time to rant at the weather. The meal we order in the restaurant is overcooked, and we are able to just eat it without making a scene or letting our excursion be ruined. But, when we've circled the block waiting for a parking place and someone pulls into it just as we get there, we can't help muttering and scowling. A few months later, this may happen again and we are able to just drive on and keep looking. It's a gradual thing. When you're cleaning out the attic, you start with what is easiest to discard and then you get down to the hard work of sorting through the boxes of photos that wring your heart with nostalgia or the items you haven't used in a while, but might want someday. Same thing here. We begin with the things that don't touch us too deeply. The things we haven't hooked into, the things we don't identify with as "self". The weather, a meal, OK. My parking spot. Tougher. My actions? Ouch!

Today, I've bumped up again against the limits of the circle I've been clearing for years. The effort I make to communicate clearly, to please and to have harmony. These are things I've hooked into big-time. And to feel that I'm being unjustly accused of not doing these things hurts. For a moment. The hurt that goes on has nothing to do with this momentary exchange, and everything to do with the mind's habit of nursing a perceived wrong. So today, I watch this pattern as it starts itself over and over. I patiently and kindly allow it to be, but within my awareness of what this is causing. What I'm feeling. What I'm suffering. And I turn the light on the "why". Not because of the words, but because of my reaching back to them again and again. Because of my creation of this wronged me and that other who did this. This is the careful sorting. I've been doing the work today. It's not easy. But if I don't abandon the work, I'll eventually discard this box, not shuffle it back into a dark corner again. The circle widens a bit at a time.

## Hamsters and Pinball

Sometimes I wake in the dark quiet hours of the night not just for the routine walk to the bathroom but because my mind has taken hold of something it unearthed and is shaking it in my internal ear. Waking befuddled, there are times when I don't know what woke me, only that I have a vague sense of unease and, when I pay attention, I notice thoughts ricocheting around like the silver balls in a pinball machine. Though peace and sleep are what I long for, there's little hope of making anything but an accidental strike against the bell of serenity while I'm in this state.

Other times upon such a wakening I find the mind has become a hamster on a wheel, industriously going round and round as if it were getting somewhere…steps in something complex I need to do, items to pack for an outing, a check list of to-do items for the next day or even the next week. These experiences are not regular for me, but they are not unusual either. And because they are not unusual they are themselves tied to habitual, conditioned responses that still lie in wait after a couple of decades of mindfulness practice. The foggy state of waking in the middle of the night provides ideal conditions for old habits to crawl out of hiding.

One nasty habit is escalating anxiety to a point of panic. Fortunately this one has such obvious bodily symptoms that I catch it quickly. It's a full on frontal attack that even sleep-fogged I know enough to sidestep. Anger and fear are more insidious. Why is this happening? Why is my husband still sleeping so soundly, oblivious to my discomfort? How awful I'm going to feel in the morning. I'll probably end up with a headache out of this. These responses initially feel as if they are purely mental. It takes effort to look more closely. I have to rub my metaphorical inner eye. I have to speak soothingly. It reminds me of earlier years of mothering when a wound-up or frightened child had trouble sleeping. Speak softly. Keep calm. Be reassuring, not demanding of this mind and body. They have reverted to that vulnerable and impulsive child's state. This determination, to be kind and patient, is my door in to the body. Here I notice the tension anger and fear can bring. The momentum that is added to the zinging thought balls or spinning hamster wheel when I throw my weight into the future, worrying about how I'll feel tomorrow, or when I push against the other, resentful of my peaceful partner.

Recently, I woke suddenly to a single word. It rang crystal clear in a young male voice: "Mom". I'm the mother of sons although neither of them lives in this house. Both are independent adults. Yet this word has so many hooks. This body woke ready to throw itself between them and harm, yet there was no threat, and indeed no call except that which my own dreaming mind had generated. The upside of this episode was how wide awake it left me. No fog. Instantly alert. I felt the pull of fear, but resolved to turn this clear attention inward. What's happening in my body right now?

Inch by inch, from toes to the top of my head I explored. Finding a knot, I mentally whispered and rocked as I would have one of my children waking from a nightmare. I softened and soothed. I was firm about turning away from the mind's desire to weave stories. "Don't know mind" is an able assistant here. I don't know where the voice came from. I don't know what it meant. I can't have an opinion. What would it be based on beyond speculation? But I do know this stoney hardness in the shoulders, this taut piano wire in the neck, this aching heart. These I can be with. These I can stroke with the breath.

Sleep comes again when I listen to what the body needs. The hamster snuggles into his bed of paper shavings, the pinging of the pinballs quietens. I have only to patiently look to the body. What's true right now?

# 48  Wants

When caught up in the moment and about to make a purchase you had not planned for, deliberately make yourself space to let the reactivity of grasping mind settle. Set the intention to return in an hour, or the next day. Often we'll find that given this delay, the attraction has lost its grip.

**Feelings**

It's not uncommon to find science-related books and magazines in our home. We all have an interest, though the particular topics of interest vary. So, recently, in the Christmas loot, *Discover*\* Magazine's issue of the top 100 science stories showed up. The title of #78 caught my eye: "Plotting the Pattern of Emotion". The surprise discovery was "...our sensations are preloaded with emotions."

This is indeed an important discovery, only it's not. It's a confirmation of what the Buddha taught some 2500 years ago. Sensation, he found in his own body laboratory, comes pre-loaded with a "feeling tone". That is, whatever enters the sensory gates, whether that be hearing, sight, smell, taste or touch, and he included thought, counting the mind as a sense gate, will be perceived as pleasant, unpleasant or neutral.

What science has been able to add to this is observation by an external party of the actual firing of brain cells, noting that neurons firing in one direction will accompany a participant's report of positive feelings, and in the other direction of negative. "Our subjective feelings" the article goes on to say, "are actually intertwined with perception."

The Buddha made it clear that we should not just accept what he said as true, but should examine our own experience. Science is the method of examination that Westerners tend to most readily accept. But each of us can confirm these external affirmations by looking closely at our own personal and private experience. Touch a horse's soft nose, and the velvety sensation is immediately perceived as pleasant. If the horse objects and bites your hand, that new touch sensation will be unpleasant. A bowl full of glowing summer fruit is a pleasant sight, and if you lean in for a sniff, you may be rewarded by a sweet and pleasant aroma. A week later in the heat, the unpleasant smell may draw your attention before you look reluctantly towards the shriveled and leaky fruit.

What is the importance of this knowledge for a person striving to live mindfully? The importance is in what happens a nano second later. We move instinctively toward what is pleasant and away from what is not. We are caught like a fish on a hook and if we are not aware of being caught we begin a chain of behaviors that lead inevitably to suffering.

Let's revisit the horse. If the horse does bite, we may well react in anger. As we might with the child who doesn't obey, the spouse who says something hurtful, the clerk who can't answer our query, the neighbor who doesn't share our views on how loud it is appropriate to play music. What is traditionally called "aversion", the instinctive pushing away of all that is unpleasant, leads to endless cases of conflict, from a scuffle in the schoolyard, to slammed doors and ultimately to violence and wars. The instinctive wish to get rid of what seems to be the cause of suffering, escalates the suffering itself through the mental anguish of struggle.

"Clinging", the instinctive movement toward, the holding onto what is pleasant, is no less painful in the long run. It is clinging that leads us to deny aging, to keep smoking because it "calms" us, to become overly possessive of a friend or lover. And when we grow old anyway, or our breathing becomes painful, or the friend or lover leaves, we exacerbate our pain in thinking mistakenly that it should have been otherwise.

One aspect of mindfulness is to train in seeing the emotional tone, the feeling tone which accompanies sensation. Without the benefit of expensive scientific equipment, each of us is in the unique position of being able to see this, when we train in looking. Over and over, life gives us the opportunity to not swallow the hook, falling into old patterns of reactivity. Instead, we train each time we see the bait, to swim around it with curiosity, letting it swing there in the water undisturbed.

* Jan/Feb 2015

## Sorting

"I've got the peace that passeth understanding down in my heart." Words of an old hymn, popular in family and kid groups, run through my mind as I sit on the floor of our bedroom this morning, coffee in hand, glancing at my watch on the rug beside me, because writing time is limited. The morning kennel routines await. It's breezy and cool again today with enough cloud to indicate that the rainy period is not yet over. But today I will have a space, if all goes as the day is planned, of nearly two hours of solitude in the afternoon. Knowing this smooths out this ragged waking time. As did sitting this morning. Watching the morning sponginess dissipate from my brain, a kind of stretching, like the bends and yoga poses I do afterward for this body.

I think of the idea we have of "mind", of "self", as permeating the body. Then another idea: of consciousness as the ether we live in, the body like an antenna tuning in to different stations. It seems I resonate with certain "messages" at certain times. Lately, to live in my body, not retreat into thought/head. And to not take myself so seriously. "Life and death are a hide and seek game" the Tibetan prayer for the dying tells me. And "game" is key here. When we play board games or card games with children and they throw things or rant and cry when they lose or some play goes against them, we tell them "It's only a game!" We mean, lighten up, have fun, enjoy the valleys as well as the hills, be there for the ride. There have been valleys lately. Worry, aging, menopause and some hard struggles in communication. And I've spent time lying on the floor of those valleys, weeping and fussing in the mud or kicking my heels in a tantrum. It is freeing and funny to look up and see the sun on the hill on the next horizon and to see the mess I've made and to just smile and trudge on, enjoying the slip and slide of moving forward.

In a few moments, the working day begins, and time will move in the strange way it has. The flurry of activities pulling us through at frenetic speed. Yet in moments (crossing the gravel drive, folding laundry, climbing into bed at night) I'm caught in the familiar as if in an eddy that never moves, just turning round and round in the same moment.

Keeping calm, good intentions in my heart and an ear open to the guidance of the universe, my toes pointed in a wished for direction, that's my task. Some of the inner joy bubbling up is really anticipation beyond the taste of space that today's two hours will bring. Change coming as we move toward retirement. In sitting some days my mind is all scattered planning. I see the potential for suffering if I cling to plans, allowing hope to become expectation. Desires color our perceptions. I reflect on khamma and lessons and try to imagine in previous lives where my head was to bring me here. Life is good. But in youth, like so many, I followed my whims without a moral centre to guide relationships. I regret and grieve some actions…yet it was all a road leading here and to this spiritual path.

Lama Surya Das, a favorite Buddhist writer of mine, says that journaling is spiritual work. I think he means the kind of reflection it makes possible. I am so often surprised by what pen and page reveal. In the going we find the destination. The connections that the page makes clear. I've been boxing up things to purge. Stuff that belonged to my parents, or to me when I was young, or even to the boys at earlier stages. Identity in boxes. The way we box up and label our own memories and mind lists in order to understand, creating the illusion of things, of something that lasts. Even me. Even me. Dad's records to the collectible shop. Scribblers and texts and novels to the Heritage Society. My grandmother's Speller. I hesitate over novels presented to my parents as kids in 1931 and 1940 and in the end keep them on my shelves. Will they matter to anyone in a few years? Sometime they will be ignominiously trashed. A twinge of regret at this truth. Simplification calls though. We are stewards and everything is on loan.

## Restlessness

It is important for me to remember right now that movement of the mind is its nature. This teaching is significant for me in these last stretches of a Canadian winter, where it seems inevitable that restlessness arises. When I was young and not a practitioner, I remember a wild sense of holding back something that seemed it would surely explode as I waited for spring. The last exams of the university year were arduous and long. The necessity of stillness and focus and study were experienced like the claustrophobic squeeze of the blood pressure cuff in the doctor's office. It was uncomfortable and I waited it out with gritted teeth.

These days restlessness has a different flavor. It has me gazing away from the pages of a good book, or finding a fine meal tasteless. It can sit sometimes like a headache just behind my eyes when the familiar thought cycle begins: there is just this and then this…and then what? That's the question that my twitching mind turns up over and over again. The question that, these days, identifies for me what's going on. The answer is not that something is missing right now. This is the answer I used to believe. Now I know that what I see in this question is a leaning into the future. Nothing specific desired. Just desire itself stirring the mind.

This is what underlies so much minor-league but persistent suffering in our lives. The mind is all desire looking for an object.

What's the difference now from 40-plus years ago when I was that ready-to-scream university kid throwing herself face down to do snow angels and bursting at the seams for something, anything to happen? Then, desire kept finding landing places because it ran free and unchecked. New clothes, a movie, a boyfriend, a trip, an amazing cheesecake, change. I thought then that there was something I needed, something I could find that would satisfy the crazy itch. And each time the landing proved to be not quite enough, I blamed it on the skirt, the actors, the guy, the chef. Never thinking to look closely at the feeling itself.

Now I know better. It's not just age, though I suppose a slowing of energy and an accumulation of experience does a little to modify and streamline this crazy dance. It's having learned to be with these unpleasant feelings sufficiently that I'm aware of their many disguises. A desire for spring won't be slacked when the snow melts. It will be followed by a desire for my hands in the earth and the smell of campfires and freshly cut grass, and a time of lazy family days. Ah...there you go. I will eventually bump up against the desire to turn back the clock. To have my kids young again. To have a replay of favorite times. And if I believe that thought, I'll be melancholy because that's a desire that can't be met.

So it isn't the thing out there. In this case, it isn't that the snow is lingering or that daylight savings time means longer dark in the mornings again, or that I still have to wear my boots in our country yard. It's the movement of the mind. That perpetual waving of the flags of wanting this and not wanting that. Look at the feeling itself, the Buddha instructed. Be mindful of this. How this wanting sucks the joy out of the moment. Plunge past it, not being derailed, and find the door in again...to the good book in my hands, the good food on my plate. Sense doors open, present in the body, not hostage to the flickering confusions of the mind.

# 49  Remembering

It's an old trick, the string around your finger to remember. But try tying a pretty bit of yarn around your wrist, or wearing a piece of jewelry, such as a *mala* bracelet to remind you of your intention to live, act, and speak skillfully. This could be for every day, or just for a day when you feel fragile and in need of a reminder of your heart's intention.

### In the Company of the Buddha

Something miraculous happened tonight and it made me weep. Second day into retreat and a day of difficult sitting: still and obedient body, unruly and scattered mind. Not sure how to approach what I knew I needed: happiness and energy as the foundation of my practice…all but lost in these last months of depression, as I sank in the murk of *dukkha*…what did I say to a friend? "Existential angst." I could see the truth of suffering, but felt stuck, unable to reach the raft of the other Noble Truths leading to its end.

I signed up for an interview but Bhante Pavaro had too many of us to get to and I took my name off the list, opting instead to put a question in the basket "Questions for the Monk". I asked about skillful use of visualization to generate and develop energy and joy.

At the beginning of the evening sitting, Bhante addressed this and I appreciated his suggestions but the miracle followed when he introduced another monk, visiting for the evening. A younger but more senior monk just returned from Thailand and soon to be going to New Zealand but here, now. What complex khammic causalities brought me here to hear him? This is a small and ordinary miracle. I am grateful.

He opened by speaking of what brings us to spiritual seeking and he had me there. Thus the tears. Dukkha. Discontent. He mentioned the three paths people follow in seeking contentment: sensuality/pleasures; existence (goals and achievements, carving out a kind of life); and spiritual seeking for something more, for the truth. Yes!

And then he addressed my question with personal examples: Buddha, Dhamma, Sangha. He described visualizing being in the presence of the Buddha…being the recipient of faith and calm. He talked of generating the feeling of a warm and open heart in the body (kindness, compassion, generosity) and how this can be the subject of meditation or the opening of one. I gratefully accepted this gift of his presence and teaching, the spark I'd hoped for in re-setting the fire. I have felt so cold and plodding and sad…but I simply broke open as he spoke with such gentle sincerity and kindness. I could feel the smile beginning in my heart.

The next day began with a calm mind and twitchy body…turning yesterday inside out. I had slept well, partly the joy at the close of the day and partly the more mundane fact that I had stuffed a face cloth in the door beside the frame to prevent the bumping that is incessant if I leave my window open a little. Still, in the first session I mostly walked, unable to switch off my physical body's rising energy.

After breakfast and a shower though, calm mind spread tendrils through this body. I settled in the next session and when I opened my eyes after a timeless time, blinking like a newly hatched chick, but moving my stiff legs like an old hen, I found an hour and a half had passed. I unwound and walked before sitting again.

I am using the Buddha reflection to begin and it is as if a hand is reaching through the fog of dukkha. Tranquility is possible and a firm and consistent return of the mind to breath and heart when it wanders. No falling away, but some distancing of sensation so bodily complaints come from far away and are not a bother for long stretches.

Walking the grounds at peace in the evening, and I catch a glimpse of one of Providence's huge rabbits, grooming himself in the courtyard, thoroughly white still against the black dirt of the newly turned spring flowerbed. Change often happens slowly, I am reminded. But I am in the company of the Buddha, of the Sangha and of the Dhamma. My feet are firm on the path.

### Time Delay

Ovens are usually equipped with a handy feature that might be called *delayed start* or *time delay*. If the cook needs to tuck a casserole into the oven early and go off to do other things, the meal waits in this suspended time period before the oven turns on and the heating process begins. In this way, you're able to use the time you have available, say early in the morning, and the meal is ready just when you need it, at the end of the day. I'm not composing an instructional manual here or even a modern cook's handbook. But I do the cooking, mostly, in my home. I am also doing the work of practicing the Buddha's Eightfold Path, one breath at a time. And there seems to me to be some useful overlap here in understanding how my practice is working these days.

In the Upasika training that I'm undertaking, I've found that the depth of my practice is rapidly increasing. That is, the mindfulness I've been working to develop over a couple of decades is becoming more than ever my set point. Notice I didn't say my behavior is suddenly saint-like! But continuity of awareness of how I am intending to behave has been ramped up several notches in only a few months time. It flags, of course, mostly when I'm tired or ill or have had my inner resources stretched by several "crises" in a row. But even then, I gotta say, I will know how I am behaving even as the behavior unfolds. I don't need someone to be hurt or angry and to act out in response. The light of awareness inside tells me as words leave my mouth or as I press the send button, or as I move away from an unpleasant encounter. I've had this happen before. What is becoming apparent to me is that this is my "set point" these days. It's a more often than not kind of thing, this awareness. I hope it lasts. But I also know all things are subject to change so it's important that I keep doing the work, and don't sit back and decide "I've got it".

But this is where I see the *time delay* metaphor applying. At least twice recently I've had this process unfold for me: Someone's behavior triggers for me an ego-aversion. *I don't like this. I want something else to happen.* That kind of thing. I am able to be with the nastiness of this feeling and let it ride through. I restrain my responses. And I know both that I am restraining them and that the problem is all of my making. That doesn't make the feelings any less uncomfortable. In one case this meant a bout of private tears, in another, keeping myself out of a conversation temporarily until I could watch the narratives my ego was weaving begin to recede into muted mumbles. Then I was able to replace the grief, in one case, and the anger, in the other, with deliberate thoughts of loving-kindness both for myself and the other.

Here's where the time delay made itself known. A few hours later, when circumstances brought up the situation again, I noticed that my original responses just didn't recur. That's all. In the hours between setting a more wholesome intention (setting the time delay on the oven, if you will) and the arising of necessity for acting (sitting down to my meal) the heat of the Dhamma had done its work.

I dunno. I'm a failed poet (though generally a pretty good cook) and I have a penchant for metaphor. Maybe this doesn't make the point I'm after. But it feels right. What I'm seeing is that I *can get it* in my head that I am causing my own suffering and that my responses are harmful to myself and others. And I can *choose* to plant other thoughts in a rather mechanical way. But then I have to trust and give it time. And my heart will get the message. Change is happening all the time. And my choices do nudge that change in the right direction. All the ingredients are there, in the making of the meal, in watching my own mind and reactions. Then I need only set skillful intentions and have patience. Something surprisingly warm and wholesome emerges.

## What's In A Name?

The name my parents gave me, "Bonnie Gay", has Celtic heritage. The first name means variously "pretty" or "good" and the middle "lighthearted, happy". All these qualities represent hopes parents could be expected to have for their first born daughter, I suppose. My last name "Ryan-Fisher" is a modern hybrid. My father's older sister used to like to tease me that she had once been a Ryan, but wasn't anymore. She told me that would happen to me too and I defiantly proclaimed that "I will always be a Ryan." Well, that's the family story. I was too young to remember the argument, but I stand by my conclusion of the time. To honor that, I keep "Ryan". It merges, of course, with my husband's family name, representing for me the merging of our lives.

Recently, however, I requested a Pali name from my teacher, Ajahn Sona, at Birken Forest Monastery. This name does not replace the one my beloved parents chose for me, nor the names of my families of birth or marriage. But, to me it marks my dedication to my teacher and the Dhamma-family I have become part of. The Upasika training I began last spring has meant even closer ties and deepening practice. I wanted to honor this turning.

The name my teacher chose for me is Sumana. After only a week, I am already fond of it. I like the whisper of the first emphasized syllable and downhill ripple of the middle to the release of the long sigh at the end. I like the curves and flow and hills and valleys of the letters under my pen. Ajahn explained it as meaning "joyful or glad".

Parsed further, the Pali prefix "Su" can mean "very", "good", or "beautiful". "Mana" means "happy", according to one source, and variously "mind, intellect, thoughts, heart" in another dictionary. Because Pali does not really distinguish mind and heart, the two are often hyphenated in translation, with reference to the "heart-mind" and its feelings or workings. So whether I opt for *good heart, beautiful mind, very happy, good thoughts*, the message in this name is clearly of a positive and uplifting nature. I find reason for a smile at the unintentional echo and inspiring suggestions in the meanings of both my Celtic birth name and my new Pali spiritual name.

"What's in a name?" Juliette famously asked in Shakespeare's play. While her conclusion left names empty of meaning, I beg to differ. In the case of a name chosen for an individual, a name may offer aspirations.

Ajahn suggested that I learn a little about the many historical Sumanas and their relationship to the Buddha. Perhaps I would find one I identified with. And indeed there are many with this name, both men and women. One that speaks to me was a highly dedicated lay disciple, who never missed an opportunity to hear the Buddha speak but who nevertheless chose to remain in her lay life devoted to the care of her aging grandmother. She ordained only as a very old woman, but is described in the *Therigatha* (poems of early Buddhist women) as completely ripe for awakening at the time of her ordination. As a wife and mother and devoted lay practitioner I am encouraged by this dual dedication and an example of one who followed the way with such devotion without renouncing worldly loves and duties.

The gentle rhythms of my new Pali name as I mentally repeat and absorb it have become a personal chant for me. A reminder of the purpose and promise of this path. The good and the beautiful and the glad. Aspirations for shaping a life free of suffering.

# 50 Thanks

Write a letter or make a phone call to express feelings of gratitude. Too often we assume others know what is in our heart. Bringing joy to another will nourish your own spirit.

**Life and Death**

Hugs and tears shared with my sister and with our brother, too seldom seen. Once again, as we were a few years ago, we're united around the illness and critical need of a parent. Somehow we all drop the so-important routines and obligations of daily life and converge here...around a sickbed.

"Is Mom still here?" we ask. She hasn't wakened since her heart attack. She's breathing...with the support of machines. The fever of pneumonia abates a little then returns. Occasionally she reflexively moves her legs and she pulls away from any touch on her sore leg, the one that has tortured her with gout for weeks now. But no blink, no word. Even her coughing is silent and eery.

Where is she if not here with this frail body now? Choosing to let go? We laugh through our pain about Mom's characteristic indecision, even now.

I chant as I hold her hand. I know my beliefs are not hers. Hope the love and intent to comfort carry despite words she won't understand if she's hearing them. Then I sing softly...*Amazing Grace*.

She's here. Not in the familiar body, warm to the touch, the curling white hair, the pulse so strong by her left ear. She's in my brother's brown eyes, in the spontaneous and intense love he radiates. She's in my sister's touch and voice, taking on too much in her quiet and practical care-taking of each of us as we camp in her home. She's in the anxiety I feel about asking others to take on my kids and duties while I watch here. All these are her legacy. The strand of life's web that is this small family. Trembling now at the changes, a foot lifting, a soul flying free again.

Back at my sister's house, the boys, my young sons and nephews, are all happy to be together, no thought of what circumstances bring this about. The house is filled with their chaos: toys, laughter, forgotten snacks.

Life is this composite of pain and joy. The adults talking in hushed voices about decisions we don't want to make, battling fatigue, struggling with patience. Yet breaking into laughter as we share stories or amusement at something the children do.

The wonderful warmth of the shower. Coffee and fruit in the morning. Shared glances with no need for words. Love running as a steady stream below the fumbling of actions, words, mistakes.

This too will pass. And somehow, moment by moment, we'll face the decisions and what needs to be done and time will go on as it always does.

Driving here I tried to remember the trips we must have made when the parents of my parents were critically ill. And my mind jumps ahead to the day my own sons will take on this role.

It's as it should be. The Tibetan prayer for the dying says birth and death are but doors. Perhaps Mom is reaching her hand to the door. If so, it is ours to love, let be and let go.

## Saying Thanks

It's snowing again. Each morning I wake remembering it's April. The calendars that hang on the walls show songbirds and tree blossoms, brightly painted buckets of flowers, translucent blue skies. But outside the window, it's a panorama of grey and white. Stark evergreens and bare-branched willows. A deep sigh is instinctive.

This reactive sigh is a good thing for it brings me back to the breath, triggering a softening of shoulders and brow. Thus I return to my new resolve to begin each day in loving-kindness. In this context, this starts with myself and the replacement of negative mind states with those that nurture and warm. A love for this earth and each day of this life. A recognition of my place in it, just one small breathing molecule in the world body and beyond. And a smile that arises when I remember that all things change. The snow will give way to sunlight. And perhaps within a few weeks the radio will broadcast warnings about fire hazards and the dangers of drought.

I take a few moments to be grateful. To choose to be happy in this time and place. Moving a few steps across a warm room, shuffling on a soft rug, I am grateful for indoor plumbing and this cosy home. Splashing water on my face and brushing my teeth, I am grateful for the well that supplies ready, clean water. Taking the first of the morning medications that are a daily ritual for me, I am grateful for modern medicine that makes living with a chronic health condition possible, for it's a truth that without modern medicine I wouldn't be here at all to sigh over the snow. And without the vigilance of various health professionals who help me monitor diet and meds, I'd be much less comfortable and healthy.

Gratitude. Not ten minutes into the day and there are so many people whose efforts have not just enhanced but made possible this good life. This scrolling through is similar to what is often suggested as a kind of "prayer" to accompany meals. The farmer who grew the food, the truck drivers who hauled it, the workers in the stores, and so on. If we can develop the habit of looking not just at the surface of the day, but at the myriad levels that hold those surfaces in place, we might be moved more often to not just gratitude, but a sense of connection. Is there one without the other?

Human beings can be a reticent bunch too often when it comes to saying "sorry" for our mistakes and "thanks" for the efforts of others. Yet, when we feel the emotion that stirs the word, the speech is automatic. I'm trying to make more effort to notice the efforts of others in the day and when another is there to express thanks to, let it be expressed. Sometimes it feels odd and maybe unnecessary to say thank you to my husband for doing the dishes, something he does every day; or to thank a friend who, thinking of me, sends information that might be relevant to my life; to take time at the supermarket to thank both the cashier and the clerk who packs my groceries; to thank someone who waits an extra moment holding open a door. But I remind myself that the words are spoken for the benefit of us both. Resolving to speak thanks makes me more likely to notice the opportunities. People are kind and generous. I'm grateful. Gratitude in the heart-mind changes the way I see the world. Even April's snows sparkle!

**Gratitude to the Dhamma**

In the practice of gratitude I have discovered one of the roots of joy. Gratitude is woven into love. Can they be separate? It seems impossible. I've found as the years of practice go by I come to love the Dhamma more and more and to feel deepening gratitude for the causal chain that brought this path into my life. Rather than being only awed and puzzled by dear Dhamma-friends whose smiles seem ever ready, whose equilibrium seems to return so quickly in the midst of life's storms, I am beginning to understand how this happens. I've got a lot of work yet to do but when I look inside and examine the impact of the Dhamma on choices I have made as well as on my own resilience and capacity for joy, I see the diverging between the life I might have had and the one I do have here and now. That might-have-been road is a darker place. The pain that lurks in those shadows is familiar to every human being.

Had I remained on that path I would have traveled differently. I know this because I followed its familiar windings for several decades before finding this middle way. I would have hunched in fear more often; I would have defied in anger. I would have done more harm to myself and others because of this fear and anger. The journey would have been a colder one, drained of the warm emotions by a sense of helplessness that arose too often. All of this because the events of this life that I feared and defied, the outside weather and wolves and thorns and obstacles, are mostly out of my control.

Of course, on this path I am traveling now that is also true. That is, there are still thorns and wolves and bad weather. But I am aware of how my fear and anger give them power over my state of heart and mind. And I've learned that it is my choice whether to curse or tremble, or to turn away from these negative mind states and replace them with what is more skillful. Gratitude itself is one of these more skillful states.

So I am grateful. This gratitude is a warming thing. When I create an inner tally of the beings who have contributed to making this choice possible for me and who support me on the journey, my load is lightened and the day brightened. From the great gift of the Buddha himself who chose to teach what he had learned, to all the teachers and practitioners who have followed over more than 2500 years.

Sending thanks is a bit like writing a love letter and keeping it silently inscribed in my heart: I'm the one to benefit.

At the end of my daily sitting I do three bows…Homage to the Buddha, Homage to the Dhamma, and Homage to the Sangha. These bows are symbolic of my deep gratitude to this life practice.

# 51  Moving Meditation

Taking a walk, keep yourself awake and alert by scanning the environment for the colors of the rainbow. Look for them in order (red, orange, yellow, green, blue, indigo, violet), building a rainbow of your own over the course of the outing.

### Who Is on Retreat?

The second morning in a retreat centre I haven't visited before. I wake twice before the morning alarm even though it is set very early. It has not been deep and satisfying sleep. I feel the beginnings of "grumpy" mind this morning when I find there are a number of people busy at the coffee station where I go to make my early tea. Yesterday I was alone, and yes, I prefer that. It was about 15 minutes earlier though, so…. There will be thoughts to watch, as planning mind formulates a schedule to meet personal preferences. It is a constant effort catching the gap between external events and the leaps the mind makes.

This morning the young woman who shows me the kettle switch I"ve been fumbling for, raises her eyes, unsmiling, to be sure I understand and my mind leaps from her neutral face to a mental formation: "She feels superior and annoyed". This mental voice that divides everything into self and other is familiar, and recognizing its persistence is humbling. Is it any wonder that confusion rules our world? Such cruelties, injustices and war-making the self-ing leads us to. How can this be wise in an evolutionary sense? Someone once told me I expect too much from evolution. It is interested only in the survival of the species, that a few make it to child rearing age. But can this impersonal force reach across species? If we were a wiser species, we would not eliminate other species from the earth on a whim. Ah...convoluted thinking. And a product of my fuzzy morning head. I should take my tea outside for a stroll. Dissolve the voices in fresh air and awareness of breath. Perhaps that is the best plan.

This wet and chilly June continues. This morning, though, a dry spell of sufficient length for walks...before breakfast and afterward. The tall, crowded-together homes on the other side of the ravine are far enough away to imagine how pure and beautiful the view must have been before their construction. It is still lovely.

First sitting this morning is clear and still. The open quality stays with me until breakfast, when there is need for a spell of quite ordinary mindfulness as the "self" pushes itself forward, hungry and demanding. I arrive with the stragglers, having gone to my room for meds first. French toast on the menu but none left in the warming bin and sounds of whipping eggs from the kitchen. It will be awhile. Pour tea and sit. Directly in my view at a neighboring table is a large young man with four slices of French toast on his plate. I see aversion arise and hear its unpleasant voice nattering in my mind. Annoyance. The story begins. Smile, breathe. Shift from targeting this stranger to noticing my own selfing and desire. Now the harsh voice of self-criticism arises. Another face of aversion. Sigh!

Later I find some whitebread French toast in the new lot and sit down to eat, but as I do so, the retreat coordinator brings a plate from the buffet to show me. Wrapped in foil, it is labelled "white bread French toast". OK. It was there all along if I'd looked further. I didn't see it. And now I feel obligated to eat this too, made particularly for me and I spin into a story about her annoyance with me since she made these special arangements. Watching the mind. Suddenly a burble of silent, relieved mental laughter and I feel calm and settled, leaning back in my seat, mere audience to this inner struggle. I recall instructions. Nothing to do with me. I don't will these voices into being. I can work to quiet them, to replace them. I can let them recede, not give them power.

Now and then over the morning I find my mind drawn to composing a thank you and apology e-mail to send to the retreat coordinator when I get home. Ah...this fragile self and all its needs. Now it is off begging for love and understanding. Poor thing. Quit your fussing and come here.

The teacher offers a metaphor to consider in meditation: Concentration is that which holds the apple still. Mindfulness is the knife that cuts through it, creating the thinnest of slices. So for me today, I foster concentration in the sitting, practicing the skill of presence, and this is useful as I move beyond the cushion. Broadening awareness as I move through the day, mindfulness looks closely, cuts through to truth.

## Retreat Strategies

I have great difficulty with drowsiness for half the morning. Whether on cushion or chair, I move from breath to dream and catch myself slumping forward. Walking is effortful. I am leaden and weary. I listen to Ayya's talk but my brain is like a sloping roof and her words fall and slide like rain. In the last hour of the morning she leaves to conduct interviews and instructs us to continue sitting and walking, striving for continuity. I do not need continuity of drowsiness but renewed energy.

I take this body outside where the sky is blue and bright, the sun blazing, the air moving in a soft breeze. I find a private stretch of grass, pressed down a little from mower or tractor tracks and I walk back and forth in the hot sun. It soothes the muscles in my neck and shoulders, my feet find their own way. I tune into movement, the swing of my legs. In awhile I move a few feet into the trees to a low wooden chair and I sit, hands on knees, for awhile gazing through the tangled limbs of an upsweeping tree where I see other retreatants walking the stone path of the little courtyard near the building, waiting for their interviews. The water of the central fountain arcs up and droplets fall like jewels in the sun. An unseen squirrel scolds me from my right and when a machine drone stops suddenly far to the left, I feel the silence like a hand on my ear for a moment. It is shady and breezy in this little space and I begin to revive, close my eyes and follow my breath. A time passes. Short? Or long? I return to my grassy walking path and move back and forth a long time. I choose a focus for each passing: The soles of my feet, the swing of my hips, the sun on my arms, tiny movements in the grass where I rest the gaze of my downcast eyes.

Later I return to the chair to sit until it is time to go into lunch and there I make simple choices good for my body and not too heavy...then I return to my room to lie down till the lengthy afternoon sit begins.

It is the kind of day where this body has demands. Knees and back rebel, and monkey mind is drawn to their sharp entreaties over and over in the early afternoon. Then Ayya invites the whole group outside where I find another stretch of grass to walk, a chair to sit on, and peace in squirrel meditation, sparrow meditation, lady bug meditation. Ease spills over at last, making the walking and sitting simple again and not hampered by either sleepiness or striving.

Gathering clouds chase me inside again for the final hour, but this cloak of ease makes the journey with me.

Ayya offers a helpful metaphor: just as a carpenter cannot see how the print of his hand is wearing away the wooden handle of his hammer, day by day, still he will notice when it has worn through. Keep up the practice and do not be despondent at seeing no fruits day by day. The hindrances will be worn through. Watching her...the fine, long-fingered hands, the quick and fleeting smile, the certainty and kindness in her manner... I am struck by yearning. Not envy. Her teaching and example are gifts and I am grateful to be here where yearning pulls me like gravity more surely to this path.

I take a long rambling walk on the grounds before the evening session. I find a corner new to me, a mound where someone has planted petunias, the color unusual in the varying greens that dominate. Back inside with the retreat group, I am clear and still for this final sitting, remembering the surprise of that vibrant color in an unexpected corner, letting each breath unfold in its unique, never to be repeated, way.

Ayya closes the day with a story of her own imagination and self-pity when reliant on alms on a solo retreat once – the lay people who had promised to bring provisions were late and she feared she'd been forgotten. I think of my own craving and self pity, self-made obstacles to practice. Retreats are often where fires are lit again and the clutter of discontent is burned away.

## Honoring the Moment

I live in my head a great deal. In walking meditation I began to see how much I do this by trying to place my awareness in the soles of my feet, in the muscles of my calves. It was like junior high drama class. Place your voice in the top of your head and down in your belly. At first it seemed silly and artificial. Later, just difficult. And only much later, possible, but never natural. So I worry about my intellectualizing of experience. Of my tendency to immediate reflection. My experiences are like folding a towel. The experience is now, laying out the towel's length, but as I've barely done this I begin to turn it back upon itself, looking at my motivations, my reactions, and then again folding the fabric upon itself and seeing these. Till the smooth length of a moment is instead a layered block. Over and over again. I have come to desire simplicity in my experience, to want to stop this folding in. But I see simultaneously the paradox of desire and aversion here. The judgment of my own judgment. But even this is "what is". Breathe. Let the fabric drop again: in a single length or back upon itself. Each is good.

Yet, it is easy so often to feel in touch with the ground of being in nature. When I walk our woods path each day with the dogs I am aware how I ease my breathing, relax into the sounds of my steps and the breath of the wind, the snuffling and rooting of each dog who accompanies me. The knocking of the woodpeckers and the scolding chatter of the squirrels. A scurrying rabbit now and then or the drumming of the grouse. I watch my feet much of the time for the trail is uneven and I notice new growth, fallen branches, the footprints of deer in the mud or snow, droppings of rabbit, deer, coyote. Last summer the trail was marked nightly by some little black bear who had claimed this territory. The trail moves in and out of woods, in sun and then in shadow. We cross two small wooden bridges over swampy areas. The first will soon fill with the brilliant yellow water flowers that my son sometimes gathers for me in bouquets. The second, over summer, will fill with tall cat tails. In nature, with animals, I often feel the reality of connection with everything that is. I imagine this is so for many people. We drop "who we are expected to be" when we are in this kind of environment. And we drop the over-thinking that complicates the moment.

Zen teacher Dogen mentions "pillars and walls" in his list of teachers. So this teaching of connection does not stop as we move into the world of mankind's making – around me now are cups and table, chairs, pens and books... no visible pillars, but certainly walls, the stuff that fills a kitchen, fills a home.

All these ordinary things. "...use a blade of grass to make a six-foot golden Buddha body..." Dogen says and I laugh, remembering a Zen Dhamma talk. A Buddha in a head of cabbage, a handful of sweet peas. The making of a Buddha is in how we regard each object and being in the world. When we see the buddha-nature in each thing, when we honor that in the way we treat each being, each object, then we make a Buddha from a blade of grass, a head of cabbage. So in my day today I make Buddhas of the food I prepare, the blankets I smooth, the little dogs I cuddle and cajole and the big ones whose ears I stop to scratch. Being in each moment and honoring what touches my path. This is practice. This feels like the verge of a deep understanding. It is not just slowing down. Being here. Experiencing my own life in the fleeting moment, but it is honoring the Buddha in what I touch. The path I walk on, the cup I drink from, the water I drink, the plate I wash, the floor and the mop, the toilet and the brush, the knife and the bread. A new glimmer, a new piece in the puzzle of understanding what mindfulness entails.

# 52  Selfing

Our sense of ownership (whether of people of roles, of views and opinions), often causes us pain. Write down on post-it notes, those things you claim and then symbolically tear them up, repeating to yourself "not me, not mine, not myself", freeing your heart.

**Who Am I?**

What is the self at all, but a dragging forward of what is familiar, like children who carry a beloved blanket until it is in tatters. It is ragged from dragging, and no longer soft and comforting to the touch, yet too precious to let go completely.

This habit of constructing and of overlaying the present with the past, even imagined pasts, and certainly imagined futures is a trap for me and for all those I love. Thinking I know them, I do not allow them to change. Thinking I know myself, I do not feel the changes happening, in fact I may even deny them.

Aging. I will soon be 54. How does aging feel? My mom used to say she didn't feel any different than she had at 20. Well, ok, I understand that on a certain level. I have difficulty grasping how quickly the years pass. I am at the stage of life when we are expected to be talking of retirement plans. On Halloween night both boys were out, and we made dinner and listened to tapes of old "Shadow" radio programs and I was thinking: "This is like this." I glimpsed what an empty house means in visceral terms. I'll miss them. But solitude is a good place for me. A natural place. I feel, there, like a fish in water. I breathe more easily. So it's not that I need to fill space. I don't imagine myself joining a bridge club and getting three little dogs, or taking in boarders. These actions would be a great divergence from the conditions now in place.

Still, I will miss the boys. The impromptu talks in the kitchen or on the stairs or while I'm folding laundry, when one of them finds me and has a plan or a passion or a worry to share. Being taunted when I lose at ping pong or can't understand a computer game. The "what if" games. Life will lose its randomness in many ways. The spices. A nourishing meal still with all the food groups but low on flavor. That's what I think now anyway. I suppose it will take time to notice the nuances of flavor that emerge without the "hot peppers" present!

When I watch my boys these days I am savoring and trying to memorize, striving to know them, the mystery of them and their way of being in the world. When I watch them my vision is full of memory, hope, imaginings. It is never pure. Never completely clean and present.

When I watch my husband, too, each vision is overlaid by years of being together. I see his parents in some movement or tone of voice, and I bow inside to the inevitable influence of our genetic heritage. I wonder to what degree I carry my own parents. The hand rubbing I catch myself doing always makes me think of Mom. The voices and faces I call up to play with the kids is my dad. But how else do they inform who I am?

And then the unanswerable question of ancestors. Not just the grandparents I knew. But all the "greats" stretching back in time. Grandparents, yes, and aunts and cousins. I see people like me in farm kitchens, on ships from Ireland, on plantations in the south. Cowboys. Were there other teachers? Writers? I imagine nuns and monks and priests, knowing my deep turning to these mysteries and the greater meaning of life.

Growing older also means the accumulation of experience, of selves in my past, that I recognize as part of this stream but feel so little common ground with now. The flighty teen, the self-absorbed young woman, the single-minded hedonist, the self that feared being one in a world of couples, the self that believed in fairy tale outcomes and perfect worlds, the self that harmed others thoughtlessly in pursuing what looked like happiness.

How did that chain bring me here to the breath? Lately, I've been in a dark place for awhile. I trust that in some way I'm moving again from the melancholy of dukkha (suffering) recognition to a place where sukkha (happiness) is noted as well. I feel that happening. And I wonder about the slow development of equanimity. Is this how it grows? Gradual awakening. Not a single moment of insight but a slow shift to the incomplete wisdom this life offers.

### Parenting and Plant Pots

It's that season again when I return to an annual, simple practice related to acknowledging impermanence. Each morning I visit the potted plants on my deck (there are many) and as I pluck away withered blossoms and shrunken leaves, I chant "All things are impermanent/ They arise and pass away/ To be in harmony with this truth/ Brings peace." Every time I do this I find that I am working not just with the short and brilliant lives of these plants, of course, but with something in my life that is more pressing, something else I am watching fall away.

This year seems to be the year for yet another transition in parenting for me. Like all transitions in parenting have been, it came on suddenly, like the flash floods I've read about in New Mexico. You know it's part of the landscape, a possibility, an inevitability even. But when it materializes, you're not always in the best place for dealing with it.

I've had the blessing, to me it seems like a blessing, of having my youngest at home for a few years beyond high school because of work and school arrangements that made this a good choice. But all things are impermanent. And now suddenly he's preparing to move out. And not just in the neighborhood but to the far end of the province. Ironically to the very city I grew up in and left in my youth. The writer in me likes this symmetry. The mother in me isn't so crazy about it. So OK, a kid's gotta do what a kid's gotta do. And this is a natural and necessary adjustment. It's just that my heart wants to hang on.

When he's down the hall it's easier for me to retain the delusion that he's safe. I remember a kind of panic the first time I took both my boys on a city outing after the arrival of the youngest. Suddenly I realized how impossible it was to keep full attention on both of them at once...the baby in the stroller and the curious pre-schooler beside me. We had some difficult moments. Parents of more than two children have shared that once you know you have more kids than arms to grab for them, you have to relax a little with this. Having never had more than two, I continued to believe somewhere in my heart of hearts that so long as they were in the vicinity it was in my power to get there in time. I retained this belief even when ordinary childhood accidents proved otherwise. Such is the state of the ordinary human mind. All evidence to the contrary, we hold on to what we wish were the case.

Practice over the years has given me an awareness of these strange mental gymnastics, and gradually it has allowed me to develop the tools to loosen the grip I have on the beliefs that don't serve me, and lessen the grasping after the rainbows I paint in the sky. So this time is no different.

What I'm doing with this transition is trying to be with it. Acknowledging the pain. Letting the tears come during morning meditation. Sending metta to this suffering self, and letting it spread wide to other mothers, other parents everywhere in this time and in times previous and to come, who have likewise had to experience this. Their children may have gone to sea at nine, as in pre-industrial England; married at twelve, as still happens in some cultures; left in their teens to travel overseas to work or explore, as youth have always been inclined to do. Whatever the circumstances, each being has his or her own journey. He is not mine to hold onto. And I can protect him only so far. My job description changes as the years pass; what is constant is only to love.

I am reminded too of the "selfing" that goes on here. Looking inward in practice we begin to see how the self is constructed. Something we claim and define, but no more solid than the air we breathe. What we claim as ours, even the people we love, we seek to protect, to control, to keep. So much of my work right now is to see this desire arising. To notice that if I see each fearful thought for what it is, it arises and passes away, with a life much briefer than the blossoms of my summer flowers. This watching and breathing and allowing of the natural process is what brings peace.

### A Writer's Wish

I wonder about the place where writing and meditation meet. These are two of the overlapping circles in the Venn diagram that represents my life.

What is inspiration, the muse that moves creativity? Is an artist's mind blank, ready to grasp an image but with no image pre-formed? What does this mean for a writer? When I sit and stare at the flickering prompt on my computer screen and no words come, I'm blank alright. And sometimes a despair hits me that I have nothing to say. Yet, it's only like the fragile skin on water and when I break through it's into the cool rush of all the things I want to say. The stories I want to write that will somehow help others struggling with life. Because we mostly forget the universality of that struggle.

We grasp onto a fairytale: the world as fair and just and kind, a place where permanent happiness is a possibility. I know my mother wanted us to believe this. Perhaps every parent wants their children to believe this. Yet, from the perspective of years now, I imagine how she must have suffered during any natural family conflicts, for the loss of her babies as we grew and left home, and during Dad's final year when there was no way she could intervene or change what he went through. My mother was not unique. Many good people are confounded by the reality of the world, and the suffering they see, the suffering they experience, because they do not want to believe in it. They do not want to accept it; they want it to be an anomaly, an abberation somehow. Yet, believing the universe is targeting "me" or some other undeserving soul with pain and disappointment that "shouldn't" happen, triggers emotional swings and anger.

The web of causality in this world of impermanence is such that all of us suffer. If nothing else, we will age and sicken and die. And along the way all of us, I believe, suffer despair, disappointments, anxiety, loss. The stories I want to write would make the universality of this clear, reaching across the illusive divisions, dispersing the fog that makes us believe, mistakenly, we are solitary, solid and alone.

What story then? I raise my pen and wait. What I find is how difficult it is not to plan, to think and choose and when I do this I go only a little way... an image, a line and then I hit a wall. I need to make myself empty of planning and choosing for the process to be possible.

Natalie Goldberg teaches not to edit. To just write the chatter down and trust that somewhere we will break through to what is real – the lightning and thunder, she calls it. I've seen this happen. Reading pages and pages of trivia in my journals and then a moment, something, that shines. Sometimes so brief. A moth burning bright in the flame and then gone. Sometimes it flows on. I'm greedy and want to be able to dip into that flow on demand.

Where the circles of a Venn Diagram intersect, there is a shaded place. The insights meditation brings, the stories I want to tell. The work of writing is plunging into this dark and taking a chance. Trying to illuminate and to share.

# Postscript

The year through which this book has taken shape has been an eventful one in my life and, therefore, in my practice. Life brought gifts, the process of preparing this book for publication being one of those. Blossoming of the practice community in my hometown was another. There were both bumps and positive turns in the lives of my grown children, and growth and celebration in our family with the birth of a grandniece and the wedding of a nephew. An ordinary life. Life also brought challenges, foremost being a frightening diagnosis for my husband, my life partner of more than three decades. As we shuffle life's usual arrangements to accommodate doing all that we can do for his treatment, some discomfort arises with simple unfamiliarity and interruption. This is the froth on the tides of fear and uncertainty that the diagnosis itself carries.

But all of these are the surface waves. Deep down has been continuing practice of mindfulness and awareness. Remembering my intent to maintain balance and a clear view of what is so, despite the buffeting of life's worldly winds: joy and sorrow, loss and gain, fame and insignificance, praise and blame.

Whether waves of experience are positive or negative, whether feelings are pleasant or unpleasant, whether the lifts and valleys are monumental or minute, my task has been "to bring the training to bear," as my teacher wisely instructs. Know this moment and what it holds, know its impact and what is needed. Each experience requires this combination of awareness, turning toward and not away, opening not closing, and then a creative response that moves toward peace, equanimity and the end of suffering.

In order to do this, I take refuge again and again in the Buddha, the Dhamma and Sangha. I make effort to choose wisely, recognizing that when the small self closes in from fear or greed, pain results. Any success in letting go of this narrow perspective nudges open the door into heaven. I've got a toe in that door. Each mindful moment makes moving through more possible.

# About the author

Bonnie Ryan-Fisher is a long-time meditator and Buddhist practitioner. In recent years she has been leading meditation and yin yoga classes in her home town of Whitecourt, Alberta. She has also undertaken Upasika training in the Theravada tradition, receiving the Pali name, Sumanā, from her primary teacher, Ajahn Sona, abbot of Sitavana, Birken Forest Monastery in BC.

Her publications are varied and numerous, both fiction and non-fiction appearing in magazines, newspapers, journals, and anthologies since the mid-80's in Canada, the U.S. and the U.K. Drawing on her experience as a former highschool and college instructor she has also produced educational materials and study guides of various kinds.

While continuing to write and mentor beginning writers through a manuscript reading service, she has found her own work naturally becoming more clearly Dhamma-related. Transcribing and editing talks by Ajahn Sona for eventual publication is one of her ongoing projects. Her blog *Mindful Moment* is the foundation of this book. Other practice-related publications include:

"Reflections on the 'S' Word" (essay) in *Zen Words: A Newsletter about Buddhist Practice, Vol 1, Issue 1*, Oct. 2004

"Seeking a Sangha" (essay) in *Zen Words: A Newsletter about Buddhist Practice, Vol.1, Issue 2*, Nov. 2004

"Beginnings" (essay) in *Zen Words: A Newsletter about Buddhist Practice, Vol.1, Issue 4*, Jan. 2005

"I Think I'm a Buddhist" (essay) in *Buddhadharma: The Practitioner's Quarterly*, Winter 2012

"Training in Mindfulness" (article) in *WestWord*, Magazine of the Writer's Guild of Alberta, Vol 35, No. 5, Sept-Oct, 2015

"Discovering the Three Jewels in Rural Alberta" (essay) in *Lotus Petals in the Snow*, Sumeru Press, 2015

# Retreat teachers who have influenced my practice

Ajahn Pavaro
Ajahn Sona
Anne Mahoney
Ayya Medhanandi
Heather Martin
Jude (on-line tutor for *Insight Meditation Course*)
Kuya Minogue
Michael Stone
Richard Shankman
Stephen Roehrig

Several anonomous lay instructors who stepped in to assist at retreats or monastics who gave visiting talks should also be listed here. I apologize for not being able to recall their individual names.

Many of my teachers have come into my life via books or online. Some are teachers, other scientists, poets, philosophers, singers. Those mentioned in the blogs are:

Aitken, Robert *The Dragon Never Sleeps*
Ajahn Amaro
Ajahn Chah
Ajahn Liam
Ajahn Sucitto
Baraz, James *Awakening Joy* (on-linecourse)
Beck, Charlotte Joko *Nothing Special: Living Zen*
Boorstein, Sylvia
Chodron, Pema *When Things Fall Apart*

Cohen, Leonard
The Dalai Lama *Living the Compassionate Life*
Darling, David *Soul Search: A Scientist Explores the Afterlife*
Decker, Eve
Dogen, Eihei
Frost, Robert
Goldberg, Natalie
Goldstein, Joseph
Gross, Rita
Hanh, Thich Nhat *The Sun in My Heart*
Hokusai (Woodblock prints)
Kornfield, Jack *The Wise Heart*
Lama Surya Das
Le Guin, Ursula *The Dispossessed*
Maclear, Kyo *Birds, Art, Life*
Major, Alice *Intersecting Sets*
Monk Kidd, Sue *When the Heart Waits*
Morrow Lindbergh, Anne *A Gift From the Sea*
Oliver, Mary
O'Reilly, Mary Rose *The Love of Impermanent Things*
Pirsige, Robert M. *Zen and the Art of Motorcycle Maintenance*
Pullman, Philip *The Golden Compass*
Ram Das
Ricard, Matthieu *Happiness*
Russell, Peter (guest speaker in *Awakening Joy* course)
Ryan, M.J. (guest speaker in *Awakening Joy* course)
Salzberg, Sharon
Sekito Kisen *The Sandokai*
Shimano Roshi, Eido *Golden Wind: Zen Talks*
Supraner, Robyn *No Room for a Sneeze*
Watts, Alan

CPSIA information can be obtained
at www.ICGtesting.com
Printed in the USA
LVHW01s0110080518
576362LV00001B/2/P